Further Praise for
Econospinning

D1279351

"*Econospinning* is right on target about the need for journalists to do a better job understanding the statistics they use. In the pre-Internet days, it was not easy for anyone to find the underlying definitions and survey details Epstein uses in this book, but he clearly demonstrates that such information is now either only a "click" away on a Federal agency web site or a phone call away from an agency expert whose name and number are available on the site."

> —Robert Parker, former Chief Statistician of the Bureau of Economic Analysis, and long-time producer of key economic indicators

"An exhaustively researched and incisive account of how newspaper columnists, policymakers, political operatives, television new anchormen and others in influential positions brazenly misrepresent economic statistics to sell us their politically tinted conclusions. Even if you don't agree with all of Epstein's opinions, his penetrating analysis and crisp but deliberate writing style makes this a fun book to read."

> —Jagadeesh Gokhale, Senior Fellow, Cato Institute

ECONOSPINNING

ECONOSPINNING

How to Read Between the Lines
When the Media Manipulate the Numbers

Gene Epstein

WILEY

John Wiley & Sons, Inc.

For general information on our other products and services or for technical support, please contact our Customer Care Department within the United States at (800) 762-2974, outside the United States at (317) 572-3993 or fax (317) 572-4002.

Wiley also publishes its books in a variety of electronic formats. Some content that appears in print may not be available in electronic books. For more information about Wiley products, visit our web site at www.wiley.com.

ISBN-13: 978-0-471-73513-7
ISBN-10: 0-471-73513-2

Printed in the United States of America.

10 9 8 7 6 5 4 3 2 1

For Rifka Laine Handelman:
My poor excuse for being an absent
grandfather over the past two years.

CONTENTS

Preface   xi

Acknowledgments   xxi

CHAPTER 1
Eldercare Fraud   1

CHAPTER 2
Two Ways to Measure Employment   18

CHAPTER 3
Bush League Economics   30

CHAPTER 4
Long-Term Unemployment Myths   44

CHAPTER 5
The Case of the Phantom Dropouts   59

CHAPTER 6
Participation Rate Follies   73

CHAPTER 7
What Does the Employment–Population Ratio Tell Us?   83

CHAPTER 8
May Average Hourly Earnings Rest in Peace   91

CHAPTER 9
Hourly Compensation and the Unemployment Rate   101

CHAPTER 10
Wages and Productivity   111

CHAPTER 11
The Record Profit Boom That Never Happened   116

CHAPTER 12
End the Monthly Madness: The Change in Payroll
Employment Data   124

CHAPTER 13
End the Monthly Madness: The Unemployment Rate   137

CHAPTER 14
Greenspan Idolatry   150

CHAPTER 15
Best-Selling Myths: *Freakonomics*   163

CHAPTER 16
Best-Selling Myths: *Nickel and Dimed*   185

CHAPTER 17
Dobbs and Jobs   193

Afterword   205

Notes   215

Index   235

PREFACE

I n the past decade, we have read and heard much about media bias. Liberals complain about conservative bias, conservatives about liberal bias, and both are partly right. Lost amid the partisan squabbling, however, is any real discussion of the quality of economic and business reporting, analysis, and commentary. How economic data is interpreted affects economic policy, business decisions, investment planning, and trading strategies for the individual and professional. And yet, in so many of these areas, the practice of economic spinning has almost become an ingrained habit. This book is an attempt to uncover what I call *econospinning* and expose its failings. If you can recognize what is flawed, then you will be able to better identify accurate analysis and reporting.

I use the term *econospinning* to refer to the sort of economic journalism that shapes the data around a predetermined story, rather than the story around the discoverable data. Who is guilty of econospinning? Sadly, virtually ever major media outlet from the *New York Times* to the *Economist* to the *Wall Street Journal* (owned by Dow Jones & Co., parent company of my own employer, *Barron's*) to think tanks that include the Heritage Foundation, the American Enterprise Institute, and the Council on Budget and Policy Priorities. No journalist is completely immune, myself included.

Econospinning thrives in economic journalism for all the usual reasons bad journalism thrives: the preference for "sizzle" over substance, compounded by ordinary human failings like sloth, ignorance, emotionalism, and opportunism. The main difference is that economics reporting tends to be far more complicated than most other forms of reporting. So it's hardly surprising that econospinning often seems the norm rather than the exception.

Take, for example, a practice that has nothing to do with partisan politics: the media's habit of headlining economic data that government sources keep trying in vain to warn them off because the figures are within the range of statistical error. While these numerical nonevents are a classic case of manufactured news, they are also rooted in the power of numbers over the human psyche. In Chapter 13 of this book, I quote an exchange between a well-known journalist and the Commissioner of the Bureau of Labor Statistics discussing why the journalist kept reporting statistically insignificant data. The journalist's comments revealed that he hadn't understood what the Commissioner was trying to say. Add the fact that the markets have an insatiable and irrational need for timely data, and it's clear that the only way for these numbers not to be reported is for the sources to stop releasing them.

Partisan politics can also be a key motivator. For example, the *Wall Street Journal* editorial board engaged in econospinning out of a clear desire to see President Bush reelected; Paul Krugman of the *New York Times* aggressively pursued it to see Bush defeated. Since I'm not privy to the innermost thoughts of reporters and opinion page writers, I have to assume they believe their own arguments. What I object to is their attempt to persuade others.

What if certain econospinners came out and said honestly that the end justifies the means—that in the service of a good cause, it's okay, even admirable, to econospin to win? While I can imagine cases in which distorting mere economic data has moral uses, I don't know of any from real life. If the physician's oath is, "First, do no harm," the journalist's should be, "First, tell no lies." Especially since getting things right in economic journalism is no easy matter.

So strong is the tendency to get things wrong, in fact, that when planning this book, I was not surprised to find the mountain of potential material was even larger than I had anticipated. If, as I believe, the frequency of econospinning is far greater than in times past, the mutually reinforcing reasons are not hard to find. They include the heavily partisan environment and the explosion in media coverage—more or less dating from that moment in 1992 when "It's the Economy, Stupid" first appeared on the wall of Bill Clinton's campaign headquarters—compounded further by the rise of blogging. We can hope that more coverage leads to more knowledge on a net basis. But the gross quantity of obfuscation expands. Also, econospinners are not limited to journalism's traditional practitioners. By the media, I exempt none who speak out on the economy, whether they call themselves reporters, professors, policy analysts, politicians, or public intellectuals.

Deciding what to exclude from the book was often as difficult as deciding what to include. For example, if journalism is the first draft of history, then history is surely one of journalism's later drafts. Since I first read the late economist George Stigler on the appalling stuff that passes for economic history by some of our most eminent historians, I've taken a keen interest in this ongoing intellectual scandal.[1] My own update of Stigler's whistle-blowing work, however, had to be sacrificed for lack of space.[2] Material that did make the final cut includes issues raised in two best-selling books about the current scene: *Freakonomics,* co-authored by University of Chicago economist Steven Levitt, and *Nickel and Dimed,* by journalist Barbara Ehrenreich.

One strategy I used for keeping the material manageable was to narrow my targets to the elite media—the intellectual trendsetters. However, if the *New York Times*—targeted frequently—is rife with error, then *USA Today*—rarely mentioned—may be even more troubled. Even that strategy had to be scrapped if any mention was to be made of cable television, where many folks apparently get most of their economic news. You'll find a long discussion of the CNBC television show, *Squawk Box,* and a chapter on CNN newsman Lou Dobbs.

The longest section in the book is devoted to data on jobs and joblessness. Since labor data gets covered most often by the media, and is of great concern to all four main kinds of potential readers of this book—policy makers, traders, investors, humanists—it warrants in-depth coverage here. It also happens to be my own favorite kind of data.

KRUGMANIA

One of my former interns, Neil Dutta, attended a debate in midtown Manhattan that Paul Krugman, the prolific *New York Times* columnist, participated in, and told me that the audience gave Krugman a standing ovation the moment he walked on stage. Then, the audience applauded whenever he made a particularly stirring remark.

You might say that in economic journalism, there's Paul Krugman, and then there's everyone else. Princeton professor, textbook author, and

xiv   PREFACE

1991 winner of the prestigious John Bates Clark medal for the best economist under 40, Krugman has been writing a regular op-ed column for the *New York Times* since January 2000. As he himself has fairly said, he now "land[s] on a million doorsteps twice a week."[3] He's an accomplished writer. Before joining the *Times,* he'd been writing monthly for the online magazine, *Slate,* while appearing bimonthly in *Fortune.* His recent collection of *Times* pieces, *The Great Unraveling,* was a *New York Times* best seller.[4] The cover of the expanded paperback edition (2004) of *The Great Unraveling* quotes the following from political commentator and attack-book author Al Franken: "Paul Krugman is a hero of mine. Read this book."[5]

Another opinion: "Op-Ed columnist Paul Krugman has the disturbing habit of shaping, slicing and selectively citing numbers in a fashion that pleases his acolytes but leaves him open to substantive assaults."[6]

When *New York Times* ombudsman (or Public Editor) Daniel Okrent wrote the preceding opinion in his final column for the paper (his 18-month tour-of-duty was just expiring), he probably did not anticipate the storm of protest from bloggers quick to defend their champion.

I had briefly corresponded with Okrent a few months before, prompted by a mutual acquaintance, Jonathan Laing, a colleague at *Barron's.* Laing, who had noticed that Okrent was apparently enamored of another economic journalist at the *Times,* David Leonhardt, had remembered that I had once cited Leonhardt for a major gaffe in one of my columns, and encouraged me to send it on to Okrent.

Instead, I wrote Okrent that Leonhardt wasn't the problem with the *Times'* economics coverage; Krugman was. At Okrent's invitation, I then sent him a few examples of what I meant. When his critical remark about Krugman appeared in print, Krugman demanded that Okrent either elaborate or publicly retract his statement. Okrent responded with criticisms that included topics he had discussed with me. Not only did Krugman respond by denying all; those who leapt to his defense included U.C. Berkeley economist Brad DeLong. I began to view Okrent as roughly in the position of the O. J. Simpson prosecutor overmatched by a dream team of pros willing to say anything to get their client off.

New Republic online editor Jonathan Chait, who sided four-square with Krugman, put his finger on the fundamental issue involved by observing:

Being too ideological or partisan is a common flaw among pundits, and it's in the eye of the beholder. Manipulating data is far more serious. Readers can judge for themselves if Krugman is playing to the liberal crowd. They can't judge whether he's using numbers dishonestly. To say he does so is to tell readers they can't trust him.[7]

Just so.

Responding to Okrent, Krugman observed, "I'm sure that a careful search through 100 or so columns will find some errors or misrepresentations. So would a careful search of anyone's work."[8]

Fair enough, which is why the errors and misrepresentations cited in this book will be: (1) repeated in more than one column; (2) specifically denied in response to Okrent; or (3) preserved in Krugman's book, *The Great Unraveling*.

Of course, these categories are not mutually exclusive.

THE FALLACY OF CREDENTIALISM

Krugman is not the only John Bates Clark Medal award winner who comes under scrutiny in this book. Another is University of Chicago economist Steven Levitt, co-author of the runaway best seller, *Freakonomics*. Credentialed or not, we're all subject to the same standard. To believe otherwise calls to mind an exchange in Lewis Carroll's *Sylvie and Bruno:*

> "Do you mean to say," said Lady Muriel, "these manikins of an inch high are to *argue* with me?"
> "Surely. Surely!" said the Earl. "An argument doesn't depend for its logical fore on the *size* of the creature that utters it!"
> She tossed her head indignantly. "I would *not* argue with any man less than six inches high!"[9]

No less absurd is the following version of the credentialist fallacy in left-leaning Eric Alterman's attack book, *What Liberal Media?* In the preface, Alterman claims to have written a work "that so perfectly contradicts conventional wisdom," and further admits, "I suppose I am a natural for it."[10] But instead of working from his nature, he later takes a "non-economist" to task for daring to disagree with a credentialed economist (all italics mine):

> Columbia University Professor Joseph Stiglitz [he writes] was the chair of Bill Clinton's Council of Economic Advisors, chief economist at the World Bank, and winner of the 2001 Nobel Prize in economics. With the possible and only *partial exception of the* New York Times' *pundit Paul Krugman, there is not a journalist alive who comes close to matching Stiglitz's credentials.*[11]

Alterman then quotes certain critical remarks from Stiglitz's recent book, *Globalization and Its Discontents,* as though they were holy writ. Alterman adds:

> And yet while these views are apparently sufficiently sensible for *a man like Stiglitz* to espouse, they meet with nothing but *undisguised contempt* from those who report and comment on this subject in America's elite media. In its July 7, 2002, edition, for instance, the *Washington Post Book Review* relegated Stiglitz's book to an "in-brief" review by a *non-economist.*[12]

Apparently, Alterman didn't think it was worth his time to actually read what a "non-economist" had to say about "a man like Stiglitz"; the *Washington Post*'s "'in-brief' review"—far from being contemptuous—read like a publisher's blurb. Since we're both New Yorkers, I e-mailed Alterman an invitation to visit my office to discuss this and related matters. I'd been planning to tell him:

> Take another Nobel Prize winner—say, Milton Friedman—whose opinions you strongly disagree with. I could list Friedman's many plaudits, before expressing shock and dismay that a "man like Friedman," whose "credentials . . . not a journalist alive comes close to matching," should have to put up with naysaying "non-economists" like . . . Eric Alterman?

Once we mutually recognized that there were too many credentialed economists we both disagreed with, we could discuss some of the substantive issues raised in his book, one noncredentialed person to another.

Alterman and I did not meet, however. After some back-and-forth about time and place (he proposing that I treat him to a steak lunch, I countering that we needed web access while we talked), he backed off on the grounds that he was "opening up" his summer home for the season.

THE PLAN OF THE BOOK

Each chapter in this book is structured around fairly simple propositions about the economy or about economic data that are then contrasted with the distortions of media coverage. Since I view it as sad enough that these distortions are so widespread, I see no point in denying ourselves the occasional fun of dissecting the twisted logic of those under scrutiny.

Chapter 1 deals briefly with a huge topic—the looming cost of eldercare in the form of Social Security, Medicare, and Medicaid. I start by laying out one of the major stories in contemporary economic journalism: According to the most plain-vanilla sources, like the bipartisan Congressional Budget Office, eldercare is on a trajectory to swallow up the federal budget. That's all. On the question of what to do about this frightening prospect, which often splits along party lines, I say nothing at all.

I then contrast this simple proposition with various forms of denial it has received in the print media, beginning with a recent article in the *New Yorker,* which has to rank among the funniest humor pieces ever run by that weekly, albeit of the unintended variety. I then focus on Krugman's coverage of the issue, which includes an episode that has to rank among the most brazen spin jobs engaged in by any *New York Times* op-ed columnist.

The *Times* had run a feature story on the front-page of its business section that highlighted a scary $44 trillion estimate of the unfunded liabilities of Social Security and Medicare. *Times* reporter Edmund Andrews made it clear that, far from associating itself with this figure, the U.S. Treasury had "swiftly disavowed" it.[13] Andrews' story was a valuable, if belated, wake-up call to *Times* readers about the prospective costs of eldercare. But Krugman responded in a column three days later by pretending the $44 trillion estimate was a U.S. Treasury-approved figure, the better to brand it as "ideologically driven."[14] He even specifically mentioned that *Times* story in the same column, as though daring the paper's fact checkers to find him out, although *Times* op-ed columnists are apparently not subject to such indignities.

To compound the irony, the misidentification of this source was one of several charges leveled by Okrent that came to the attention of *Times* Editorial Page Editor Gail Collins. To determine whether Okrent might have been right in this case, all Collins had to do was compare a feature story in her own newspaper with Krugman's version of the same facts.

Chapter 2 is the first in a series of chapters on jobs and joblessness. One of Okrent's charges—that Krugman had confused data from the Establishment and Household surveys to score a political point—provides the opportunity to introduce these two very different surveys that together make up the monthly employment report released by the Bureau of Labor Statistics. Here again, despite Krugman's flat denial of his error,[15] and U.C. Berkeley economist Brad DeLong's unfortunate attempt to defend Krugman against Okrent, the confusion is obvious to journalists who cover this data regularly.

Chapter 3 continues to probe the depths of the Household and Establishment Survey data in order to highlight the different ways in which the two surveys track employment. But in this chapter we'll see a case of spinning the numbers in the service of politics by the Heritage Foundation, American Enterprise Institute, and the editorial board of the *Wall Street Journal*.

Chapters 4 through 7 might collectively be titled, "In Defense of the Unemployment Rate." I consider in turn the compendium of fallacies in support of the abiding myth that the unemployment rate is no longer a proper measure of the rate of unemployment.

Chapters 8 through 10 cover a related question: How do we measure the earnings of labor? I begin by explaining (Chapter 8) how the most widely cited measure has been effectively repudiated by its own issuing agency, the Bureau of Labor Statistics. I then explain (Chapter 9) how a far superior measure, also released by the Bureau, closely tracks a measure of labor market tightness based on the unemployment rate. Finally (Chapter 10), I explain how the same measure also tracks long-term gains in productivity.

Chapter 11 tells the recent story of profits and profitability, mainly contrasted with the way that story has been told by the British newsweekly, the *Economist*.

Chapters 12 and 13 are addressed not just to the media, but to Wall Street, taking brief aim at the CNBC morning show, *Squawk Box*. Monthly figures on the economy all too frequently melt into air, so vulnerable are they to revision and volatility. To make this point (Chapter 12), I use real-time data on payroll employment—what was known at the time—instead of the revised data that economists often confuse with the real-time figures. Even the three-month and six-month trends are so rife with false signals that they obscure more than they clarify. The 12-month trend provides the best trade-off between timeliness and accuracy. That stricture applies to most monthly figures, with the exception of ratios like the unemployment rate (Chapter 13).

The monthly employment report happens to be the biggest market mover of all the major economic reasons. So in Chapter 13, I draw on what we've learned about false signals to ask a bottom-line question: "Does the monthly employment report move the bond market in the right direction?" Judging from the results of two limited track records, I offer an admittedly tentative response, "Probably not." But it's not the fault of the employment data. Blame it on the way data are interpreted. Had the markets focused solely on the 12-month trend in payroll employment, and the 6-month trend in the unemployment rate, the false signals would have been eliminated in favor of the true.

This discussion of the unemployment rate gives me the opportunity to shine a light on a never-before-told story about how President Richard Nixon got a few Jews fired over at the Bureau of Labor Statistics because he didn't trust them to measure this indicator properly.

Chapter 14 tries to set some of the record straight on former Federal Reserve Chairman Alan Greenspan, mainly contrasted with the idolatrous coverage of *Wall Street Journal* reporter Greg Ip. Chapter 15 looks under the hood of the mammoth best seller, *Freakonomics,* and Chapter 16 of the by now semiclassic, *Nickel and Dimed.* Chapter 17 reviews CNN newscaster Lou Dobbs' position on outsourcing and globalization to conclude that his coverage is, at bottom, jingoistic.

And finally, in an Afterword, I briefly discuss two issues—solutions to the healthcare crisis, and rising income inequality—that each require book-length treatments in their own right.

MY EXPOSITION

Throughout this book, I quote copiously from those I take issue with. This is deliberate. I know that when I read criticism of someone else's work, I often feel frustrated that the target was not given enough of a hearing before the critic pounced. To make the quotes easier to follow, I have highlighted in italics words and phrases the reader should be especially aware of. So unless it says [italics in original], italics are always mine.

I also resort frequently to the bane of economic books, charts, and tables, to make my arguments. You can't believe what I say unless you can see the evidence, and the charts and tables—all carefully labeled and captioned—are where you'll find much of it.

I had dreamt of writing a book that could be a definitive guide to rooting out econospinning in all its forms. But not even a work of encyclopedic length could slay the hydra-headed monster. So I opted instead to cover the most pressing topics and most influential media outlets and writers. If you find this book to be no more than a useful corrective to certain misconceptions about the economy, then writing it was worth the effort. If it sharpens your ability to discriminate between good and bad coverage of the economy, I'll be gratified. If it excites your interest enough to want to learn more about the use and abuse of data, or stirs you enough to consider economic journalism as a career, I'll feel overjoyed.

ACKNOWLEDGMENTS

I t's unfortunate you'll be criticizing Paul Krugman," said the agent who eventually rejected my book proposal. "Norton publishes him, and they'd be perfect for you."

Another agent wrote me, "You're biting the hand that feeds you," but would I please keep her in mind in the event that I had a book idea with commercial potential?

A third agent told me she might be able to place my book proposal with a "conservative house," until she learned that both the *Wall Street Journal* and the *Economist* would also come under scrutiny.

"But," I protested, "the best-seller list is filled with books that criticize the media, and you're telling me I can't even get mine published?"

The problem, she explained, is that I wasn't proposing a liberal attack on conservatives, a right-wing attack on the left-wing, a left-wing attack on the . . . I got the point.

Which is all by way of thanking John Wiley & Sons' Editorial Director Pamela van Giessen for taking on this equal opportunity work of media criticism.

Thanks to those who read and critiqued parts of this manuscript— Bureau Labor Statistics Supervisory Statistician and Branch Chief Kirk Mueller, former *New York Times* Public Editor Daniel Okrent, former Bureau of Economic Analysis Chief Statistician Robert Parker, and other professionals who chose to remain anonymous because of their institutional affiliations. Thanks also to Jason Benderly and Karen Anderson of Benderly Economics for teaching me so much about the careful use of data.

Thanks to my brilliant research assistants, Michael Gorun, Jen So, and Deborah Zwi, and to John Won of the *Wall Street Journal* for doing the charts.

Thanks to my *Barron's* editors Ed Finn, Rich Rescigno, and Phil Roosevelt, who have all taught me how to write better; to former *Barron's* editor-in-chief Alan Abelson, for turning me into a weekly columnist; and to Shirley Lazo, for a thousand-and-one kindnesses.

Thanks to literary agent Kate Epstein, not for representing me (as my daughter, she cited "conflict of interest"), but for coaching me at crucial moments; and to son-in-law Ethan, daughter-in-law El, and grandchild Rifka merely for being who they are.

Finally, thanks especially to my son Jim, my warmest critic and sternest admirer, who read and critiqued the manuscript through many drafts. If it weren't for Jim, this book would have taken half as long to complete—and would have been only half as good.

ECONOSPINNING

Eldercare Fraud

A t *some point* in the future, American society *may* have to decide to devote *somewhat more* of its collective resources to the care of the elderly, or else it will have to require the elderly to get along with *somewhat less*. But, as Bush himself has now admitted, this is not a problem that *privatization* [of Social Security] can solve."[1]

It was hard to say, on reading this, which part was more disturbing: the casual dismissal of the frightening cost of elderly entitlements; the apparent assumption that these costs strictly involved Social Security; or the fact that these inadvertent confessions of ignorance were made by *New Yorker* Editorial Director Hendrik Hertzberg. Bush had just been quoted as having "admitted" that his "privatization" plan for Social Security could not "solve" the solvency problem of Social Security. He had said nothing about solving the problem of *caring for the elderly,* most of which was accounted for by the Medicare and Medicaid programs.

Hertzberg's main focus in this March 28, 2005, editorial was on the more limited question of the Social Security trust fund. President Bush had recently declared that Social Security had no trust fund as part of his failed attempt to sell his privatization plan. Counterarguments had been appearing in the *New York Times, Boston Globe, St. Louis Post-Dispatch,* and *Washington Post.* Hertzberg's particular denial of "the trust-fund-as-myth contention, . . . of Bush's echo chamber of conservative op-edders and think-tankers"[2] happened to be more detailed than most, while also outdoing the others for unintended humor.

If Hertzberg was a minor player in this saga of denial, *New York Times* columnist Paul Krugman was a plot mover. Both had difficulty separating the facts involved from their obvious disgust with the policies and proposals of President Bush, and both even improvised certain facts to better support their arguments. But while Hertzberg's breach was relatively innocuous—and inadvertently funny—Krugman's involved misrepresenting an informative article on the soaring cost of eldercare that had appeared in his own newspaper. Krugman's own line of argument often took the form of bait-and-switch: bait the reader with the problem of rising eldercare costs while switching to the Bush tax cuts, the Bush spending increases, or the Bush privatization plan for Social Security.

The whole story would be amusing, in fact, if it weren't ultimately so serious. Contrary to Hertzberg's denial, "American society" is already devoting an ever-increasing share of its "collective resources to the care of the elderly" in the form of Social Security, Medicare, and Medicaid. And unless something is done, these programs will either be as large as the federal budget itself, or the elderly will have to "get along with" *considerably* less.

That's the premise of this chapter. In the course of reviewing the record, I further argue that no form of bait-and-switch is justified: elderly entitlements would be a source of urgent concern no matter how you feel about President Bush's other policies and proposals, and no matter what your views are on the long-term solution to the healthcare crisis.

THE PREMISE DEFENDED

The best source on the subject of elderly entitlements is the bipartisan Congressional Budget Office (CBO). The CBO has released projections for the share of gross domestic product claimed by federal spending on these three programs with no major change in policy. But instead of merely extrapolating past trends, CBO analysts make an optimistic assumption about the future. The per capita cost of Medicare and Medicaid has been rising faster than per capita gross domestic product ever since these programs were first created. Following the lead of the Medicare trustees, they assume an incremental growth of only 1%—by far the slowest on record.[3]

Even so, by 2050 the combined cost of Medicare, Medicaid, and Social Security will claim 19% gross domestic product (GDP), compared with about 8% today. The first two would be the fastest growing. But Social Security will still account for an estimated 6.4 percentage points of that 19%, or about a third.[4] The December 2005 CBO on "The Long-Term Budget Outlook" also points out that "Federal revenues have averaged 18.7% of GDP for the past 10 years and 18.3% for both the past 20 and past 30 years."[5] If that continues, then at 19% of GDP, the cost of those three programs alone will eventually push the federal budget into deficit. All other spending by the federal government claims about 12% of GDP; and outlays by states and localities, another 10%. Assuming those shares hold, we're looking at a rise in government spending between now and 2050, from about 30% of GDP (12+8+10) to 41% (12+19+10).[6]

Beyond 2050, the same assumptions would cause that 19% to continue to climb.

Some might say that's okay. Others might ask whether we have a right to impose that burden on future generations. In any case, this outlook is a far cry from the *New Yorker*'s "somewhat more, somewhat less" way of putting it.

Bear in mind that the problem will not go away with the passing of the baby boomers. Even with respect to Social Security, the role played by demographics has been much exaggerated. According to a CBO Policy Brief called "The Future Growth of Social Security: It's Not Just Society's Aging," 45% of the projected increase in costs is due to an "increase in the *real value* of . . . benefit checks."[7] The reason is that payments to beneficiaries are determined by their wages and salaries, which tend to reflect increases in living standards.

Hence the proposal of Concord Coalition president Peter Peterson that new Social Security benefits be indexed to prices. That would mean the next generation of retirees get the same value as the current generation, but not any more.[8]

While I prefer to cite the latest research on this looming crisis, the essentials have been known for years. We can at least wonder if the

December 2003 Medicare drug bill would have passed in its present form if these scary scenarios had been widely understood. But then *New Yorker* readers were being told as late as March 2005 that "at some point in the future," the elderly "may" have to make do with "somewhat less" if they aren't given "somewhat more."

Let's begin this saga of denial with Hertzberg's defense of the Social Security trust fund, before turning to Krugman.

TRUSTING THE TRUST FUND

The fact that George W. Bush might have some personal knowledge of trust funds would be one good way to highlight the irony that as President Bush, he recognized the fraudulence of the Social Security trust fund. He could tell the difference between trust funds for rich folks like him and the one his government had palmed off on the taxpayer. And yet Hertzberg boldly begins on that very note, speaking of "this ingenious financial tool, through which part of a family fortune can be protected for its intended beneficiaries," including "George W. among other Bushes."[9]

The key point Hertzberg manages to ignore is that the "family fortune" can only be "protected" through investment in assets—securities like stocks and bonds that are claims on the wealth and income of those *outside the Bush family*. Imagine how the Bush offspring would have felt upon discovering that their trust funds contained nothing more than I.O.U.'s signed by the dad. To the Bush family as a whole, there would be no trust fund, because there would be no assets. Or to put it in a more roundabout way, the sons would be free to think of the dad's I.O.U.'s (presumably, made out to them) as assets. The dad, on the other hand—the guy who owes the money—would have no choice but to think of the I.O.U.'s as liabilities. To the Bush family as a whole, then—both father *and* sons—the assets are canceled out by the liabilities. The effect is a wash. There are no assets on net.

Now imagine that, instead of being flush with cash in his own right, the dad himself were deep in debt, and you've come very close to conjuring up the Social Security trust fund. In this case, the Social Security system is the son and the U.S. Treasury is the dad. To Social Security, there is a trust fund, with real assets. But these assets are claims on the income of the U.S. Treasury. So from the Treasury's standpoint they are liabilities. To the U.S. government as a whole, then, the effect is also a wash. Social Security's assets are offset dollar for dollar by the Treasury's liabilities. If the assets belong to the U.S. taxpayer, then so too do the liabilities. George W. Bush was merely telling us that if we think our government has treated us the way his dad treated him, we should all think again.

Yet, Hertzberg and others defend the use of the term with all the zeal of government flaks. They should try reading a CBO policy brief called "Comparing Budgetary and Trust Fund Measures of the Outlook for Social Security" where the CBO analysts remark (in the second paragraph): "[The Social Security Trustees] treat transfers from the government's general fund to the trust funds and the reserves of the funds as resources to pay benefits. However, those transfers and fund reserves are *simply* the result of *credits exchanged* between Treasury accounts—and thus reflect the *government's commitment* to pay the benefits but *not necessarily the means* to do so."[10]

How could this "commitment to pay" be backed by the "means to do so"? Simple: treat Medicare, Medicaid, and Social Security like any other health-coverage-and-pension program by funding the liabilities with stocks and bonds—just as states, municipalities, other national governments (and, of course, private corporations and insurance companies) routinely do. Wherever the liabilities are "fully funded," taxpayers do not have to worry about paying them. The commitments are backed by real assets—claims on the income of others. The U.S. taxpayer, by contrast, faces financial commitments that are backed by U.S. Treasury bonds, which are claims on the taxpayer's income.

Notice how the foregoing sentence can read, "The U.S. taxpayer, by contrast, faces financial commitments"—and stop there, and still mean the same thing as the longer version.

When a *New York Times* editorial observed that "if the [Social Security] trust fund is a joke. So is the full faith and credit of the United States,"[11] the editors had it backward. The fact that the full faith and credit of the United States is no joke is the very reason the joke is on those who take the trust fund seriously. The U.S. Treasury will fully and faithfully pay those debts, which makes them liabilities to the U.S. taxpayer.

Hertzberg brings the *Times*' argument to a new level. Here's the whole paragraph:

The trust-fund-as-myth contention is a staple of Bush's echo chamber of conservative op-edders and think-tankers. Whether there is any truth to it is an interesting, as he might say, question. (It's worth noting, by the way, that, if the trust fund is a myth, then its prospective shortfall is a myth too.) The trust fund, which has close to two trillion dollars in it at the moment, is frequently derided as an accounting fiction. *In fact,* it consists of a growing pile of U.S. Treasury bonds of a special type, *embossed* and *beribboned* and *neatly stacked in a vault* in West Virginia. Unlike standard Treasury bonds, these do not fluctuate in value. By the same token, they cannot be traded on the open market, which is why many of Bush's ideological allies dismiss them as mere pieces of paper, without inherent worth.[12]

Social Security's "prospective shortfall" is indeed a myth which myths like the trust fund help create. The prospective *cost* of programs like Social Security, Medicare, and Medicaid is the only reality worth dealing with. And those "ideological allies" seem to be ignoring the fact that there are plenty of legitimate assets that cannot be traded on the open market.

But is Hertzberg really saying the bonds are assets because they're "embossed and beribboned and neatly stacked in a vault"? Perhaps the *New-Yorker*-ish resort to vivid imagery explains why these factual claims were left to stand in a magazine with a world-class reputation for fact checking. It turns out that Hertzberg got the "West Virginia" part right, but nothing else.

According to an Associated Press story (confirmed by Bureau of Public Debt spokesman Pete Hollenbach), the bonds are in the bottom drawer of a file cabinet "in a pair of white loose-leaf notebooks" with "plastic page covers." Hollenbach adds that this paper has no legal status anyway: the bonds legally consist of electronic book entries, like all Treasury securities. But the file cabinet is definitely in West Virginia.[13]

"It is theoretically true," continues Hertzberg, "that the Treasury, with Congress's permission, could refuse to redeem these bonds when the time came. . . . Of course, the Treasury could also refuse to honor the bonds held by foreigners. These, too, are pieces of paper. . . . The entire economy runs on promises—that is, trust—which is why paranoid survivalists convert their assets to guns and cans of tuna fish."[14]

Hertzberg is right. When the Social Security Administration (SSA) starts redeeming the bonds (in about 15 years), the Treasury will have to pay up. But taxpayers will ultimately have to be trusted, since the "trust fund" is in any case expected to run dry some time in the 2040s. And benefits could still be cut: the SSA would simply redeem the bonds in return for new bonds (rolling them over), in effect redeeming them at a slower rate.

Testifying before the House Budget Committee on "The Economic Costs of Long-Term Federal Obligations," CBO Director Douglas Holtz-Eakin remarked, "*Every dollar* of federal spending has a *cost.* It makes *no difference* if the payment is charged to the general fund, a *trust fund,* or an enterprise fund."[15]

MISREPRESENTING A SOURCE

The trust-fund fallacy played a key role in Krugman's first bout of denial on the soaring cost of eldercare in general. It was also a clear case of misrepresenting a source—although the source being misrepresented turned out to be flawed in its own right.

Krugman's March 20, 2003, column at least began by framing the discussion in what seemed to be fair terms:

> Many commentators are reluctant to blame George W. Bush for [the] grim [fiscal] outlook, preferring instead to say something like this: "Sure, you can criticize those *tax cuts,* but the real problem is the *long-run deficits of Social Security and Medicare,* and the unwillingness of either party to reform those programs."[16]

But, he continued, while "it seems more reasonable to blame long-standing problems for our fiscal troubles than to attribute them to just two years of bad policy decisions . . . there's only one problem with this reasonable, balanced, non-shrill position: it's *completely wrong.* The Bush tax cuts, not the retirement programs, are the *main reason* why our fiscal future suddenly looks so bleak."[17]

He bases that statement "on a new study" from the Center on Budget and Policy Priorities "that compares the size of the Bush tax cuts with that of the prospective deficits of Social Security and Medicare. The results are startling."[18]

In the age of Internet, the study is easily retrieved. And what truly startles is that it does not do what Krugman claims. It compares the "prospective deficits" of Social Security and *part* of Medicare to the "size of the Bush tax cuts." It does not attribute even so much as a dollar's worth of costs to either Medicare Part B (physician's care) or to the new drug benefit (Part D), then a near certainty to pass Congress in some version. It includes only the "prospective deficit" of Medicare Part A (hospital care). If it had covered "the prospective deficits of Social Security and Medicare," as Krugman claimed, the "results" would have swung the other way.

To justify the omission, the authors of the study—Peter Orszag of the Brookings Institution, and Richard Kogan and Robert Greenstein of the Center on Budget and Policy Priorities—try, in effect, to turn a fault into a virtue. They restricted the choice to Social Security and Medicare Part A because these are the only programs that have "dedicated trust funds." The "prospective deficits" they calculated are based on future costs, but only after each program was duly credited with the value of the assets in its trust fund. Since Medicare Part B has no trust fund, they could not follow that same procedure.[19]

But so far, how that could be an excuse for ignoring Medicare Part B? As we have already seen, if the trust funds are assets to the programs to which they are "dedicated," they are liabilities to the U.S. Treasury itself. So to credit these programs with their trust funds already amounts to rigging the results, since the cost of the Bush tax cuts and the cost of these programs will both be fully borne by the Treasury. In other words, the use of a faulty procedure for Social Security and Medicare Part A can hardly justify not following a more valid procedure for Medicare Part B. Why can't its prospective deficit be calculated without benefit of a trust fund?

The answer, according to the authors, is that similar deficits would then have to be figured for all other federal programs!

As they explain in a long footnote [italics theirs]:

> Under federal law, Medicare Part B, like most government programs, is supported primarily by general revenues rather than by a dedicated trust fund. Calculating an *actuarial deficit* in Part B thus is akin to computing a "deficit" in the Defense Department or in other parts of government that are supported by general revenues; such a "deficit" has little meaning unless it is calculated for *all* federal programs taken together, relative to all projected general revenues.[20]

In other words, you can't project the long-term costs of entitlement programs for the elderly until you've done a similar job on farm subsidies and the future cost of the Iraq war!

Orszag, Kogan, and Greenstein are surely being disingenuous. They must know full well that budget analysts routinely use terms like "mandatory" and "discretionary" to categorize different kinds of federal spending, and they don't need to guess where Social Security and Medicare are filed. To be consistent, they ought to propose that such terms be abolished forthwith, lest anyone get the impression that some programs are more discretionary or mandatory than others.

They should also object to the following remark by Holtz-Eakin of the CBO in congressional testimony on the "Economic Costs of Long-Term Federal Obligations" when the prescription drug benefit for Medicare was about to become law: "While five- or 10-year projection horizons may be *adequate* for some budget decisions, they are *especially deficient* when evaluating the implications of changes in *entitlement programs.*"[21]

The whole point about entitlements is that, once the promises are made, they are difficult to back out of, especially when the beneficiaries are the elderly. When Director Holtz-Eakin informed congress that "CBO is developing the capacity to provide long-term projections for Social Security and Medicare to more accurately estimate future commitments under those programs,"[22] no one thought to ask him why he singled those out to the exclusion of all the others. Nor did anyone doubt that he meant all of Medicare, not just Part A.

And as for "dedicated trust funds" being the touchstone for what you do and do not include—well, I haven't met Orszag, Kogan, or Greenstein, but I find it hard to imagine them suggesting this to the CBO director with a straight face.

The authors at least made it clear that they had excluded a large part of Medicare. Krugman, for his part, had misrepresented their findings. When an economics columnist writes about the "deficits of Social Security and Medicare," he can only be referring to all of Medicare, especially if he later declares, "Without those tax cuts, the *problems of an aging population* might well have been manageable."[23]

Finally, Orszag, Kogan, and Greenstein are ambivalent enough about their findings to begin with a statement that sounds faintly like the one Krugman just called "completely wrong": "The Administration," they write, "is *correct to identify* the projected deficits in Social Security and Medicare as important problems requiring attention from policy-makers. But it is a mistake to exclude the Administration's own tax cuts from discussions of the projected long-term fiscal imbalances that face the nation."[24]

BRAZEN MISREPRESENTATIONS

A year after misrepresenting a source that was itself rather suspect, Krugman misrepresented a story that appeared in his own newspaper.

The March 2, 2004, story by *Times'* reporter Edmund Andrews performed a valuable service by presenting key facts and figures on "the looming shortfalls" of Social Security and Medicare. The story provoked an immediate response from Krugman, who cited it specifically in his March 5, 2004, column, so we have to assume he had read it. Those who had not read it but read Krugman's version would have gotten a very different impression of those same facts and figures. Those who read both Krugman and Andrews might have been shocked by Krugman's distortions.

What motivated Krugman? Well, first, he obviously did not like the frightening "$44 trillion" estimate of those "looming shortfalls," so he pretended it came from the "ideologically driven" U.S. Treasury.[25] But Andrews had made it painstakingly clear that the U.S. Treasury had "disavowed" the figure.[26] Second, Krugman must have felt that by making it seem that it took "great care" to discern which part of the $44 trillion came from Social Security—as though he were thwarting a subtle effort at dissembling—he could make a smoother transition to the Bush tax cuts. This time, no part of Medicare got placed on the other side of the ledger: the Bush tax cuts were compared only with Social Security.

Andrews' account of the genesis of the $44 trillion figure is worth quoting:

> In 2002, two senior economists at the Treasury Department were asked by Paul H. O'Neill, then the Treasury Secretary, to come up with a comprehensive estimate of the federal government's long-term fiscal problems. The total, calculated by Kent Smetters . . . and Jagadeesh Gokhale . . . was an *almost unthinkable $44 trillion.*

That projection was *swiftly disavowed by the administration.* Rob Nichols, *a spokesman for the Treasury Department,* said the White House never intended to use the study in its official budget forecast. "They were doing what they called *an independent paper,"* he said.

Mr. Gokhale, now a senior fellow at the Cato Institute, *recalled matters differently.* "At some point, late in the game, it was decided that it *wouldn't be in the budget,"* he said. "In my opinion, if they had reported these numbers, they would have gotten a lot of credit."[27]

In fact, this story about the Treasury's suppression of the $44 trillion was already stale news. Economists Jagadeesh Gokhale and Kent Smetters had published an op-ed article in the July 17, 2003, *Wall Street Journal* that specifically indicted the Bush administration for ignoring their figures.[28] The article had been timed to accompany the publication of their book on the subject, *Fiscal and Generational Imbalances.*

The $44 trillion had also been mentioned in *The Price of Loyalty,* Ron Suskind's account of former Treasury Secretary Paul O'Neill's travails,[29] which Krugman himself had written about sympathetically in a January 2004 column.[30] O'Neill, in fact, had sided with Gokhale and Smetters. So not only did Krugman have ample opportunity to know the circumstances—both from reading Andrews' story and Suskind's book— one might even think he would make common cause with Gokhale and Smetters against the Bush administration.

The whole dispute turned on whether a 75-year projection was long enough. Gokhale and Smetters had run afoul of the Treasury by insisting that the cut-off was arbitrary and irresponsible: it implied that the problem would go away in the 76th year, when it actually got worse. Thus they were telling a kind of grisly bad news/good news joke. The bad news: The current tab is $44 trillion. The good news: To cover the next 75 years, only $17 trillion need be left on the table.

The numbers would have been even greater if Social Security and Medicare had not been credited with their share of the payroll tax. The method also caused Social Security to be a disproportionately smaller share of the total than the CBO's more straightforward method. Gokhale and Smetters had no desire to hide this fact, stating in the "Introduction" to their book that all but $7 trillion of the $44 trillion came from Medicare.[31] And in his own story, *Times* reporter Andrews had written that "Most experts say the problems of Social Security are much smaller" and later, that "Medicare's condition is more ominous."[32]

Now get ready for Krugman's version. Its tone seems odd. Gokhale and Smetters were never mentioned, or even vaguely referred to. Leading off with the statement that Social Security is "in pretty good financial shape," he suddenly declared that:

> Other reports, however, appear to portray a system in deep financial trouble. For example, *a 2002 U.S. Treasury study* described on Tuesday in the *New York Times,* claims that Social Security and Medicare are $44 trillion in the red. What's the truth?[33]
>
> Here's a hint: While even right-wing politicians insist in public that they want to save Social Security, the ideologues shaping their views are itching for an excuse to dismantle the system. So you have to read alarming reports generated by people who work at ideologically driven institutions—a list that now, alas, *includes the U.S. Treasury*—with great care.
>
> First, two words—"and Medicare"—make a huge difference. According to the *Treasury study,* only 16% of that $44 trillion shortfall comes from Social Security. Second, the *supposed shortfall* in both programs.[34]

We'll resume quoting Krugman in a minute. But notice that he portrays himself as penetrating a subtle plot to suppress the fact that Social Security is "only 16%" of the $44 trillion, and that he attributes the figure to the "ideologically driven" U.S. Treasury—the very same institution that, in the *Times'* story, had "swiftly disavowed" it! This made it possible to brand the $44 trillion the "supposed shortfall."

To pick up the quote where we left off:

> Second, the supposed shortfall in both programs comes mainly from projections about the distant future; *62%* of the combined shortfall comes after 2077.
>
> So does the *Treasury report* show a looming Social Security crisis? No.[35]

Again, no one had spoken of a Social Security crisis, looming or otherwise. Andrews had spoken only of "the looming shortfalls of the *two* retirement programs," making it clear that Medicare was by far the more costly. But the false note of melodrama helps set the stage for Krugman to declare in the next paragraph, "The Bush tax cuts are a much bigger problem for the nation's fiscal future than the Social Security shortfall."[36]

But now rewind: If "62%" of that $44 trillion occurs "after 2077," doesn't that mean 38% comes earlier? Since 38% of $44 trillion is nearly $17 billion, and since most of that must come from Medicare, isn't that $17 billion rather a worry? But Krugman manages to ignore it (in astonishing fashion) by focusing only on the post-2077 portion. "Medicare," he writes:

> though often lumped in with Social Security, is a different program facing different problems. The projected rise in Medicare expenses is mainly driven not by demography but by the rising cost of medical care, which in turn mainly reflects medical progress, which allows doctors to treat a wider range of conditions.
>
> If this trend continues—which is by no means certain when we are considering the *very long run*—we may face a real *long-term* dilemma that involves all medical care, not just care for retirees, and is as much moral as economic. It may *eventually be the case* that providing all Americans with the full advantages of modern medicine will force the government to raise much more money than it now does. *Yet* not providing that care will mean watching poor and middle-class Americans die early or suffer a greatly reduced quality of life because they can't afford full medical treatment.
>
> *But* this dilemma will be there regardless of what we do to *Social Security.* It's not even clear that we should try to resolve the dilemma *now.* I'm all for taking the *long view;* when the administration makes budget projections for only five years to hide known costs just a few years out, that's an outrage. By all means, let's *plan ahead. But* let's set *some limits.* When people issue ominous warnings about the *cost of Medicare after 2077,* my question is, Why should fiscal decisions today reflect the possible cost of providing generations *not yet born* with medical treatments *not yet invented?*[37]

Fine, but what about pre–2077?

This odd exercise in denial appeared in somewhat different form in a January 2005 on-line article of Krugman's that he referenced in one of his columns. Here again, he made statements like, "In 2100 Medicare may be paying for rejuvenation techniques"; and "What do you think the world will look like in 2105?" and, "I doubt that anyone really believes that it's important to look beyond the traditional 75-year window."[38]

All in the service of not looking through it.

WAYS TO DESCRIBE THE TRUTH

By the time Krugman published a long article in the March 10, 2005, *New York Review of Books*[39]—ostensibly a review of a thoughtful book by Laurence Kotlikoff and Scott Burns called *The Coming Generational Storm*—he had evolved to another position. Based on an earlier version of the CBO's projections, he did indeed call the prospective costs of Medicaid and Medicare a source of real concern.[40]

But, he insisted, when it came to dealing with this problem, Social Security dollars were off the table. Why that should be the case when Social Security accounts for half the cost of elderly entitlements now, and will still account for about a third 45 years from now, is never made clear.

"*One way* to describe the truth," he writes, "is to say that there is no program called Socialsecuritymedicareandmedicaid: these are separate programs with separate problems."[41] Krugman gives three main reasons for describing "the truth" in this way, and while all are overstated, none is entirely wrong. First, he maintains that rising Social Security costs are driven by "the aging of the population," while never mentioning the CBO report, which revealed that to be only about half true ("The Future Growth of Social Security: It's Not Just Society's Aging"). Second, he points out that the "scary" projections of Medicare and Medicaid are not based on demographics, but on the assumption that healthcare spending would continue to rise faster than GDP, while never mentioning that the figures also make the optimistic assumption that the trend will slow considerably.

Finally, he points out that most of the rising cost is accounted for by Medicare and Medicaid. But not only is that statement exaggerated—as we have seen, Social Security will still account for one-third of the total costs by 2050—it's even somewhat arbitrary. To see why, just ask what would have happened to Social Security costs if Medicare and Medicaid had not been created. Social Security, which preceded these other two programs by nearly three decades, was surely conceived to help cover all living costs of retired folks, healthcare included. Without these two programs, Social Security's present and future obligations would be much larger. In fact, Medicaid even pays most of the living costs of seniors who cannot take care of themselves, with Social Security picking up a relatively small part, as anyone with a parent in a nursing home (like me) knows firsthand.

But if Krugman's is "one way to describe the truth," there are other ways, such as: there is a program called Socialsecuritymedicareandmedicaid. That way can become useful when we consider that the soaring cost of all three parts will mainly go to entitlement programs for the elderly; that the total cost threatens to swallow up the federal budget; that whatever savings can be realized by one part could provide relief to another; and that there might be ways to realize nontrivial savings in the part called Social Security.

Instead, Krugman gets back to his real concern—Bush and his privatization plan. "The administration's rationale for privatization," he writes, "is that it is needed because Social Security is in crisis. As we've seen, that's a huge exaggeration, and many of the things President Bush says—such as his assertions that the system will be 'flat broke, bust' when the trust fund runs out—are just plain false."[42]

But of course, if privatization will detract from the system's ability to pay on its promises, it would only be worse if Social Security really is in danger of going "flat broke, bust"—just as it would be worse if Socialsecuritymedicareandmedicaid were in similar danger.

In response to a letter from authors Kotlikoff and Burns—who rightly complained that their book had been ignored—Krugman wrote: "I stand by what I said in the review. Nobody should ignore the demographic *problem,* which is real and substantial. But exaggerating it, and pretending that the quite different health care *problem* is part of the same syndrome, only distorts the policy debate."[43]

I'll give him this: While his own role in distorting the policy debate persisted, it had certainly diminished. After all, he had just used the word "problem" twice in the same paragraph. But how seriously he took the problem was not quite clear.

Not until a year later.

Closing the Door

The March 23, 2006, issue of the *New York Review of Books* ran another long article by Krugman (co-authored with his wife and Princeton colleague Robin Wells) called, "The Health Care Crisis and What to Do About It." On certain aspects of what not to do, the article was also explicit: do nothing—at least, "not today"—about the soaring cost of elderly entitlements.

What Krugman *would* do is to replace our "current complex mix of health insurance systems" with a "single-payer system" similar to that found in Taiwan and Canada.[44] He would even go beyond that model to the "next step"—"honest-to-God socialized medicine, in which government employees provide the care as well as the money," similar to the Veteran's Health Administration in the United States. If we go that route, "the savings would be so large that we could cover all those currently uninsured, yet end up spending less overall."[45]

While I don't find that last part convincing, to explain why would go beyond the scope of this chapter—and indeed, of this book (see final chapter). But even assuming we should do what he proposes, why do nothing about elderly entitlements? He again declares that "there is no program called Socialsecuritymedicareandmedicaid," with the same objective of getting Social Security dollars off the table. And as for making Medicare and Medicaid "tomorrow's issue, not today's,"[46] a certain element of denial still remains.

While Krugman does acknowledge the "crushing burden" of "excess cost growth"—per capita costs of Medicare and Medicaid rising faster than per capita GDP—he points out that "without this excess cost growth," the rise would be "significant . . . but not overwhelming, and could be addressed with moderate tax increases and possibly benefit cuts."[47] True, but nowhere does he mention the hopeful assumptions on which that excess cost growth is based.

According to the CBO figures on Medicare, "costs per enrollee . . . rose 2.9 percentage points faster than per capita GDP over the 1970–2004 period."[48] More recently, from 1990 through 2004, this excess cost growth slowed to 1.9 percentage points. (The Medicaid figures are distorted by demographic factors.) One might expect the forecast would be based on that slowed rate of 1.9 percentage points. But as the CBO makes clear, the "crushing burden" of which Krugman speaks assumes a near halving of that figure to just 1 percentage point a year on a sustained basis. That's how the CBO projects that Social Security, Medicare, and Medicaid will account for 19% of GDP by 2050, more than swallowing up federal revenues as we know them. Should anything less fortuitous happen, the crushing burden would be even more crushing.

These grim realities, of which Krugman says nothing, seem to conflict with the vision of Medicare set forth in his article. "The core of the system" they want, write Krugman and Wells, "would be government insurance—'*Medicare for all*,' as Ted Kennedy puts it." They go on to explain:

> Although it's rarely described this way, Medicare is a *single-payer system* covering many of the health costs of older Americans. (Canada's universal single-payer system is, in fact, also called Medicare.) And it has some though not all the advantages of the broader single-payer systems, notably low administrative costs.[49]

With Medicare thus anointed as a less costly system, why rush to rein in its costs?[50]

The CBO, by contrast, which apparently lacks Krugman vision, keeps counseling against delay. Regarding "changes to the Social Security and Medicare programs," the CBO declares at one point, "*sooner is better than enacting them later* because future beneficiaries would have longer to prepare, because the revisions could be less drastic, and because the changes could enhance economic growth."[51]

Meanwhile, Krugman's tendency to deny goes beyond his work on elderly entitlements. It has spilled over into narrower disputes about the use of data, as we'll see in Chapter 2.

Two Ways to Measure Employment

I n a column of May 25, 2004, Krugman derided the Republicans' in-flated claims about the recent pickup in job growth, comparing the "sustained employment growth" of the "Clinton years" with the "dismal job numbers" the "Bush administration [had] presided over."[1] The numbers Krugman kept citing were accurate, and were drawn appropriately from the "Establishment Survey" data, updated monthly by the Bureau of Labor Statistics (BLS) in its "Employment Situation" report.

But when Krugman declared in the same column that "a mere return to Clinton-era job growth" was not "enough"—and then promised to "do the math" to show how much would be "enough"—his confusion mounted rapidly. To set the math up, he threw in a statement about "employment" having to "rise by about 140,000 a month just to keep up with a growing population" that referred to the Household Survey data, also updated monthly by the BLS in that same employment report. The numerical result Krugman got from having done "the math"—that "President Bush needs about *four years* of job growth at last month's rate"—could only have come from having hopelessly confused the 140,000 from the Household Survey with data from the Establishment Survey.[2]

No one unfamiliar with the Household and Establishment Surveys could possibly make sense out of Krugman's "math." But spotting his confusion required nothing more than basic familiarity with the two surveys—making his subsequent denials all the more disturbing.

A year later, departing *New York Times* ombudsman Daniel Okrent faulted Paul Krugman for "blending, without explanation" in that same May 25, 2004, column, "numbers from the Household Survey and Establishment Survey—apples and oranges—apparently in order to make a more vivid political point about Bush."[3] Krugman responded, "In fact, I used consistent data. I don't know what your problem is." He then told Editorial Page Editor Gail Collins that Okrent was "just wrong," adding: "All the numbers in that 5/25/04 column come from the same (establishment) survey."[4]

Okrent identified the number that came from the Household Survey: Krugman's reference in that column to "the 140,000" jobs needed "just to keep up with a growing population."[5] Krugman responded: "Now Mr. Okrent claims that he was only referring to my assertion that the economy needs to add 140,000 payroll jobs per month, which for some reason he thinks comes from the household survey. (It doesn't.)"[6]

The formal name of the Household Survey is "Current Population Survey." Since Krugman had written that "employment . . . must rise by about 140,000 a month just to keep up with a growing *population*,"[7] he had already left himself a broad hint about the source of the number. *Times* Editorial Page Editor Gail Collins, for her part, might have asked any of several economists at the Division of Labor Statistics of the BLS to read the column (Steven Hipple for example), and tell her the source of the 140,000.

As though to add to the confusion, U.C. Berkeley economics professor Brad DeLong, who posted parts of the Okrent-Krugman exchange on his web site, weighed in with an odd observation of his own which seemed calculated to support Krugman, but which effectively took a third view. I will return to it later.

The propositions underlying this chapter are of the most basic sort. To untangle the confusions in Krugman's column, I will explain the difference between the Household Survey and Establishment Survey data in that mother of all economic reports, the BLS's monthly report on the

"Employment Situation." The employment report gets cited by the media more than all other economic reports combined; its power to move markets is greater than all others combined. Accordingly, the myths and fallacies perpetrated in its name will take up the next 12 chapters of this book, with Krugman's writings coming up more often than anyone else's because his writings speak to it so frequently and because he is the most prominent of economic analysts read by millions every week.

ESTABLISHMENT AND HOUSEHOLD DATA

One way to survey the job situation is to ask the people; another is to ask the employers. The BLS does both. Its monthly Household Survey asks a representative sample of 60,000 households about the job status of all residents over the age of 16.[8] Its monthly Establishment Survey asks a representative sample of 400,000 government and private establishments (excluding farms) to report the number of jobs currently on the payroll.[9] Narrower in scope, but more in-depth for what it does cover, the Establishment Survey was—typically—the source of the first part of the BLS's lead statement on the April 2004, Employment Situation: "Nonfarm payroll employment increased by 288,000 in April"[10] The Household Survey—also typically—was the source of the second part: "and the unemployment rate was about unchanged at 5.6 percent."[11]

The Household Survey is much broader in scope precisely because it asks people, not employers, about the job situation. Krugman's statement about the "140,000" read, in full: "And employment is chasing a moving target: It must rise by about 140,000 a month just to keep up with a growing population."[12] That could only come from the Household Survey because it both explicitly and implicitly refers to measures that only the Household Survey covers, and because *140,000* is a figure that plausibly reflects the underlying trend in these measures.

The measures implicitly referred to in the statement—which explain the link between "employment" and the "growing population"—include *unemployment, labor force,* and that huge negative category, *not in labor force.*

When you survey the job situation by asking people, you will naturally create categories that go beyond the narrow purview of *nonfarm payroll employment* in the Establishment Survey. You begin with the population eligible for employment: the *civilian noninstitutional population,* where *civilian* excludes the armed forces and *noninstitutional* mainly excludes people in prison, mental institutions, hospitals, and nursing homes. They must also be *16 and over*—the cutoff age used to be 14.

By surveying a representative sample of this employment-eligible population, you can then create two broad categories: the *employed*—respondents who say they have jobs, including the self-employed; and the *unemployed*—jobless respondents who want a job and are actively looking. You can combine the employed and unemployed into an even broader category called the *labor force.* And since those remaining are jobless respondents who are not actively looking, they can be placed in a negative category: *not in labor force.*

So the *civilian noninsitutional population 16 and over* exhaustively consists of those in the *labor force* and those *not in* [the] *labor force,* while the labor force exhaustively consists of the *employed* and the *unemployed.*

Now, when Krugman wrote that "employment . . . must rise by about 140,000 a month just to keep up with a growing population,"[13] he was using, unwittingly or not, all of the above concepts. A longer version of this statement can be summarized as follows: (1) Growth in the employment-eligible population (*civilian, noninstitutional, 16, and over*) will naturally lead to growth of both the labor force and of those not in the labor force. (2) If the labor force part of this growth runs about 140,000 a month, then either the employed, the unemployed—or both employed and unemployed together—will increase by 140,000. (3) So employment "must" rise by the full 140,000 a month to prevent an increase in the unemployed.

Why assume "140,000"? Well, if the increase in the *civilian noninstitutional population* runs about 2.5 million a year—a plausible figure—that averages to about 210,000 a month. Of that 210,000, the share that chooses to participate in the labor force—the *labor force participation rate*—is plausibly about two-thirds. (So the other third ends up as *not in labor force.*) Two-thirds of 210,000 is 140,000—the monthly increase in the labor force that can be expected. But participating in the labor force is not an automatic ticket to employment; you could end up unemployed. So unless *employment* rises by the full 140,000 rise in the labor force, there will be an increase in unemployment.

It's not an exact number. It's just an approximation, again based on the assumption that (1) the population deemed eligible for employment grows by about 2.5 million a year, or 210,000 a month and (2) about two-thirds of that eligible population chooses to participate in the labor force, which means (3) the labor force can be expected to grow by two-thirds of that increase, or by 140,000 a month.

Krugman, remember, denied that this statement had anything to do with the Household Survey. So we can only assume he got it from another unnamed source (with, presumably more information than he). That source must have been making assumptions based on recent and expected trends. When Krugman's May 25, 2004, column first appeared, the Household Survey showed growth of the civilian noninstitutional population 16 and over had run 2.2 million over the previous 12 months, but over the next 12 months it ran nearly 2.7 million. The 24-month average is only slightly shy of 2.5 million.[14] As for the labor force participation rate, from 65.9% in April 2004, it ticked up to 66.0% 12 months later—still short of 66.7%, or two-thirds.[15] But since 66.7% is closer to the accepted "norm" of the 1990s, it was widely expected to recover to that level.

So Krugman's source could plausibly have assumed a 2.5 million annual increase in the employment-eligible population, or 210,000 a month, and labor force participation rate of two-thirds, which would have given him a monthly increase in the labor force of 140,000.

Now read Krugman's statement again: "And employment is facing a moving target: it must rise by about 140,000 a month just to keep up with a growing population." Using Household Survey concepts, we can elaborate on it further. The "moving target" is the "growing population." Since the "growing population" will drive an increase in the labor force of 140,000, employment "must rise" by that much *just to prevent* the unemployed from increasing. If, say, the employed rise by only 100,000, there will be an increase of 40,000 in the unemployed. If the employed rise by, say, 160,000, the unemployed will decrease by 20,000. But if the employed rise by that same 140,000, unemployment will stay flat.

Not too hard, is it? The only hard part is to figure out what this sentence was doing in the middle of a discussion of the Establishment Survey data.

As mentioned, the headline figure from the Household Survey is the unemployment rate—the percentage share of the labor force that is unemployed. In April 2004, with the unemployed at 8.2 million and the labor force at 146.8 million, the unemployment rate came to 5.6%:[16]

$$\frac{8.2}{146.8} = 5.6\%$$

The labor force of 146.8 million was broken down this way:

Employed	138.6
Unemployed	+ 8.2
Labor force	146.8

Note: Numbers are in millions.

The employment-eligible population (222.8 million) was broken down as follows:

Labor force	146.8
Not in labor force	+ 76.0
Civilian noninstitutional population (16 and over)	222.8

Note: Numbers are in millions.

And finally, the *labor force participation rate*—the share of the eligible population that choose to be in the labor force—came to 65.9%.

$$\frac{146.8}{222.8} = 65.9\%$$

Is it always wrong to mix data from the Household and Establishment Surveys? No, not at all. In fact, Chapter 3 deals specifically with the BLS's own quite legitimate apples-to-apples comparison between the data on nonfarm payroll employment tracked in each of these surveys. And in a later chapter, I combine the rise in employment from the Establishment Survey with the decline in the unemployment rate from the Household Survey to help shed light on the tightening situation in the job market. But Krugman's attempt to mix the data from these surveys yielded statistical gibberish.

In the press release that accompanied the April 2004, employment report—which Krugman cited in that column—there is a heading that reads: "Industry Payroll Employment: (Establishment Survey Data)." Under that heading, the first sentence begins as follows, "Total nonfarm payroll employment increased by 288,000 in April to 130.9 million."[17]

By rounding the April tally to 130.9 million, the BLS let it be known that the 288,000 increase is overly precise. But sticklers for such false accuracy could readily find in the tables provided that the job count in April was indeed 288,000 higher than the job count in March, down to the nearest thousand:[18]

	Total Nonfarm Payroll Employment
April 2004	130,902
March 2004	− 130,614
Difference	288

Note: Numbers are in thousands.
Source: Bureau of Labor Statistics.

DOING THE MATH

You are now ready for Krugman's full explanation of the "math" he did— or at least as ready as anyone familiar with the data would be. You are about to read the two paragraphs in the May 25, 2004, column that lead up to that surprise reference to the 140,000, followed by the paragraph itself. So far, he'd only quoted Establishment Data—for which, remember, the April increase had been 288,000 jobs, to a total of 130.9 million. Contrasting recent performance with "the Clinton years," he wrote:

> And a mere return to Clinton-era job growth isn't enough: after all those years of poor job performance, we need extra-rapid growth to make up for lost time.
>
> Here's one way to look at it. The job forecast in the 2002 Economic Report of the President assumed that by 2004 the economy would have fully recovered from the 2001 recession. That recovery, according to the official projection, would lead to average payroll employment of *138 million* this year—7 *million* more than the actual number. So we have a gap of 7 *million* jobs to make up.
>
> And employment is chasing a moving target: it must rise by about *140,000 a month* just to keep up with a *growing population.* In April, the economy *added 288,000 jobs.* If you *do the math,*

you discover that President Bush needs about *four years of job growth at last month's rate* to reach what his own economists consider *full employment.*[19]

The question is, once we "do the math," how do we get "four years"?

The confusion over this "math" not only stems from the surprise Household Survey reference to "140,000 a month . . . to keep up with a growing population." It's further compounded by the sudden use of the term "full employment," which is also a Household Survey concept. Look it up in the glossary of Paul Samuelson's well-regarded economics text, *Economics,* and you'll find that it refers to "that level of employment at which no (or minimal) involuntary *unemployment* exists."[20]

We can bend over backward to try to confirm Krugman's claim that "all the numbers" came from the Establishment Survey with the following strategy. We'll ignore the reference to "full employment" and treat that 140,000 as a throwaway figure irrelevant to his findings. But we can only do that if we can get Krugman's "four years" by just using the Establishment Data cited in his column.

We can't. When we "do the math," we can only work with the math we're given. The BLS press release (quoted earlier) that stated "Total nonfarm payroll employment increased by 288,000 in April to 130.9 million" also made it clear that a 288,000 increase means just that—no more, but no less. So "four years of job growth at last month's rate" of 288,000 means 288,000 gets added every month. Accordingly, for 130.9 million to rise to that "official projection" of 138 million would require a 7.1 million increase, or slightly more than Krugman said. But at 288,000 a month, it would take 24.7 months, or a little over two years.

In fact, when I asked the most data-savvy economist I know—Jason Benderly of the Vail, Colorado-based Benderly Economics—to interpret that third paragraph, he took it for granted that *all* the data referred to the Household Survey, even including the 280,000 jobs that had been added. Try reading it again in this light:

Employment is chasing a moving target: it must rise by about *140,000 a month* just to keep up with a *growing population.* In April, the economy *added 288,000 jobs.* If you *do the math,* you discover that President Bush needs about *four years of job growth at last month's rate* to reach what his own economists consider *full employment.*

What else could he be citing but the Household Survey data if reaching "full employment" required employment to rise by 140,000 a month "to keep up with a growing population"?

It took Benderly about 10 seconds to do this math. "The unemployment rate," he reported, "would be close to zero." Here's why.

Remember we said that with a labor force increase of 140,000, if employment rose by 160,000, the unemployed would fall by 20,000. Based on the same labor force increase of 140,000, with employment gains of 288,000, unemployment will decline by 148,000. And over the stipulated four years, or 48 months, the cumulative decline will run 7.1 million.

But how many unemployed were there to begin with? Remember we said that in April 2004, there were 8.2 million. Based on this math, there would be 7.1 million fewer by April 2008, leaving 1.1 million. The unemployment rate would be 0.7%, by far the lowest ever recorded. No economist would expect that kind of "full employment," not even in his wildest fantasies. But if full employment is defined as reaching an unemployment rate of 4%, then given these figures, full employment could have been achieved in 15 months (see the Box).

What if It Was All Household Data?

We said that if all these figures came from the household data, the result would be just as absurd. Here's the math in more detail.

The labor force rises by 140,000 per month, or 6.7 million over 48 months. The employed rise by 288,000 per month, or 13.8 million over 48 months.

	Labor Force	Employed
April 2004	146.8	138.6
	+ 6.7	+ 13.8
April 2008	153.5	152.4

Note: Numbers are in millions.

Notice how much the gap between the employed and the labor force has shrunk, leaving very few unemployed?

In each case, the labor force minus the employed equals the unemployed:

	Labor Force	−	Employed	=	Unemployed
April 2004	146.8	−	138.6	=	8.2
April 2008	153.5	−	152.4	=	1.1

Note: Numbers are in millions.

With the unemployed at 1.1 million, the unemployment rate has shrunk to an unheard-of 0.7%.

But if "full employment" is defined as an unemployment rate of 4%, then given these same numbers, it would take only 15 months to reach full employment.

The labor force rises by 140,000 per month, or 2.1 million over 15 months. The employed rise by 288,000 per month, or 4.3 million over 15 months.

	Labor Force	Employed
April 2004	146.8	138.6
	+ 2.1	+ 4.3
July 2005	148.9	142.9

Note: Numbers are in millions.

Subtracting the employed from the labor force, we get 6 million unemployed:

$$148.9 - 142.9 = 6.0$$

Dividing the unemployed by the labor force, we get an unemployment rate of 4.0%.

$$\frac{6.0}{148.9} = 4.0\%$$

Since neither set of consistent numbers yields Krugman's result, how could he get it? Only by doing exactly what Okrent charged: "blending, without explanation, numbers from the Household Survey and the Establishment Survey." If you subtract 140,000 per month from 288,000 per month, you get 148,000 or 7.1 million in four years. That 7.1 million plus the April 2004 payroll count of 130.9 million equals 138 million.

This method of figuring does not, to steal a phrase, even make good nonsense. As mentioned, that 288,000 gain in nonfarm payroll employment must be taken as is. To subtract 140,000 from it is to mix "apples" with "oranges," just as Okrent charged. But it is consistent with Krugman's figures. To reach what he called the "official projection" of "138 million" meant "a gap of 7 million jobs to make up," which did take four years.

DELONG'S CONFUSION

U.C. Berkeley economics professor Brad DeLong posted parts of the Okrent-Krugman controversy on his web site, adding the following remark about the "140,000 a month":

> Note: To my—certain—knowledge, that number appears in *neither* the household nor the establishment survey: it's an estimate of the current trend growth rate of payroll employment driven by rising population.[21]

This unfortunate statement is worth quoting—and dissecting—only because it comes from a credentialed economist who claims to be "certain" of his "knowledge."

For starters, if "neither" survey was the source of the number, what was? DeLong doesn't say. Instead, he offers up a definition, calling it "an estimate of the current . . . growth . . . of payroll employment driven by rising population."[22] If these words read, "an estimate of the current . . . growth . . . of [the labor force] driven by rising population," he would have been much closer to Krugman's text. But in any case, he had effectively admitted that it either comes from both the Household and Establishment Surveys, or more sensibly, from the Household Survey alone.

For where do the figures on "rising *population*" come from if not the Household Survey—which is formally called the "Current *Population* Survey" and is conducted for the BLS by the Bureau of the Census? Nor is this just any population, but the *population eligible for employment according to the Household Survey definition.*[23] In 2005, for example, the civilian noninstitutional population 16 and over was estimated at 292.4 million, against a total U.S. population of 297.6 million.[24] The number of folks from that rising population that will seek employment depends on another Household Survey figure—the labor force participation rate. And the 140,000 estimate comes from plausible figures for both the increase in population and the labor force participation rate.

Also, when DeLong said "payroll employment" (and not the labor force) is "driven by a rising population" he raised two puzzling questions. First, why would he make it just "payroll employment"—which normally refers to the nonfarm, wage-and-salary jobs tracked by the Establishment Survey—and not all forms of employment tracked by the Household Survey, including self-employment? Second, and far more seriously, why would he assume that *only* employment is "driven by" population growth, as though people who enter the labor force in search of work automatically avoid *unemployment*?

When Krugman observed that "employment *must* rise by about 140,000 a month just to keep up with a growing population,"[25] it could not have meant that employment inevitably keeps up—still less, is "driven by"—a growing population. Krugman was, after all, hardly taking an optimistic view of the job outlook.

A year later, when the controversy erupted, Krugman wrote: "Now Mr. Okrent claims that he was only referring to my assertion that the economy *needs* to add 140,000 payroll jobs per month, which for some reason he thinks comes from the household survey. (It doesn't.)"[26]

Ignoring the same odd reference to "*payroll* jobs," we can ask why "the economy *needs* to add 140,000 . . . jobs per month." Again, it "needs" to do so to avoid an increase in unemployment because (to paraphrase DeLong) 140,000 is the "estimate of the current trend growth rate of" *the labor force* "driven by rising population."

Finally, did Okrent "for some reason" think this "comes from the Household Survey"? (It does.)

Bush League
Economics

"T he last jobs numbers to be reported before the Presidential election
are in," began the October 11, 2004, editorial in the *Wall Street
Journal,* "and predictably John Kerry is spinning them as 'disappointing.' Well, if this is a disappointment, most people would probably like to
have four more years of it."[1]

The *Journal* editors were about to take on a tough case. In fact, even
though "most people" could plausibly want "four more years" of job
gains at the previous year's rate, few could wish for an extended repeat of
the full three years and nine months since Bush took office.

To make matters worse, the *Journal* editors were arguing that Kerry
could interpret the results as "disappointing" only by citing the Establishment Survey data. But the source they kept pointing to—the
Household Survey—actually provided a quicker refutation of their
shaky argument.

Recall the "iron law" of labor force math explained in Chapter 2.
The labor force consists of the employed and the unemployed. So if the
increase in the labor force is not matched by an increase in employment,

there will be a rise in unemployment. Accordingly, before high marks can be given to any period of job growth, the first question to ask is whether the job growth was at least enough to cover the growth of the labor force. If the unemployment rate rose, we can be sure it was not enough. In fact, despite relatively slow growth of the labor force—putting less pressure on the growth of jobs—the unemployment rate rose fairly steadily through most of Bush's first term: from 4.2% in first quarter 2001 to highs above 6% by third quarter 2003. When the *Journal* editorial appeared, the unemployment rate had fallen back to 5.4%. But that was hardly enough to off-set the dismal performance of the earlier period.[2]

To place most of the blame for the earlier period on the Bush administration made no more sense than to give it most of the credit for the marked improvement since then. Hopefully no one would want the job market to be influenced so decisively by whoever occupies the White House, the *Wall Street Journal* editors least of all. But the pressures and passions of partisan politics can apparently make econospinners of us all.

Compare, on the other side of the divide, Paul Krugman's sensible remark in more serene days (August 16, 2000): "Business cycles have very little to do with the administration that happens to be in office,"[3] with his feisty posture a few years later (August 10, 2004): "Many apologists . . . claim that presidents don't control the economy. But that's not what the administration said when selling its tax policies,"[4] or with this extended metaphor several months earlier (October 24, 2003): "[Bush administration] officials are trying to convince the public," Krugman declared, "that if, after several years of dismal performance, *they can achieve one year of job creation* at a rate below the average rate *Bill Clinton achieved over eight years,* this will constitute a great economic victory."[5]

Nearly a year later, in fact, the *Journal* editors were trying to convince us that the entire period of job growth on Bush's watch had been victorious enough to be worth repeating.

In this chapter, we deepen our understanding of the difference between the Household and Establishment Surveys by focusing solely on measuring jobs, the one area that is supposed to be the Establishment Survey's specialty. When that *Journal* editorial appeared, nonfarm payroll employment tracked by the Establishment Survey was still below the level of first quarter 2001, when Bush first took office. Bush had become, in the words of the *New York Times,* "the first president since Herbert Hoover in 1932 to go into an election with a net decline in jobs over a single term."[6] The pro-Bush media responded with several rejoinders, all of them variations on the same theme: The Establishment Survey is not all that it's cracked up to be; the jobs data in the Household Survey sheds light that has heretofore been underappreciated.

Was any of it true? Once you stripped away the myths and distortions, very little remained. Even if the Household version of the story were given maximum weight, job growth since Bush took office was still below par. But the controversy did make one long-lasting contribution. As we'll see, it helped inspire the Bureau of Labor Statistics (BLS) to launch an apples-to-apples comparison between employment data in the Household and Establishment Surveys.

We'll take the various bouts of econospinning in turn, culminating in the *Wall Street Journal* editorial, while delving more deeply into the Establishment and Household Surveys.

SELF-EMPLOYMENT MYTHS

As mentioned, the Establishment Survey is restricted to nonfarm wage-and-salary ("payroll") employment, while the Household Survey covers all kinds, including agricultural employment and self-employment. So the pro-Bush media mined the Household Data for positive trends the Establishment Data had missed. It turned out that agricultural work—which also includes "forestry, fishing, and hunting"—had been relatively flat over recent years (2.2 million in 2005 versus 2.3 million in 2001).[7] The category that did show some signs of life was the self-employed.

Anyone interested in this job count should first be aware of the BLS's definition of *self-employment*. It not only affects the Household Data but the Establishment Data as well. To be counted in the self-employment category, your business has to be unincorporated. The wording of the Household Survey questionnaire is specific on this point. Respondents who say they spent the recent period employed are asked, "Were you employed by government, by a private company, a nonprofit organization, or were you self-employed?" Those who name any of the first three are classified as wage-and-salary workers. Those who answer "self-employed" are then asked, "Is this business incorporated?" Respondents who answer "yes" are *also* categorized as wage-and-salary workers. Only the "no" respondents are counted as self-employed.[8]

The rationale, of course, is that people who work in an incorporated business are on salary with that corporation, and whatever ownership interest they may have in the company is incidental. The Establishment Survey deals with the self-employed in much the same way. Its survey questionnaire specifically states that the establishment's employee count should exclude "proprietors, owners, or partners of *unincorporated* firms," while "salaried officials of *corporations*" should be included.[9]

So *unincorporated* self-employment is the only category tracked by Household Survey that the Establishment Survey omits. And cynics might observe that this form of "self-employment" can often be a code word for unemployment. Those of us who've known certain "freelance writers" and "independent consultants" during hard times—or worse, been one of them ourselves—can't help agreeing. These same self-employed folks will drop the pretense as soon as they have an offer of a steady paycheck. That may help explain why there was no increase in self-employment during the jobs boom of the late 1990s. Even if we assume the entire increase since Bush took office was nothing but a tribute to the resurgence of the entrepreneurial spirit, its contribution to the overall picture was too small to make a difference.

That point was unfortunately obscured in a December 1, 2003, *Wall Street Journal* story headlined, "Self-Employed Boost the Economic Recovery."

"For the past 18 months," wrote reporter Jon E. Hilsenrath, "more and more Americans have been going off to work on their own. Self-employment has increased by 400,000 in the past year alone, according to a monthly survey of American households conducted by the Labor Department."[10]

Hilsenrath had to have been referring to the Household Survey Data on nonagricultural self-employment. But why cite the "past year" or even "past 18 months" if the longer haul is your real focus? "If more people are striking out on their own," continued Hilsenrath, "then their job status in some cases wouldn't show up in the government's measure of employment levels at established businesses, which is *down 2.4 million since* the recession started in *March 2001.*"[11]

That last reference was to the Establishment Survey data. But if March 2001—two months after Bush took office—was to be the base-period, the increase in nonfarm self-employment was suddenly much diminished. Since March 2001, it was up only 100,000, from 9.4 million to 9.5 million. While a fairer comparison that smoothed out volatility would have put the increase since first *quarter* 2001 at 200,000, it was hardly worth mentioning against an Establishment Data decline in payroll employment of more than 2 million.

By using November 2001 as the base period, a March 2004 Heritage Foundation study managed to put the increase in self-employed at 650,000. But here, too, the choice of base period seemed rigged: Heritage economist Tim Kane made it clear that his topic was the "illusion of 2.2 million 'lost jobs' *since President George W. Bush took office.*"[12] By that point, the increase in self-employment since Bush took office was 300,000 at most.

But Kane also claimed there were hundreds of thousands of additional self-employed the Household Survey had somehow missed:

> The *problem* with CPS [i.e., Household Survey] counts of self-employment is that the workforce is evolving. It is *by no means clear* that *Americans understand self-employment* in the same sense that *the government does.* For example, a worker who leaves the IBM payroll and switches to a full-time consulting role with IBM is likely still to consider himself or herself an IBM employee. Certainly, the worker's family is likely to misidentify the worker's role as employed rather than self-employed. Likewise, partners at a limited liability company (LLC, a new company form) often consider themselves traditional employees.[13]

Kane did not seem to know that, since LLCs are corporate entities, the Household Survey counted them as wage-and-salary workers by definition. And if there really were many former employees turned independent consultants who mistakenly thought they were still employees, then they, too, would be counted as wage-and-salary workers. The idea that if these folks were not counted as self-employed, they somehow weren't being counted, was a delusion.

THE ESTABLISHMENT SURVEY REPUDIATED

An article in the September 26, 2003, *Wall Street Journal* went on the offensive against the Establishment Survey itself. The plunge in payroll employment tracked by the Establishment Survey was not to be believed, said Carnegie Mellon professor Allan H. Meltzer, because Establishment Survey methods led to a serious undercount at this stage in the business cycle: The Survey's employment count did not reflect the millions of new jobs created by start-up businesses. Because it was up-to-date on employment in start-up business, the Household Survey was more accurate.[14]

Dr. Samuel Johnson famously blamed one of his own errors on "ignorance . . . pure ignorance." By comparison, Professor Meltzer's ignorance was only about 98% pure—there were particles of truth in what he said—but Dr. Johnson hadn't made his ignorance the excuse for confusing an issue of national importance (just for getting a dictionary definition wrong).

Starting with the particles of truth in Meltzer's argument, he rightly observed that "in our dynamic economy, old firms die and new ones are born," while adding that the Establishment Survey "learns about deaths quickly, but it takes longer to learn about births."[15] True, the Establishment Survey, which goes out to a broad sample of business establishments, cannot reach new firms that did not exist when the sample was drawn. So jobs created by these firms will be missed, leading to a potential undercount in the employment tally. It is also true that the Household Survey has an advantage in this respect. Since the respondents are people, not establishments, they can tell the field interviewer they work for start-up businesses sooner than the start-up businesses can report it to the Establishment Survey interviewer.

If that's all you knew, your findings could be just as sweeping as Meltzer's. The Household Survey was more than just a valuable supplement to the Establishment Survey by tracking other kinds of employment. It even beat the Establishment Survey at its own game. The Household Survey data on nonfarm wage-and-salary workers were the only accurate source at this stage of the business cycle because it was the only source fully up-to-date on new jobs created by start-up businesses. Since the Establishment Survey version of this same data—which showed a plunge in nonfarm payroll employment—lagged far behind, it could now be ignored.

Assuming Meltzer was right, the next logical step would have been to put the Household Data under the spotlight to see what it was really saying. But Meltzer was wrong. The Establishment Survey data on nonfarm payroll employment are still more reliable than similar data from the Household Survey—based on key facts about the way the Establishment Survey really works that Meltzer ignored.

To begin with, in January of each year, the BLS compares the employment tally from the Establishment Survey as of the previous March with the tally from its Quarterly Census of Employment for the same month. The BLS then revises the Establishment Data accordingly in a process that is called *benchmarking*. The Quarterly Census amounts to a "universe count" of wage-and-salary jobs because it is based on the administrative records of state unemployment insurance programs. It does not miss jobs created by new firms because all firms must be registered with unemployment insurance as a matter of law.

So when you examine the Establishment Data on employment as a historical series, you are no longer looking at sample-based data, but at a fairly complete "universe count" of paycheck jobs from March to March of each year. (Cash jobs in the underground economy are another matter.) While the months in between are still approximations, they have been adjusted to reflect the March tallies. For example, if the March total for one year comes to 130 million and the March total for the following year to 132 million, the totals for the 11 months in between will have to track the 2 million increase, even if they meander on the way.

Since he apparently did not know about the benchmarking, Meltzer displayed a chart showing how Household Survey and Establishment Survey employment had "fluctuated over the past 40 years." He then proceeded to attribute the differences in trend to the influence of start-ups: "After every recession," he observed, "the difference increases because many new firms start. . . . The difference narrows in long expansions such as the 1960s and the 1990s as the Labor Department learns about the new firms."[16] But none of this could apply to the Establishment Survey's historical data because those data are no longer based on a sample. They are based on a universe count, which fully reflects start-ups.

But how timely would the Establishment Data have been when Meltzer's article appeared on September 26, 2003? Quite timely, in fact, if his own timing had not been odd. A week later, he would have had up-to-date figures through March 2003. While the benchmarking for the previous March is not done formally until the following January, the BLS routinely preannounces the planned revision in its employment report for September, due to be released October 3. Had Meltzer waited, he would have learned that a small *downward* revision to the March 2003 employment tally was forthcoming—which meant that, if anything, the BLS had been *overcorrecting* for missed start-ups.

Which brings us to the final key fact about the way the Establishment Survey really works. The BLS has long been aware of the problem of missed start-ups, probably since the Establishment Survey's inception. It has built-in methods of boosting the Establishment Survey's monthly tally to correct for the downward bias. The automatic mark-up used to be called the "bias adjustment," while known colloquially in the bond trade as the "plug factor"; today's more sophisticated methods have more technical names. Sometimes employment gets boosted by more than is necessary to compensate for the undercount—which the downward revision to March 2003 seemed to indicate.

Since Meltzer's article got reprinted by the American Enterprise Institute a few weeks later, he would have had ample opportunity to revise it in light of these facts. Based on the September 2003 jobs report, he would have had no good reason to question the Establishment Survey data.

The Establishment Survey's tally of payroll employment was still down about 2.5 million from first quarter 2001. Only by making heroic assumptions could you blame even a small part of the shortfall on missed job creation from new firm start-ups. The BLS had just reported that the March 2003 tally was due for a small downward revision against the universe count that fully reflected start-ups. So if the Establishment Survey was somehow understating gains in employment for this reason, it had to be blamed entirely on the six months' worth of data since March 2003—April 2003 through September 2003—which had not yet been benchmarked.

But now remember that the BLS automatically boosts its monthly estimates to try to compensate for the downward bias. How far off the mark, then, could the six months' worth of data really be? The biggest upward revision from the benchmarking had boosted monthly employment gains by an average of 40,000. Apply that figure to the past six months, and you've got an extra quarter-million jobs. Double it, and you've still added only a half-million jobs—still far short of the 2.5 million goal.

With a little informed reasoning, Professor Meltzer would have known enough to tell the American Enterprise Institute to cancel the reprint altogether.

An Apples-to-Apples Comparison between Household and Establishment Data

We have seen that if the Household Survey really was telling a more accurate version of the employment story, it could not have been due to the influence of start-ups. But how different was that version anyway? We have also seen that, when it came to the main category tracked by the Household Survey that the Establishment Survey ignores—unincorporated self-employment—the gains were relatively small. The only question that remained, then, was whether they diverged on the huge category of employment they both tracked: nonagricultural wage-and-salary jobs.

That question was answered with striking clarity by early April 2004, when the BLS first released its apples-to-apples comparison between the two surveys. The agency faced only one real obstacle to laying the data side by side. The Establishment Survey counts jobs, not people; the Household Survey counts employed people, not jobs.[17] One survey asks establishments to count the number of jobs on the payroll, and jobs with two different establishments can often be held by the same person. The other survey asks people to say whether they have a job, and some hold more than one.

But ever since the Household Survey was redesigned in 1994, it began tracking these "multiple job holders." So all the BLS had to do was boost the count of nonfarm wage-and-salary workers by the number of multiple job holders among these workers—and its apples-to-apples comparison between the Household and Establishment Data became a reality as shown in Figure 3.1.

First, notice the amazing convergence before we consider the divergence. From 1995 through 1997, the two were virtually the same number. By mid-2003 through 2004, the two were virtually the same number again. Far from disagreeing, the two versions were strikingly confirming each other. So if there was anything to disagree about, it was not over where they were, but over where they'd been. After tracking each other through 1997, the Establishment version began to rise faster than the Household version through the boom of the late-1990s. By first quarter 2001, the gap between the two had widened to more than 2 million. Then came the economic bust—and the Establishment version began to *fall* faster than the Household version, leading back to convergence by mid-2003.

Figure 3.1

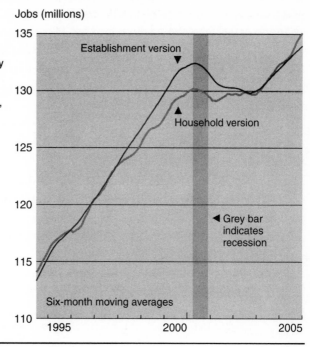

Overlapping Trends

The Household and Establishment Survey versions of nonfarm wage-and-salary, or "payroll" employment, were virtually the same number from 1995 through 1997, and from mid-2003 through mid-2005.

Jobs (millions)

Establishment version

Household version

◀ Grey bar indicates recession

Six-month moving averages

Source: Bureau of Labor Statistics.

But if where they'd been was to be the issue, the Establishment version's recent peak could not be denied. As we have explained, the historical data are benchmarked to a universe count from March to March of each year. The Household version, by contrast, is permanently based on a sample for which no universe count exists.

The BLS economists considered various explanations for the historical divergence between the two series, but rejected every one as inadequate.

PRE-ELECTION ECONOSPINNING

We turn now to the *Wall Street Journal* editorial of October 11, 2004, with which we began. Before we examine it in detail, let's go over the jobs data from both surveys that would have been known at the time.

Regarding the Establishment Survey job count, the BLS had just announced in its September 2004 report that its planned benchmark revision to the March 2004 tally would run a positive 236,000. Now assume (as in the earlier exercise we imagined for Meltzer), that the six months' worth of data since March 2004 had understated job gains by a cumulative half-million. Taken together, these figures raised the September 2004 tally by 700,000. But no matter what base period you used since Bush took office, the gains were insignificant.

Based on the BLS's apples-to-apples data, the Household and Establishment versions were still at virtually the same level. But as noted, the trends were very different, with the Household version showing a 2 million increase during Bush's tenure. Throw in the Household Survey's rise of about 400,000 in unincorporated self-employment over the same period, and you got a combined increase of 2.4 million. But that still came to an average monthly gain of less than 60,000 over this period—dismal by any standard.

So much for the facts about job gains. Another key fact was known by then. The BLS had done a study to determine if the universe count to which the Establishment Data were benchmarked still captured jobs created by start-ups ("business births") on a timely basis. Perhaps the study had been commissioned in response to Meltzer's article. In any case, since it found that "no lag has emerged in capturing" new firms, it concluded that "the universe count for benchmarking [Establishment Survey] estimates remains complete."[18]

Now try reading the following six paragraphs of the *Journal* editorial without interruption, as any *Journal* reader would have to. See if you can spot the myths we've already encountered, and the few we haven't. No words are omitted. Italicized phrases are meant to highlight false statements, innuendos, and confusions. I have numbered each paragraph to make it easier to refer back to them later:

(1) Friday's jobs data brought some new information that is *far more interesting* than the headline figure. The Bureau of Labor Statistics *finally confirmed* what we and others *believed all along,* that its "establishment survey" underestimated the number of jobs created from March 2003 to April 2004. The *government bean-counters* offered a *preliminary upward revision of 236,000,* and *some believe* the final correction early next year will be between *300,000* and *400,000.*

(2) It turns out that this economic expansion is different from those in the past, but not in the way that many thought. *New jobs* are being created as usual, but they are *different kinds of jobs.* The U.S. economy is undergoing a structural change as more people *become self-employed* or *form partnerships,* rather than working for large corporations.

(3) This transformation confounds the government's employment surveyors because they rely on the payroll data of about 400,000 existing companies. These figures are *then compared to the number* of workers who were *paying into state unemployment insurance programs* in the previous year. This provides a fairly accurate picture of employment *as long as* the same proportion of employed people continues to work for *existing companies.*

(4) But when a higher ratio of people make their livelihood as *independent consultants* to their old company, or as *power sellers on eBay,* they don't show up in the establishment survey that provides the most widely used employment figures—at least not until the *benchmark figures are revised long after the fact.*

(5) These jobs do, however, show up right away in the "household survey." The government collects this data from workers rather than companies, and while it is more volatile month-to-month due to the smaller sample size (60,000 households), *over the past three years* it consistently told us that *something unusual is happening.* If *you believe the payroll figures,* the U.S. still has to create *700,000 more new jobs* before it will return to the *peak pre-recession level of 2001.* But according to what individual Americans are saying, we've already surpassed *that level* by *two million jobs.*

(6) No doubt some employers are more cautious in adding new workers because of the rising cost of health care and other benefits. But this also helps explain why companies "contract out" *more jobs to entrepreneurs and the self-employed* that don't show up in the payroll survey.[19]

For starters, there are howlers that lead us to question if the editors are even vaguely familiar with the way these surveys work. For example, in Paragraph 3 they do not seem to realize they are referring to the benchmarking process when they speak of payroll employment "figures" being "compared to the number of workers . . . paying into . . .

unemployment insurance programs." When the editors add, "this provides a fairly accurate picture *as long as* the same proportion . . . continues to work for existing companies," you wonder if they really understand what they've just written. Even apart from the fact that the BLS had just taken pains to verify that all new companies are captured on a timely basis, wouldn't they imagine that most new companies are in the unemployment insurance data?

Similarly, they don't seem to realize the "preliminary upward revision of 236,000" in Paragraph 1 *is* the preannounced benchmark revision—the same revision that they later state only occurs "long after the fact" (Paragraph 4). If they did know, they'd realize the benchmarking does not come very "long after the fact" at all.

The confusions about the 236,000 are compounded by the questionable innuendos in Paragraph 1. If "government bean-counters" "finally confirmed" what "others believed all along," *Journal* readers would probably think some kind of unique admission had been forced out of those unimaginative statistical bureaucrats. Readers would hardly know that such preannouncements are a routine part of every September jobs report, that this upward revision to the annual tally was relatively small, and that the previous benchmarking had involved a downward revision.

As for the belief by "some" that "the final correction" would be a lot higher than 236,000 ("between 300,000 and 400,000"), the vagueness of the reference only confirms the editors' ignorance of the facts. The figure was based on the Quarterly Census of Employment, which was in turn based on unemployment insurance data that were already known. For this reason, no preannounced benchmark revision differs from its "final correction" by very much (nor did this one).

Even small verbal errors telegraph the editorial writers' lack of familiarity with statistical employment reports, as in "benchmark figures are revised" (Paragraph 4). When figures are benchmarked, they *are* revised. Then there are the various references in Paragraph 2 to "different kinds of jobs," "self-employed," and "partnerships"; in Paragraph 4 to "independent consultants" and to "power sellers on eBay"; and in Paragraph 6 to "entrepreneurs" and again to "the self-employed." As mentioned, if these people are incorporated, they are picked up in wage-and-salary employment by both the Household and Establishment Surveys. If they're unincorporated, they're picked up as self-employed by the Household Survey. Either way, they're picked up.

Finally, the references in Paragraph 5 to the Establishment Survey's "payroll figures" running 700,000 below "the peak pre-recession *level* of 2001" and to the Household Data having "already surpassed *that level* by two million" are false and misleading. *Journal* readers would think the Household Survey had surpassed by 2 million "the peak pre-recession level" of the Establishment Survey. But it hadn't. What the Household Survey had surpassed by 2 million was its own peak pre-recession level, which had been far lower than the peak on the Establishment Survey.

Readers would also think that the Household count was currently running far ahead of the Establishment count, when the two were actually running neck and neck.

But the *Wall Street Journal* editorial was right about one point not yet quoted: The September 2004 unemployment rate of 5.4% was "well below the long-term average."

More about that in the next few chapters.

Long-Term
Unemployment Myths

W hen Daniel Okrent faulted Paul Krugman for misusing the data on lengthening unemployment spells, the Princeton professor confessed to being "startled" that Okrent considered his "use of 20-year comparisons of long-term unemployment a case of numerical abuse," adding that "it is standard practice to use those data exactly the way I did."[1]

Krugman was right about the last part. He and others had been saying for quite a while that longer unemployment spells gave the lie to the lower unemployment rate. I quote from his *Times* column:[2]

> The measured unemployment rate of 5.9 percent isn't that high by historical standards, but there's something funny about that number. . . . Such measures as *the length of time it takes laid-off workers to get new jobs* continue to indicate the worst job market in 20 years.[3] (December 30, 2003)

The only seemingly favorable statistic is the unemployment rate, which has recently fallen to 5.6 percent, the same as in November 2001. But how is that possible, . . . ? . . . Other indicators continue to suggest a grim job picture. In the last three months, more than 40 percent of the unemployed have been out of work more than 15 weeks. That's the worst number since 1983, and a sign *that jobs remain very hard to find*.[4] (February 10, 2004)

But wait—hasn't the unemployment rate fallen since last summer? Yes, but . . . 40% of the unemployed have been out of work more than 15 weeks, a 20-year record.[5] (March 12, 2004)

The official unemployment rate is 5.2 percent—roughly equal to the average for the Clinton years. But . . . every other indicator shows a situation much less favorable to workers than that of the 1990's. . . . Average duration of unemployment—a rough indicator of *how long it takes for laid-off workers to find new jobs*—is much higher than it was in the 1990s.[6] (April 18, 2005)

The core proposition of this and the next three chapters is fairly simple: Contrary to what Krugman and others have been saying, the relatively low unemployment rates of the past few years have been roughly accurate, and rough accuracy is about all you can expect of such figures. In this chapter, we examine the data that points to longer spells of unemployment, and find it was partly a matter of a distorted trend (there was no "20-year record"), but mainly a reflection of demographics—something that any economics reporter should have picked up on. Once you give those factors their due, whatever remains of this story is hardly enough to shed doubt on the validity of the unemployment rate itself.

We'll also highlight a related irony. Just as longer unemployment spells shed false light on recent unemployment rates, the same data could falsely indict the "full-employment" economy of the late-1990s. The Bush-era critics passed up their chance in the Clinton era to show that jobs were "hard to find" by trotting out these figures—although it's just as well: They would have been no more correct in either case.

To help establish at the outset that I'm hardly endorsing long-term joblessness, here's an analogous argument to what follows about something far worse. Why do the figures show that more Americans keep dying of cancer? Mainly because cancer is a disease of the old, and old people make up the fastest rising share of the population. One reason there are more elderly is that people are surviving other diseases that would have killed them before they could live long enough to die of cancer. But we would hardly propose reversing that progress so that deaths from cancer could decrease.

And we certainly wouldn't call the data on deaths from cancer a "rough indicator" of "how hard" it is to survive cancer. What we can cite is death rates from cancer based on age (age-adjusted death rates), a figure that controls for this demographic trend.

Similarly, why has unemployment duration been on the increase? In this case, the main demographic is not age, but gender: The gap between men and women in the workplace has narrowed, as measured by such related trends as education, experience, steadiness of employment, and salary. Age has also been a factor: The (middle-) aging of the workforce has further boosted career-mindedness among both men and women—or what some labor economists have called an "increase in labor force attachment."

Career-minded workers tend to be unemployed less often than their more casual counterparts, but spend more time looking when they are jobless. So their duration of unemployment is greater. We would hardly propose making workers less career-minded to reduce jobless duration.

If methods of gathering cancer data had improved—causing a "break" in the trend—this analogy would be even better. There has been a break in the data on jobless spells.

THREE QUESTIONS

Say you notice a trend in the Household Survey data that interests you half as much as unemployment duration trends did Krugman. Before you start attributing it to any single cause, you ask at least three garden-variety questions that any economic journalist should know to ask:

1. Did the 1994 redesign of the Household Survey questionnaire distort the trend in any way, just as it did many other data series?
2. Was the trend influenced by the rise in the rate of women's labor force participation—and by the simultaneous narrowing of the work-related gender gap?
3. Was the trend influenced by the (middle-) aging of baby boomers?

In this case, the answer is yes to all three.

On the effects of the redesigned questionnaire, a March 1995 paper by BLS economists Anne Polivka and Stephen Miller revealed that pre-1994 data suffered from a downward bias.[7] Data on unemployment duration by age and sex—a few clicks away on the BLS web site—reveals that most of the increase in jobless spells has been driven by demographics. A quick search turns up a 2001 study that tries to make sense of these trends, co-authored by then-BLS Commissioner Katherine Abraham, called "Changes in Unemployment Duration and Labor-Force Attachment."[8]

The results anticipate the answer to a fourth question: *When did the trend begin—the time you first noticed it, or long before?*

In Krugman's version, the trend was a Bush-era phenomenon. But it was already making itself plain by the late-1990s, which is what prompted Abraham's study. When the unemployment rate first hit a 30-year low of 4.0% in first quarter 2000, Krugman called for slower economic growth to hike it back to "4.5 if we're lucky, to 5 if we aren't" to prevent the return of inflation.[9] So strong was he in this belief that those who disagreed were either "being deliberately dense" or were "just doing what comes naturally."

But before advocating a worsening of labor market conditions, Krugman might have been troubled by the rather glaring absence of a 30-year low in the duration of unemployment to match the 30-year low in the unemployment rate. According to the available data, the share of the unemployed who were jobless more than 15 weeks was not even at a 10-year low in first quarter 2000; and 10 years ago, in first quarter 1990, the unemployment rate had averaged more than 5%.

So if the George W. Bush-era Krugman could write, "Average duration of unemployment—a rough indicator of how hard it is for laid-off workers to find jobs—is much higher than it was in the 1990s," that 4% unemployment rate could have inspired his Clinton-era counterpart to observe, "Average duration of unemployment—a rough indicator of how hard it is for laid-off workers to find jobs—is higher than it was 10 years ago under President George H. W. Bush."

But not if he had asked and answered our three questions.

1. The Data Effects of the Redesigned Questionnaire

Our Clinton-era Krugman would have quickly found evidence that pre-1994 data suffered from a downward bias. In 1994, the BLS and Bureau of the Census introduced a radically redesigned version of the Household Survey questionnaire. Old questions had been dropped and new ones added; virtually every question that remained had been reworded; and the field interviewers' manual had been revised, especially the section on updating the length of unemployment spells. All this was bound to bring various breaks in the data, which the agencies fully expected. In fact, to help estimate these breaks, the new version was run in tandem with the old the year before it was introduced.

As part of their comprehensive attempt at interpreting and estimating the effect of these breaks, BLS economists Anne Polivka and Stephen Miller concluded that the old survey had underestimated the length of unemployment spells by a substantial margin. According to their calculations, the way to make pre-1994 data comparable was to readjust it upward by 16.9%.[10] Once you apply this adjustment factor (Figure 4.1), the historical pattern makes more sense. The year 2000 is now lower than it was in 1990, and at least no higher than it was in 1980. A more plausible pattern.

Figure 4.1

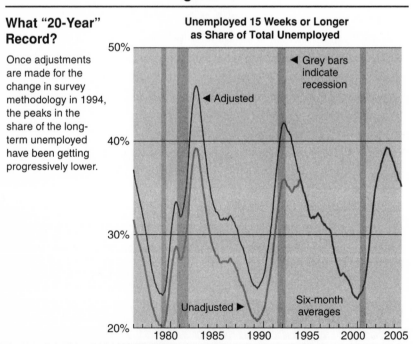

What "20-Year" Record?

Once adjustments are made for the change in survey methodology in 1994, the peaks in the share of the long-term unemployed have been getting progressively lower.

Unemployed 15 Weeks or Longer as Share of Total Unemployed

◄ Grey bars indicate recession

◄ Adjusted

Unadjusted ►

Six-month averages

Source: Bureau of Labor Statistics.

And as for the three post-recession highs, the adjusted data also make more sense. Since the unemployment rate peaked at progressively lower rates from 1982 to 1992 to 2003, you'd expect to find progressively lower peaks on the long-term unemployment share. The idea that this share could be higher in 2003 than in 1992 seemed anomalous. Since it was apparently due to downward bias in the pre-1994 data, Krugman's constant reference to a "20-year high" was simply wrong.

2. The Data Effects of Separating Men from Women

Separate the women from the men and the whole story changes completely.

Once pre-1994 data are upwardly adjusted for men, the historical pattern looks tame. The year 2000 is now noticeably lower than both 1990 and 1980; the progressively lower peaks (1982 to 1992 to 2003) are even more pronounced; and while the 2003 peak does show some upward drift since 1994, it's relatively unremarkable, as we see in Figure 4.2.

Figure 4.2

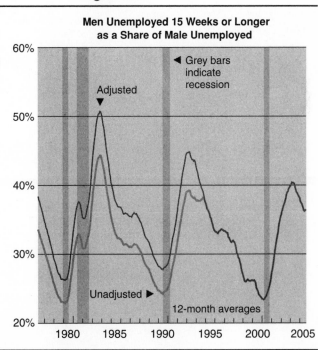

A Tale of Two Sexes: I

Once adjustments are made for the change in survey methodology in 1994, the peaks in the share of long-term unemployment among male workers have been trending down...

Men Unemployed 15 Weeks or Longer as a Share of Male Unemployed

◀ Grey bars indicate recession

Adjusted ▼

Unadjusted ▶

12-month averages

Source: Bureau of Labor Statistics.

While the pattern of unemployment duration for men looks tame, it is not so for women (Figure 4.3). Even after a huge upward adjustment to pre-1994 data, based on Polivka and Miller's figures (nearly twice as great as it was for men), the year 2000 is still above 1990. And instead of declining, the peaks of 1982, 1992, and 2003 almost replicate each other.

So we are now dealing with two trends, one for women and one for men. But run the two trends together (Figure 4.4), and the story is no longer about divergence, but convergence. Until the early-1990s, the share of unemployed women who were jobless more than 15 weeks was much lower than it was for men—but since the late-1990s, it's been almost as high. While the women's trend has the effect of reducing the overall level, it's been the main reason for the upward drift.

If we apply Krugman's mind-set to this pattern, we start to sound silly. If unemployment duration is nothing but a "rough indicator of how long it takes laid-off workers to find new jobs,"[11] then the pattern suggests that the preferential treatment women enjoyed over men was re-

Figure 4.3

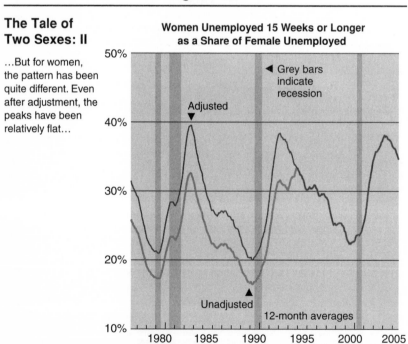

The Tale of Two Sexes: II

...But for women, the pattern has been quite different. Even after adjustment, the peaks have been relatively flat...

Women Unemployed 15 Weeks or Longer as a Share of Female Unemployed

◄ Grey bars indicate recession

Adjusted ▼

Unadjusted ▲

12-month averages

Source: Bureau of Labor Statistics.

Figure 4.4

The Tale of Two Sexes: III

...And if you put the trends for men and women together, you find that what has really been happening is that the gap between the two has narrowed.

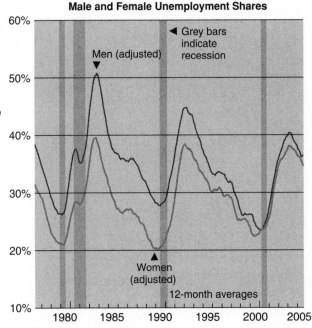

Male and Female Unemployment Shares

Men (adjusted)

◄ Grey bars indicate recession

Women (adjusted)

12-month averages

Source: Bureau of Labor Statistics.

cently lost. Since that's almost totally at odds with everything else we know about women's changing status in the workplace, there must be a more plausible reason for this trend.

That the trend was an ironic reflection of the progress women had made in the workplace is a story that had already been told in a 2001 study by then-BLS Commissioner Katherine Abraham and academic economist Robert Shimer. By the 1990s, women were pursuing careers as never before—displaying, as Abraham and Shimer put it, "stronger attachment to the labor force." And while career-minded workers are less likely to be unemployed than more casual workers, they spend more time looking when they are jobless. Their unemployment rates are lower, but those who are unemployed go through longer jobless spells.[12]

So the closing of the duration gap has a great deal to do with the narrowing of other kinds of gender gaps. "*Most of the secular increase in unemployment duration,*" write Abraham and Shimer, "*is accounted for by women, whose unemployment duration has risen to approach the male level.*"

Table 4.1   Percentage of Labor Force with a
                College Degree

	1 *Women*	2 *Men*	1–2 *Gap*
1990	24.5	28.0	−3.5
2000	30.1	31.2	−1.1
2004	32.6	32.3	+0.3

Source: Bureau of Labor Statistics.

But "at the same time," they add, "women's unemployment rate has *declined* toward the men's rate since 1980." This conflicting pattern "suggests the possibility that increases in women's *attachment to the labor force* may be responsible." Since workers with "a stronger attachment to the labor force . . . are unlikely to quit their jobs . . . , they can build up stable employment relations with a minimal incidence of unemployment [which] reduces their unemployment rate." But since they also "tend to stay unemployed when they lose a job, rather than dropping out of the labor force," this "may also raise [their] unemployment duration."[13]

Abraham and Shimer cite various measures that confirm the narrowing of the "labor-force-attachment gap" between men and women, including data on turnover and job tenure. Related kinds of gender gaps have continued to narrow since these economists first published their data. Education is one example as shown in Table 4.1. Earnings are another, as shown in Table 4.2.

Table 4.2   A Narrowing Earnings Gap

Year	Women's Earnings (as % of Men's)	Wives Earning More Than Their Husbands (%)
1990	71.9	19.2
2000	76.9	23.3
2004	80.4	25.2*

Source: Bureau of Labor Statistics.
*2003.

3. The Influence of Age on the Data

So the answer to our first two garden-variety type questions is yes, def-initely. First, pre-1994 data on unemployment duration do suffer from a downward bias. Second, and more important, the upward drift that re-mains after we correct for the bias has little to do with jobs being "hard to find." It's mainly about the greater career-mindedness of women.

In light of all that, the third garden-variety question about the in-fluence of age on the data is almost unnecessary. To whatever extent the upward drift in unemployment duration really is a sign that jobs are "hard to find." It's not enough to shed doubt on the unemployment rate itself.

But what *about* the middle-aging of the baby boomers? Has it still been a factor? Here, too, the answer is yes, definitely. Since workers over 40 tend to be more career-minded than workers under 40, they are less likely to be unemployed, but spend more time looking when they are jobless. Since the youngest baby boomer was born in 1964, by 2004 the youngest boomer had turned 40. The result was the middle-aging of the labor force. For example, with respect to the male labor force, 51.1% of male workers were 40 and older in 2004 to 2005, up from 43.4% in 1994 to 1995. So for male workers as a whole, you'd expect to see lower rates of unemployment accompanied by longer rates of unemployment duration from the age effect alone.

That's exactly what you do see. While the unemployment rate for all male workers was lower in 2004 to 2005 than in 1994 to 1995 (5.4% versus 5.9%), the share who were unemployed more than 15 weeks was higher (37.1% versus 35.8%).[14] But when you look at male workers *bro-ken down by age,* most of this effect gets washed away.[15]

I focus solely on men because their trend is not complicated by an in-crease over time in labor force attachment. I focus on the period since 1994 because that trend is not complicated by the downward bias in pre-1994 data. For each age group (Table 4.3), I matched 12-month periods when the unemployment rate was exactly the same. Notice that in most cases, the share who were unemployed more than 15 weeks in these matched periods was virtually the same.

Now, notice that while higher age groups tend to have lower unem-ployment rates, a greater share of their unemployed is jobless for more than 15 weeks. Since these higher age groups have gotten more numerous, the

Table 4.3 Unemployment Rates and Long-Term Unemployment Shares for Men

Age	12-Month Period	Unemployment Rate (%)	Share Unemployed 15 Weeks and More (%)
16–19	1/94–12/94	19.1	22.3
	6/04–5/05	19.1	24.2
20–24	3/94–2/95	9.7	29.1
	10/04–9/05	9.7	31.3
25–34	9/94–8/95	5.2	36.3
	5/04–4/05	5.2	37.1
35-44	1/94–12/94	4.5	44.1
	9/03–8/04	4.5	44.3
45–54	7/94–6/95	3.7	44.9
	5/04–4/05	3.7	45.5
55+	6/95–5/96	3.5	45.3
	10/04–9/05	3.5	45.4

Source: Bureau of Labor Statistics.

aging of the baby boomers has simultaneously lowered the overall unemployment rate while raising the overall length of unemployment spells.

THE LONG-TERM UNEMPLOYMENT RATE

There is a bottom line to all this, and it's called the long-term unemployment rate.

The BLS tracks six different unemployment rates on a monthly basis, of which the official unemployment rate is only one, and the long-term unemployment rate is another. While the official unemployment rate (U-3) is the share of the labor force that is jobless and recently looking, the long-term unemployment rate (U-1) is the share of the labor force that is jobless and recently looking for more than 15 weeks. So if U-3 reflects the average worker's risk of being jobless, U-1 reflects the same worker's risk of being jobless for an extended period. Both U-1 and U-3 tend to fluctuate in tandem with each other. But if the long-term rate looked unusually high compared to the official rate, it would indicate that the official rate had been downplaying the problem of joblessness in this crucial respect. As Figure 4.5 shows, no such unusual highs have been noticeable (see the Box on p. 56).

U–2, also shown in Figure 4.5, is another more focused indicator of the pain of joblessness: It tracks the number of unemployed who have lost their jobs, also calculated as a share of the labor force. Generally speaking, most of the unemployed are not "job losers." Most are usually new entrants or re-entrants into the labor force, while a small number quit their last jobs voluntarily. But if U–2 were unusually high compared to the official rate, it would also indicate that the official rate was downplaying the problem of joblessness.

For the most part, the *trend* in both U–1 and U–2 tells us little that U–3 doesn't already reveal.

Figure 4.5

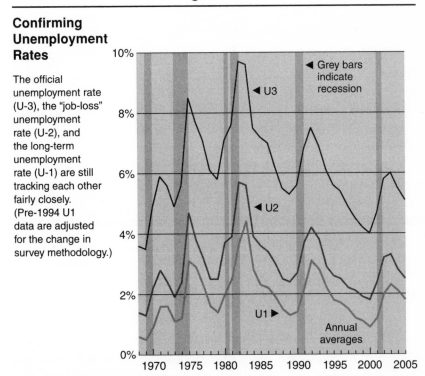

Confirming Unemployment Rates

The official unemployment rate (U-3), the "job-loss" unemployment rate (U-2), and the long-term unemployment rate (U-1) are still tracking each other fairly closely. (Pre-1994 U1 data are adjusted for the change in survey methodology.)

Source: Bureau of Labor Statistics.

The Long-Term Unemployment Rate as Bottom Line

We've said that workers with greater labor force attachment are more likely to spend time looking when they are unemployed, but less likely to be unemployed in the first place. One bottom line to all this is the long-term unemployment rate.

In the following table, columns 1 and 2 lift data directly from Table 4.3. The only difference is, the share unemployed 15 weeks or more has been turned into a decimal rather than a percentage, the better to multiply it by the unemployment rate to get the long-term unemployment rate.

Long-Term Unemployment Rate

Age	(1) Unemployment Rate (%)	(2) Share Unemployed 15 Weeks or More	(1) × (2) Long-Term Unemployment Rate (%)
25–34	5.2	0.371	1.9
45–54	3.7	0.455	1.7

Source: Bureau of Labor Statistics.

As the table shows, even though middle-aged men spend more time looking than younger men when they are unemployed (column 2), since they're less likely to be unemployed to begin with (column 1), their long-term unemployment rate is lower (last column).

KRUGMAN'S RESEARCH CREDO?

On the issue of the long-term unemployed, Daniel Okrent faulted Krugman for only one gaffe: ignoring the break in the data from the 1994 redesign of the survey questionnaire. To which Krugman responded:

After Mr. Okrent directed me to [the study by BLS economists] Polivka and Miller, I checked it out; it's a 1995 research paper which *suggested* that the 1994 redesign of the Current Population Survey questionnaire *might* have raised estimates of long-term unemployment. It wasn't an official statement that pre-1994 comparisons are improper, and the BLS didn't consider the questions raised in the paper serious enough to warrant a warning for consumers of its data. Like most such consumers, I don't go hunting for research papers suggesting possible problems with the numbers unless the BLS says there's reason to be concerned; otherwise, it would be impossible to *get my work done.*[16]

That last part might have been flagged by *Times* editor Gail Collins: No informed "consumer" of BLS data can afford to be so concerned about the niceties of what is and is not an "official statement."[17]

There are a lot of smart people at the BLS. But the first six letters of the word *bureaucracy* are also the agency's first name. So its inconsistent practices are hardly surprising. For example, BLS data on the self-employed show a sudden plunge from 1966 to 1967—the year the BLS decided to exclude the self-employed who work for their own corporation. Effective in 1967, only the *unincorporated* self-employed were covered by the data. But try finding a mention of this where the data appear on the BLS web site.[18]

Krugman wrote, "Like everyone else I rely on the advisory offered on the Bureau of Labor Statistics web site on comparability, which *warns about series that have changed definition* such [as] that for *discouraged workers.* There is no warning about using duration-of-unemployment data."[19]

And none about using the self-employment data, either. For other pitfalls of relying on the BLS to do the "warning" for us, take Krugman's mention of "discouraged workers." In fact, the warning on the web site simply takes the form of providing no data prior to 1994, when the redesigned questionnaire took effect. As we explain in the next chapter, Polivka and Miller found that the more restrictive definition of "discouragement" in the redesigned questionnaire brought a plunge in the discouraged worker count from 1993 to 1994.[20] But they also report a very similar definitional change imposed on involuntary part-timers—people who work part-time but would like full-time work—which also brought a downside break in the data.

On the BLS web site, data on the involuntary part-time go back to 1955, and from late 1993 to early 1994, it looks as though the numbers fell off a cliff, mainly because of the change in definition. But try finding any such "warning" on the web site. With Krugman's methods, the plunge would be reported as real. And if such "problems with the numbers" make it "impossible" for him to "get [his] work done," there is a solution: He should spend more time doing it.

The Case of the Phantom Dropouts

Remember baseball manager Casey Stengel's well-known dictum, "You could look it up"?

The labor force has continued to grow over the past few years, but not as fast as the eligible population age 16 and over. So the share of the population either working (employed) or actively looking for work (unemployed) has declined. Now, this decrease in the *labor force participation rate* could be due to an unusual increase in the *hidden unemployed*—people who do not show up in the official unemployment count for one reason or another, but who might be counted as unemployed according to a broader definition.

For answers, we can *look it up*. The Bureau of Labor Statistics (BLS) keeps detailed data on the hidden unemployed, all of it a few clicks away on the BLS web site.[1] After scrutinizing this data, you find that, whatever measure you use—from the narrowest to the broadest—slowed growth in the labor force could *not* have been due to unusual growth in the hidden unemployed.

Is that surprising? From a record high of 67.3% in first quarter 2000, the labor force participation rate hit a 17-year low of 65.8% by first quarter 2005. Since then, it's inched back up to 66%. The labor force increased, but those not in the labor force increased by more (see Table 5.1).

Had the participation rate stayed at record levels, the labor force in first quarter 2005 would have been nearly 3.4 million greater. But nonparticipants would still have numbered more than 70 million, and no one has ever suggested that most of them belong to the hidden unemployed. So why assume that hidden unemployment explains the 3.4 million?

Unless, you've looked it up.

Krugman certainly knew the BLS has been assiduously tracking the hidden unemployed for many years based on his comments about the "change" in the "definition" of "discouraged workers" in his reply to Okrent[2] that we discussed in Chapter 4. But the puzzle is why he did not look the data up himself. Instead, he and others took it as an article of faith that hidden unemployment explained the entire decline in the labor force participation rate. Krugman even assumed he knew what sort of hidden unemployed these nonparticipants were: They had left the labor force because they had "given up looking."[3] But, of course, slowed growth in the labor force could be due to an unusual number of people leaving, or an unusual number not entering in the first place. It's like being asked to explain slowed growth in world population and instantly answering "more deaths," without even considering that "fewer births" might be the reason.

In any case, hidden unemployment does not have to consist exclusively of people who left the labor force. It can include those who never joined.

Table 5.1   Labor Force Participation Rate Peak versus Recent Low

	First Quarter	
	2000 Peak	2005 Low
Labor force	142.4	148.1
Not in labor force	69.2	76.9
Civilian population	211.6	225

Note: Numbers are in millions.
Source: Bureau of Labor Statistics.

The basic proposition of this chapter (and the next two) is the same as in Chapter 4: The relatively low unemployment rate of the past few years has been roughly accurate, which is all you can expect from any such measure. The myth of phantom dropouts had the same punch line as the myth of the long-term unemployed: The official unemployment was misleading because it minimized the problem of joblessness. But here the indictment was even more direct. If all these people hadn't "stopped looking," Krugman insisted, the official unemployment rate would be much higher.[4]

At times, the two stories were mutually supportive: "We don't know why *so many people have stopped looking for jobs,* but it probably has something to do with the fact *that jobs are so hard to find: 40% of the unemployed have been out of work more than 15 weeks, a 20-year record.*"[5] Other Krugman charges and references to the phantom dropouts included:

A 5.7 percent unemployment rate doesn't sound that bad, but an *unusually large number* of workers *have given up searching for jobs.*[6] (September 20, 2002)

The measured unemployment rate isn't all that high, but that's *largely* because *many* people have given up looking for work.[7] (August 15, 2003)

The measured unemployment rate . . . isn't that high by historical standards, but there is something funny about that number. An *unusually large number* of people *have given up looking for work,* so they are no longer counted as unemployed.[8] (December 30, 2003)

But wait—hasn't the unemployment rate fallen. . . ? Yes, but that's *entirely the result of people dropping out of the labor force.*[9] (March 12, 2004)

Measured unemployment isn't bad by historical standards. . . . But unemployment statistics only count those who are *actively* looking for jobs.[10] (April 18, 2005)

According to Krugman, the number of people who are no longer "actively looking" came to about 3 million, which we can infer from the way he recomputed the unemployment rate:[11]

If [so many people] . . . hadn't dropped out, the official unemployment rate would be an eye-popping 7.4%, not a politically spinnable 5.6%.[12] (March 12, 2004)

The labor force participation rate—the fraction of the population either working or actively looking for work—has fallen sharply under Mr. Bush; if it had stayed at its January 2001 level, the official unemployment rate would be 7.4%.[13]

To get such an "eye-popping" unemployment rate, you follow this procedure:

1. Assume the labor force participation rate in 2004 is the same as it was in January 2001.
2. Calculate a hypothetical labor force by applying that January 2001 percentage to the eligible population in 2004.
3. Compare that hypothetical labor force to the actual, smaller labor force, and you get a difference of about 3 million.
4. Assume the entire 3 million difference shows up as unemployed.

We'll have more to say about such numerical games in Chapter 6 (Participation Rate Follies). Meanwhile, let's note that increases in the labor force on that scale have happened in the past. If the past is any guide, most or even all of that 3 million increase would more likely show up as employed.

But not if you apply Krugman's circular logic. If 3 million folks left the labor force because they stopped looking, then the same 3 million would be unemployed if they had not stopped looking.

By following Casey Stengel's dictum (look it up), however, we find that Krugman's 3 million dropouts are the statistical equivalent of weapons of mass destruction. We also find no unusual increase in the hidden unemployed, whether they dropped out or had not joined in the first place.

MEASURES OF THE HIDDEN UNEMPLOYED

"The intent of asking about discouragement," explains the BLS, "is to measure individuals who have *given up looking*."[14]

In a July 1998 *Monthly Labor Review* article called, "Persons Outside the Labor Force Who Want a Job," former BLS economist Monica D. Castillo writes that the first "concepts and definitions to account for those persons outside the labor force who wanted a job"[15] were made part of the monthly Household Survey in January 1967. "These measures were introduced," she writes:

> [out of the] recognized . . . need to collect more information . . . on so-called "discouraged workers"—that is, persons outside the labor force who were not currently looking for a job because they believed their job search would be in vain. Some analysts referred to such persons as the *"hidden unemployed."*[16]

But while the redesign kept the old criteria for "discouragement," it added two new ones that had a devastating effect on the data.

To qualify as a discouraged worker in the pre-1994 version, jobless respondents who said no to having looked for work over the past month (and therefore didn't qualify as "unemployed") must have (1) said yes to currently wanting a job, "full or part-time," and (2) given a "job-market related reason" for not having looked over the past month. Acceptable reasons for discouragement included "lacks schooling or training," "employer thinks too young or old," or simply, "could not find work" or "thinks no work available."[17]

To qualify as discouraged in the redesign, respondents also had to answer yes to these two questions: "Did you look for work at any time during the last 12 months?" and, "Last week, could you have started a job if one had been offered?"[18]

The questions seemed reasonable enough. Yet, according to BLS economists Polivka and Miller in their study of the 1994 redesign, fully half of those who previously qualified as discouraged could not answer yes to both questions.[19]

But at the same time, the BLS also created a new category of hidden unemployed. Most of those who answered yes to both questions gave reasons other than discouragement for not having looked for work over the past month. Sometimes the reasons were practical, such as child-care responsibilities, transportation problems, or school attendance. These people were added to the discouraged to make up a new category called *marginally attached*.

Finally, what about the respondents who said yes to wanting a job, but could not answer yes to both questions introduced by the redesign?

The BLS has classified them as simply, "persons who currently want a job."

In 2000, the discouraged ran 0.3 million and the marginally attached (which included the discouraged) was 1.2 million. By adding to the marginally attached another 3.2 million people who either hadn't looked for work over the past year, weren't available to start work right away, or both—but currently wanted a job nonetheless—the agency got a tally of 4.4 million persons who currently want a job.[20] (For that latter category, BLS economist and quipster Steven Hipple's version of the pertinent questions in the Household Survey read: "Did you dream about a job? And if you dreamt about one, did you dream about starting one someday?")

I cite 2000 data on discouraged workers for the same reason I cited 2000 data on long-term unemployment. Krugman celebrated that year as the very zenith of the "full employment" economy, when the unemployment rate reached a "30-year low" of 4.0%. But if you add back in the 4.4 million persons not in the labor force who currently wanted a job—or even just the 1.2 million marginally attached, you could get an unemployment rate that was eye-poppingly large.

In this case, another garden-variety question comes up: *Compared to when?* Most of what's meaningful about time-series data—data measured over time—depends on how a set of figures compares with its own past. (That's why, whenever some media representative calls me about his client's latest statistical concoction, I don't have to bother evaluating it; even if it's well designed, it won't be usable for another 10 years.) As we'll see, the BLS tracks such hidden unemployment rates on a monthly basis.

But for the moment, let's give Krugman's 3 million its best shot at being verified.

Discouraged workers as a category apply most directly to Krugman's workers who had "given up looking." As mentioned, a September 1993 article about the redesign in the *Monthly Labor Review* stated, "The intent of asking about discouragement is to measure individuals who have *given up looking.*" These are the people who offer a "job-market related reason" for why they haven't looked for work over the past month.[21]

And Krugman wrote, "There are *millions* of Americans who would be *looking for jobs* if more jobs were available."[22]

The marginally attached as a category casts a broader net, surely including people who were never in the labor force to begin with, or who might have participated sporadically, in the manner of high school and college students. As for the broadest classification—persons who currently want a job—one might expect it to include virtually everyone who, in BLS economist Hipple's joking terms, ever dreamt about working.

So if Krugman is right that 3 million people "stopped looking" during Bush's first four years in office, you'd expect the tally for at least one of these categories to have risen by at least 3 million over the same period. Table 5.2 shows what actually happened.

Notice that the first two categories—discouraged and marginally attached—are too small even in absolute terms to accommodate Krugman's 3 million. Even the "want-a-job-now" number rose by only 500,000—not to mention that, by 2005, all three figures had declined.

You could try defending Krugman's 3 million despite these results. For example, you might try arguing that if 4.4 million nonparticipants said they wanted a job in 2000, other circumstances could have diminished their number to 1.9 million by 2004. The reason the figure ended up being 4.9 million instead (you'd further argue) was that their numbers were swelled by Krugman's 3 million. But you'd have to ask yourself, *"What* other circumstances could have made so many people lose interest in working?" (Yes, there is plenty of turnover; they're never the same people, but that needn't concern us here.)

Or you might object that some of Krugman's 3 million who stopped looking no longer wanted a job by 2004. But you'd have to ask yourself, "How many could that be?"

But wait. The BLS does track another category of hidden unemployed: involuntary part-timers. Since these people have jobs, they are part of the labor force. But since they would prefer full-time work, the BLS lists them as "persons at work part-time for economic reasons."[23]

Table 5.2 The Hidden Unemployed

	Discouraged	Marginally Attached	Want a Job Now
2000	0.3	1.2	4.4
2004	0.5	1.6	4.9
Increase	0.2	0.4	0.5

Note: Numbers are in millions.
Source: Bureau of Labor Statistics.

Their measured ranks fell by about a fifth when the 1994 redesign introduced a new question similar to one put to those who want a job. It reads, "Last week, could you have worked full-time if the hours had been offered?"[24] Given the remarkable sensitivity of the data to such seemingly obvious questions, I can't help wondering what the effect would have been had they also been asked if they'd actually looked for full-time work over the past year or so.

But the increase over time is all that matters. The data show their numbers rose by 1.4 million from 2000 to 2004 (4.5 million versus 3.1 million). However, since other BLS data show that part-timers work an average of half-time, the real impact on hidden unemployment is about half that number, or 0.7 million.

When added to the increase in persons who want a job, we get 1.2 million (0.5 million + 0.7million), still far short of our 3-million goal. The part-time employed were not the people Krugman had in mind anyway. And before we ask, *Compared to when?* we must also ask, *Relative to what?*

HIDDEN UNEMPLOYMENT RATES

In this case, the number of unemployed is relative to the labor force.

Since population keeps growing over time, the labor force keeps growing. So we scale the number of unemployed against the labor force. Otherwise, we could prove that unemployment is a worse problem today than in the early days of the Great Depression.

That's where the BLS's hidden unemployment *rates* come in. I've said that the BLS tracks six different measures of unemployment, of which the official unemployment rate (U–3) is only one. The others serve as watchdogs on the official rate, ready to cry foul if any of them go off the charts. As mentioned, U–1 and U–2 target subsets of the unemployed (the long-term jobless and job losers, respectively) that feel special pain.

U–4 through U–6 are broader measures meant to reflect the hidden unemployed: U–4 adds the discouraged to the unemployment rate; U–5 adds the marginally attached. And U–6 adds both the marginally attached and the involuntary part-time. The BLS does not have a separate measure that adds the want-a-job total to the unemployment rate. Prob-

Table 5.3 Hidden Unemployment Rates

	U-3	U-4	U-5	U-6	U-7
2000	4.0	4.2	4.8	7.0	6.7

Note: Numbers are percentages.
Source: Bureau of Labor Statistics.

ably the agency believes this figure overstates hidden unemployment. But the lack is easily remedied; the BLS encourages us to "roll our own." So I've constructed U-7 accordingly (see the Box on pp. 68–70). Table 5.3 shows how U-3 through U-7 looked in 2000.

U-6 and U-7 may look eye-popping, but *compared to when?* It would be handy to check these unemployment rates against the last time the official unemployment rate (U-3) ran 4.0%. But that was 30 years ago, when these figures were not available.

However, if we track the proportionate declines in our watchdog unemployment rates, we find they all verify the official rate. For example, U-3 fell by a little over a third since 1994 (from 6.1 % to 4.0%), and all others fell by at least a third over the same period.

For 2004, we have the advantage of previous periods when the official unemployment rates were similar. In 2004, U-3 averaged 5.5%, virtually the same as in 1996, at 5.4%. If Krugman was correct that "Every other indicator [apart from the unemployment rate] shows a situation much less favorable to workers than that of the 1990s"[25] then one or another of these hidden unemployment rates should have reflected it.

Notice in Table 5.4 that they are all about the same, with the sole exception of U-7, which was running slightly lower in 2004 than in 1996. Had we compared 2004 with 1995, when the unemployment rate averaged 5.6%, 2004 would have looked even more favorable.

Table 5.4 Hidden Unemployment Rates Compared

	U-3	U-4	U-5	U-6	U-7
2004	5.5	5.8	6.5	9.6	8.5
1996	5.4	5.7	6.5	9.7	9.1

Note: Numbers are percentages.
Source: Bureau of Labor Statistics.

Hidden Unemployment Rate Math

The main thing to know when you're building broader measures of the unemployment rate is that whatever you add to the unemployed (numerator) should be added to the labor force (denominator). So if the official unemployment rate (U–3) is equal to the unemployed as a percentage of the labor force, the discouraged worker unemployment rate (U–4) is equal to the unemployed plus discouraged workers, as a percentage of the labor force plus discouraged workers.

The only exception to this rule is when calculating U–6, whose key component is involuntary part-timers. In that case, since involuntary part-timers are already in the labor force, they are only added to the numerator.

Based on data for calendar year 2005, if the unemployed came to 7,591 and the labor force to 149,320 (both numbers in thousands), the official unemployment rate (U–3) equaled:

$$\frac{7,591}{149,320}$$

or 5.08%, rounded to 5.1%.

If discouraged workers came to 436 (in thousands), the discouraged worker unemployment rate (U–4) equaled:

$$\frac{7,591+436}{149,320+436}$$

or

$$\frac{8,027}{149,756}$$

or 5.36%, rounded to 5.4%.

Similarly, if the marginally attached—a category that includes discouraged workers—came to 1,545 (in thousands), the marginally attached unemployment rate (U–5) equaled:

$$\frac{7,591 + 1,545}{149,320 + 1,545}$$

or

$$\frac{9,136}{150,865}$$

or 6.06%, rounded to 6.1%.

And if those who wanted a job—a category that includes the marginally attached—came to 4,985 (in thousands), then the "want-a-job" unemployment rate (U-7) equaled:

$$\frac{7,591 + 4,985}{149,320 + 4,985}$$

or

$$\frac{12,576}{154,305}$$

or 8.15%, rounded to 8.2%.

U-6 is equal to the unemployed plus the marginally attached plus the involuntary part-time, as a percentage of the labor force plus the marginally attached. If in 2005 the involuntary part-time came to 4,350 (in thousands), then U-6 equaled:

$$\frac{7,591 + 1,545 + 4,350}{149,320 + 1,545}$$

or

$$\frac{13,486}{150,865}$$

or 8.94%, rounded to 8.9%.

(continued)

Again, involuntary part-timers ("part-time for economic reasons") are not added to the labor force because they are already counted in the labor force.

Finally, since involuntary part-timers generally work half-time, the BLS used to calculate U-6 by adding back only one-half the involuntary part-time, which in this case would give you:

$$\frac{7,591+1,545+(0.5)4,350}{149,320+1,545}$$

or

$$\frac{7,591+1,545+2,175}{149,320+1,545}$$

or

$$\frac{11,311}{150,865}$$

or 7.5%.

Since these hidden unemployment rates are also called *Measures of Labor Underutilization*, adding back only half the involuntary part-time probably makes more sense. But since all these measures are only useful when compared against their own past measures, the method used makes little difference, so long as the method is consistent over time.

THE HIDDEN UNEMPLOYED AS A SHARE OF ALL NONPARTICIPANTS

Another kind of hidden unemployment rate would be to take these figures as a share of all nonparticipants. Since the discouraged, marginally attached, and want-a-job-now's are all not in the labor force, what share of the not-in-the-labor-force total does each account for? Again, you are

Table 5.5   Hidden Unemployment Shares

	Discouraged	Marginally Attached	Want a Job Now
2004	0.6	2.1	6.4
1996	0.6	2.3	8.2

Note: Share of non-in-labor-force total. Numbers are percentages.
Source: Bureau of Labor Statistics.

not in the labor force if you are part of the eligible population, but neither have a job nor have looked for work over the past month. Here, too, I compared 2004 with 1996 (see Table 5.5).

Notice that the hidden unemployed accounted for the same or a lower share of total nonparticipants in 2004. Note also that if 6.4% wanted a job in 2004, the vast majority 93.6%—did *not* want a job, either full- or part-time.

The miniscule share accounted for by the *discouraged* (0.6%) makes it all the more ironic that journalists keep using the term as though virtually all labor force nonparticipants are discouraged workers. The British newsweekly the *Economist* called the unemployment rate "currently misleading, because . . . *discouraged workers* have stopped looking for work."[26] All it meant was that the labor force had declined. Media Matters Action Network ran a heading that read, "Discouraged Workers Stop Looking for Jobs," to introduce a story about an increase in "the number of adults considered 'not in the labor force.' "[27]

Someone should tell the Media Matters folks that more than 99% of the "number of adults considered 'not in the labor force' " are considered *not* discouraged.

HIDDEN UNEMPLOYMENT RATES ARE USEFUL

One reason I think the discouraged and marginally attached are relatively small in number is that the definition of official unemployment is so liberal. A little-known fact is how low the bar is set for "actively looking."

All a respondent need do is say yes to having made a single effort to look for a job over the past month. And that single act can literally include sending in one resume, or filling in one application, or making a single phone call to a friend or relative about a job. Not everyone would agree that such minimal effort constitutes an "active" job search.

Since the criteria for qualifying among the hidden unemployed are even easier, it's not surprising that their attachment to the labor force is not as great as that of the officially unemployed.

That was BLS economist Monica Castillo's finding in her *Monthly Labor Review* article, "Persons Outside the Labor Force Who Want a Job." Castillo reports on follow-ups of all three want-a-job, not-in-the-labor-force categories, and then compares the results with similar follow-ups of the officially unemployed.

She found that only about 45% of the not-in-the-labor-force populations had joined the labor force the following year, while 75% of the unemployed were still in the labor force by then. Similarly, while 50% of the unemployed had found employment the following year, only about 30% of the not-in-the-labor-force categories had done so.[28]

But what if similar follow-ups had been done of the vast majority of nonparticipants who say no to wanting a job in the first place? As mentioned, those not in the labor force account for about a third of the eligible population; and of these, about 7% are in one or another of the want-a-job categories. If follow-ups had been done of the 93% remaining, the results probably would show that proportionately fewer had joined the labor force the following year. So if the labor force attachment of the hidden unemployed is less than that of the officially unemployed, it's still greater than that of other nonparticipants.

There is another reason to believe the hidden unemployed consist of meaningful categories: Whenever there is an increase in official joblessness, there is generally a proportionate increase in hidden joblessness. The question is whether hidden joblessness has increased disproportionately. And as we have seen, there is no evidence that it has.

The BLS has another term for the six measures of the unemployment rate it tracks monthly: *Alternative Measures of Labor Underutilization.*

More about that in the next chapter.

Participation Rate Follies

A *large number of people* have, for some reason, *dropped out* of the official labor force." Krugman wrote, adding: "Those with a downbeat view of the jobs picture argue that the low reported unemployment rate is a statistical illusion, that there are *millions of Americans* who would be looking for jobs if more jobs were available."[1]

As we saw in Chapter 5, those "millions of Americans" should have been found in one of the nets cast by the Bureau of Labor Statistics (BLS) to capture the hidden unemployed. In this case, since these folks "would be looking for jobs if more jobs were available," they would have shown up in the smallest net of all, "discouraged workers"—defined as those who are not looking for "a job-market related reason," including "no work available."[2]

But far from running in the "millions," the monthly total of discouraged workers ran less than a half-million. It also accounted for about the same share of the labor force (0.3%) the last time the unemployment rate had been at a similar level, in early-1997.[3] The same was true of the broader measures of hidden unemployment: the marginally attached, those who say they want a job, and the involuntary part-time. Any of these measures could have turned the "low unemployment rate" into a "statistical illusion" by showing an unusual pattern over the recent period. None obliged.

Besides, the official unemployment rate had been steadily inching down for the past two years. So if those phantom millions really existed, wouldn't they have spoiled the party by then? While Krugman seemed to have been harboring doubts, he had found a powerful ally: The Boston Federal Reserve had just published a study that vindicated his "downbeat view."

"Economists who argue there's something wrong with the unemployment numbers," Krugman continued, "are buzzing about a new study by Katherine Bradbury, an economist at the Federal Reserve Bank of Boston, which suggests that *millions of Americans* who *should be* in the labor force aren't."[4]

Called "Additional Slack in the Economy: The Poor Recovery in Labor Force Participation During this Business Cycle," Bradbury's study estimated labor force slack based on various scenarios for restoring participation rates to previous levels. "The current labor force shortfall ranges from 1.6 million to 5.1 million," she concluded, noting that "the addition of these hypothetical participants would raise the unemployment rate by *1 to 3-plus percentage points*."[5]

There's that eye-popping rate again.

Those "buzzing" over the new study apparently included the editors of the *Economist*, who made it the subject of an "Economics Focus," the British weekly's own highly respected series on economic theory and research.

The underlying argument of this chapter is the same as the past two: The low unemployment rate of the past few years has been approximately accurate. Here we focus more directly on the use and abuse of labor force participation rates to discredit the unemployment rate, while delving more deeply into BLS concepts discussed earlier. What does "discouragement" really mean? And why does the BLS call its six measures of the unemployment rate *Alternative Measures of Labor Underutilization?*[6]

We'll start with the *Economist*'s version of the story, before turning to the Boston Federal Reserve's study itself.

DISCOURAGED WORKER FALLACY

Unlike Krugman or Boston Federal Reserve economist Bradbury, the unnamed author (*Economist* articles have no byline) of this particular "Economics Focus" ("It's the Taking Part That Counts"—July 28, 2005) not only mentions "discouraged workers" but also specifically identifies them with declines in labor force participation. In the process, he or she gets the economic focus wrong:

> Looking for work is a full-time job. Many job-hunters quit, despairing of ever landing their quarry. Some of these *"discouraged workers,"* as economists call them, fall back on the earnings of a partner or spouse, some go back to school, and others discover disabilities that qualify them for government benefits. Since they have dropped out of the labour force, they also drop out of the unemployment numbers.
>
> *They show up instead as declines in the "labour-force participation rate."*[7]

The author goes on to estimate the increase in "discouraged workers" at more than 2.7 million by using the same method Krugman used to estimate 3 million dropouts from the labor force (Chapter 5). If the participation rate had remained at its 2001 peak, the labor force would have been 2.7 million greater. So the increase in discouraged workers is put at 2.7 million, even though the BLS counted less than a half-million discouraged workers in all.

Now, the author could have disagreed with the BLS's definition and methods, but he or she should have explained why. More likely, he or she was simply unaware of a category the BLS had been tracking since 1967—and had revised substantially in 1994, with the redesign of the Household Survey questionnaire. Even on the author's own terms, it makes no more sense to assume that 2.7 million "job hunters quit" than it did for Krugman to assume there were 3 million dropouts. All the math can really tell us is that the increase in the labor force would have been 2.7 million greater had the participation rate stayed at its 2001 peak. Beyond that, it tells us nothing about whether an unusual number (1) chose to leave or not join or (2) for what reasons.

More to the point, only the BLS's definition of discouragement—
and of hidden unemployment generally—can address the question with
which the article begins: "Are 5.1 million Americans missing from the
unemployment figures?" By probing nonparticipants about various degrees of desire to *join* the labor force (regardless of prior experience), it
creates a pool of candidates who *might* be "missing from the unemployment figures." There might be plenty of nonparticipants who, according
to the *Economist*'s definition, have "fall[en] back on the earnings of
a . . . spouse" or "discover[ed] disabilities that qualify them for government benefits." But unless these same nonparticipants can at least say yes
to wanting a job, they are hardly candidates for joining the labor force. If
they can also say yes to having looked for a job over the past year and to
being ready to start one now—and if then add they haven't looked over
the past month for a "job-market related reason"—then they are even
more likely candidates, and are properly defined as "discouraged."

Consider a demographic group whose declining participation rate
probably would reflect "discouragement" as the *Economist* defines it—
men ages 25 to 54. In 2000, the labor force participation rate of these
"prime-age" males was 91.6%, down from 97.0% in 1960. If we do the
same math as previously shown, we find that if their participation rate
had not fallen from 1960 levels, the labor force in 2000 would have been
3.2 million greater. In 2000, jobs were considered so plentiful, no one
would have been writing learned articles on discouragement, the *Economist* included. The BLS, in fact, counted only a quarter-million discouraged workers that year, which already sounded high. But another 3.2
million would have been discouraged on the *Economist*'s own terms.

For decidedly downbeat reading, in fact, try a recent BLS study
called "What Do Male Nonworkers Do?" BLS economist Jay Stewart
writes:

> We know that male nonworkers are less likely to be married and
> are more likely to live alone or with relatives than are employed
> men; that they are more likely to receive government transfer
> payments than working men; that the amount of unearned in-
> come they receive increases with age; and that income from
> other household members accounted for 52 percent of income in
> households with a nonworking man, compared with 31 percent
> for the overall sample.[8]

Stewart finds that most of a nonworking man's day is spent in "leisure activities and personal care."

But the BLS economist does not call these nonworkers *discouraged* or part of the *hidden unemployed,* presumably because he knows what those categories require: at least some evidence of a desire to participate in the labor force.

"In past recoveries," the *Economist* observes, "all but the most *discouraged workers* had taken heart by now, tempted back into the labour force by rising jobs and wages. What is different this time around? Ms. Bradbury digs deeper among *the discouraged,* sifting their numbers by age and sex."

No, that's what Bradbury fails to do.

WHEN ECONOMIC SLACK HAS NO MEANING

By identifying declines in labor force participation with "slack in the economy," Bradbury makes a related error.

When we speak of "slack" in the use of plant and equipment, we take it for granted that these inanimate objects must participate in their own utilization. But you can't take such liberties with human labor. True, Bradbury never assumes that every member of the eligible population must participate. But her calculations of labor force "shortfalls" are based on the assumption that past decisions to participate are somehow binding on the population of 2005. These are not even the same people. But even if they were, since the decision to participate is voluntary, the same people are always entitled to change their minds.

So when Bradbury speaks of *slack,* the term has no meaning. She would have been on more solid ground had she used the BLS "Measures of Labor Underutilization" instead. There you can speak of labor being *underutilized* because the data are based on the expressed desire to participate, whether by the officially unemployed (U-3), discouraged workers (U-4), marginally attached (U-5), part-timers who want full-time work (U-6), or those who say they want a job (U-7).

But then, instead of being called "Additional Slack in the Economy," the title of her study would more aptly have been, "Little or No Additional Slack in the Economy."

When Bradbury's study appeared in July 2005, the official unemployment rate (U–3) ran 5.1% through second quarter 2005, having fallen steadily from mid-2003 quarter highs of 6.1%. U–4 through U–7 all showed similar declines over this period. For example, the discouraged worker unemployment rate, U–4, had fallen to 5.4% from 6.4%.[9]

Bradbury was mainly concerned about the effects on the slack of lower labor force participation since the 1990s. If the official unemployment rate (U–3) was somehow obscuring the problem, the way to find out would be to compare the other measures with a period in the 1990s when U–3 was at virtually the same level. One plausible choice would have been second quarter 1997 (see Table 6.1). In 2005, the official unemployment rate was only a tenth-of-a-percentage point higher. What about the other measures?

Notice, in Table 6.1, that only U–4 is higher than its 1997 level by as much as two-tenths (part of it due to rounding). Consider how high U–4 might have gone if you take Bradbury's math literally. The Household Survey counted 420,000 discouraged workers in second quarter 2005, up from 357,000 in second quarter 1997—an increase of 63,000. But if the second quarter 2005 labor force participation rate had not declined from its second quarter 1997 level, there would have been 2.3 million more labor force participants—a "shortfall" of 2.3 million. Had these 2.3 million swelled the ranks of discouraged workers, then U–4 would have been 6.8% in second quarter 2005, not 5.4%.

That would have been a clear sign that labor really was being seriously underutilized in ways the official unemployment rate obscured. And Bradbury's finding of "slack in the economy" would have been plausible.

Table 6.1 Alternative Measures of Labor Underutilization

Second Quarter	U-3	U-4	U-5	U-6	U-7
2005	5.1	5.4	6.0	9.0	8.4
1997	5.0	5.2	5.9	8.9	8.6

Note: Numbers are percentages.

Cyclical Determinism

Why did Bradbury define slack in this way? It was mainly because her analysis suffered from a form of cyclical determinism.

True, some trends may be so strongly influenced by expansions or contractions in output (cyclical forces) that you can venture statements about where they should be, or even predictions about where they are headed, assuming the relevant phase of the cycle lasts. But are labor force participation rates really among these trends? Cyclical forces do influence participation rates. As an expansion gathers steam, labor force participation will tend to increase, both because more people are drawn into the labor force by expanding job opportunities and because others already in the labor force might delay their original exit plans. As the economy contracts, the reverse tends to happen.

But structural changes have swamped cyclical trends before, and there was no telling whether they might do so again. We've mentioned the long-term decline in participation of prime-age men. The participation rate of 16- to 24-year-olds had more recently plummeted to lows not seen since the early-1970s—and when or whether it would rebound was anybody's guess.

The pattern for prime-age women is even more intriguing. After climbing steadily through every decade since the 1950s, their participation rate rose more slowly in the 1990s and then flattened in 1997. That was unprecedented. In the past, the uptrend had slowed or flattened during or just after recession. But it had never failed to soar in the middle of a boom. And 1997 was right in the middle of the greatest boom in the labor markets since the late-1960s.

For these prime-age women, the cyclical influence had been swamped by a structural change. Break the trend down to narrower age categories, and you find the backup tends to be concentrated among the younger women. So it's just possible that younger women are making different career decisions from those made by their older counterparts.

In any case, to try to predict where these and other trends are going is foolhardy. But Bradbury tried it anyway.

"To the extent that the explanations for this sub-normal participation rebound are *cyclical*," she wrote, "additional workers would be expected to join the labor force *in the coming weeks and months*." To clarify how many "additional workers" she meant, she added, "That is, the *substantial numbers* of potential workers who might still (re)enter the labor market can be seen as representing . . . *slack* that is not reflected in the unemployment rate."[10]

A glance at the historical record should have told her she was making a rather extravagant bet on the dominance of cyclical factors.

In the 1990s, the biggest increase in the overall labor force participation rate over a *12-month* period ran 0.5%. In the 1980s, the 12-month record was 0.8%, and that was in 1986, at the tail end of the baby boom.[11] Bradbury's figures show that she was in effect predicting a cyclical rebound of anywhere from 0.7 to 2.2 percentage points in a fraction of that time.

At least eight months after Bradbury's paper was released, the participation rate was absolutely flat[12]—an easy observation with the benefit of hindsight. But even at the time, it would have been just as easy to project plausible outcomes like the one that actually did happen.

Bradbury stipulated that it was all based on "the extent" to which "explanations for the sub-normal participation rebound are cyclical." But if she had seriously considered the possibility that "explanations for the sub-normal participation rebound" were structural in some way, then at least one of her various scenarios would have projected a flat pattern. None did.

There was one noncyclical trend, however, that both Bradbury and Krugman tended to accept as given. That was the increase in labor force participation by people over age 55, even through the cyclical downturn of 2001 and 2002. The one they challenged was the absence of cyclical rebound in the participation rate of people under age 55. To appreciate Krugman's penchant for having it both ways on such matters, consider how he sorted out these various trends. After summarizing the "upbeat view" ("that labor force participation has fallen for reasons that have nothing to do with job availability"), he observed:

> That's where Dr. Bradbury's study comes in. She shows that the upbeat view doesn't hold up in the face of a careful examination of the numbers. In fact, because older Americans, especially older women, are more likely to work than in the past, labor force participation *should have risen,* not fallen, over the past four years.[13]

Overall participation rates "should have risen" because the decline in participation by those under 55 shouldn't have happened. It shouldn't have happened because it defied the cyclical trend. Based on Bradbury's "careful examination of the numbers," *that* trend is destiny. Structural influences—on young people, for example, or on prime-age women— are not worth considering. But if "older Americans" defy the cyclical trend by becoming "more likely to work than in the past," *that* secular trend is also destiny—as though "careful analysis" had not already given way to wishful thinking.

A March 2006 study of the same topic—this one from economists with the Federal Reserve Board in Washington—took a very different view. "Participation rates for newer cohorts of adult women appear to have flattened out after more than three decades of steady rise," observed the authors, "while new cohorts of men continue to be less inclined to participate in the labor market than their predecessors." Also, "teenagers and young adults are remaining in school longer and are reducing their labor force attachment whether in or out of school."[14]

The net conclusion: "Most of the decline in the participation rate during and immediately following the 2001 recession was a response to business cycle developments." But as for "the continued decline in participation in subsequent years and the absence of a significant rebound in 2005, appears to reflect other, more structural factors."[15]

It does appear that way. But when it comes to predicting what people will do next, you never can tell.

ARE THERE 2.3 MILLION MORE UNEMPLOYED?

Finally, say there was a sudden jump in the labor force, just as Bradbury predicted. Would most of it really show up as an increase in the unemployed?

In a May 1999 study called "The High-Pressure U.S. Labor Market of the 1990s," labor economists Lawrence Katz and Alan Krueger asked if there were any special circumstances that led to the surprisingly low unemployment rate of 4.5% in 1998.[16] The aging of the labor force was the major one. They calculated that if the age composition of the labor force was the same as in the mid-1980s, the unemployment rate would have been 4.9% instead.

But what also interested them was the one million increase over the same period in the number of men behind bars. To estimate how much higher the unemployment rate would have been if these men were free, they begin by assuming that 600,000 of them would be participating in the labor force. They then estimated that 38% (about 230,000) would be unemployed, while the other 62% (about 370,000) would be employed.[17] Based on these figures, the overall unemployment rate would be nearly two-tenths of a percent higher.

But notice what Katz and Krueger did not assume: that the 600,000 increase in the labor force would result in 600,000 additional unemployed. The greater supply of labor does result in more unemployment. But for men who would otherwise be in prison, it also results in 370,000 jobs that wouldn't otherwise exist.

Bradbury, by contrast, assumed that even if law-abiding people entered the labor force in droves, the increase in the unemployed would be one for one.

If, instead of running 66.1%, the labor force participation rate were 67.1%—its record high from 1997 to 2000—the labor force would be greater by 2.3 million. How many would show up as employed? Just for starters, probably a greater share than Katz and Krueger's prisoners, and based on the historical record, probably close to all of them.

To figure the impact, say the increase happens over 12 months. Added to the normal yearly increase from population growth (about 1.6 million), the labor force would rise by 2.6%.

Such an increase is hardly unprecedented. In the 56 years since 1948, the labor force has risen by 2% to 3.3% 15 different times.[18] In 12 out of those 15 cases, the unemployment rate reacted by either staying about the same or actually declining. In the other three cases—1970, 1974, and 1975—the unemployment rate did rise, but in each of those years, the economy was already in recession or barely recovering.

So unless those circumstances apply this time around, there would be no reason to expect the unemployment rate to rise simply because the supply of labor has jumped.

However, younger workers (ages 16 to 24) might account for a disproportionate share of the influx, and they tend to suffer higher unemployment rates than average. So there might be some boost to the unemployment rate of the sort that concerned Katz and Krueger.

What Does the Employment-Population Ratio Tell Us?

I f you want a *single number* that tells *the story*," Krugman wrote, "it's the percentage of adults who have jobs."[1] The "story," of course, was the usual one about the weakening labor market ("jobs are still very scarce, with little relief in sight"). Taken as a "single number," however, the decline in the "percentage of adults who have jobs," or employment-population ratio (EPR), can only tell a misleading story.

As in this case.

This short chapter is the fourth to reinforce the argument: The relatively low unemployment rate of the past few years has been approximately right, notwithstanding the fantasies of Krugman and others about long-term unemployment, labor force "dropouts," and labor force participation rates already covered in previous chapters. This chapter deals with the often-mentioned EPR, which turns out to be old wine in new bottles. The EPR is essentially a mixture of two other Household Survey indicators that have already told their stories:

the labor force participation rate and the unemployment rate itself. A decline in the EPR might be due to a decline in the participation rate, rise in the unemployment rate, or to a combination of both. The EPR can tell no coherent story until we've distinguished one effect from the other.

To understand the dynamics involved, think of a diagram consisting of two concentric circles: The labor force participation rate is the inner circle (civilian labor force) within the larger outer circle (civilian population). Within that civilian labor force circle, there is one very large slice, consisting of "employment," and one relatively small, consisting of "unemployment."

Membership in the civilian population circle is largely involuntary, since all you have to be is over 16, and not be a part of the armed forces, prison, or some other confining institution. Membership in the civilian labor force circle is more discretionary. Those who choose labor force participation will prefer "employment," and likely get it, although "unemployment" is not completely avoidable.

Now, increase the population circle in relation to the labor force circle, while holding both the labor force and the employment/unemployment shares constant. The labor force as a share of the population—the labor force participation rate—declines. Both the number of unemployed and the unemployed as a share of the labor force—the unemployment rate—stay the same. The number of employed also stays the same. But because the population has increased, the EPR—the employed, instead of the labor force, as a share of the population—also declines.

Now, hold both the population and labor force circles constant while shifting the balance within the labor force circle between employment and unemployment shares in favor of unemployment. The labor force participation rate stays the same. Both the number of unemployed and the unemployment rate increase. And because the number of employed has decreased, the EPR again declines (see the Box).

In both cases, the EPR fell. While the second case indicated a weakening labor market (a higher unemployment rate), the first (a lower labor force participation rate) was less clear. We'd have to inquire further. Does the actual decline in labor force participation over the past few years reflect worker discouragement? As we have seen, nothing in the Bureau of Labor Statistics's (BLS) comprehensive data suggests that it does.

The Labor Force Participation Rate, the Unemployment Rate, and the Employment-Population Ratio: An Example

In Scenario I, a fall in the EPR is accompanied by an unchanged unemployment rate. In Scenario II, the EPR falls by proportionately less, but is accompanied by a rising unemployment rate.

In Scenario I, the population and labor force circles begin at 30 and 20 with the employment and unemployment segments of the labor force at 19 and 1. In the second period, the population circle rises to 32, while all others remain the same:

Scenario I

	Period	
	First	*Second*
Civilian population	30	32
Civilian labor force	20	20
Employed	19	19
Unemployed	1	1

The unemployment rate remains flat, at 5% ($\frac{1}{20}$). But because the population rises, the EPR falls from 63.3% ($\frac{19}{30}$) to 59.4% ($\frac{19}{32}$).

In Scenario II, population and labor force circles remain the same, but unemployed rise from 1 to 2, while the employed fall from 19 to 18:

Scenario II

	Period	
	First	*Second*
Civilian population	30	30
Civilian labor force	20	20
Employed	19	18
Unemployed	1	2

Source: Bureau of Labor Statistics.

(continued)

The unemployment rate doubles from 5% ($\frac{1}{20}$) to 10% ($\frac{2}{20}$). The EPR falls from 63.3% ($\frac{19}{30}$) to 60.0% ($\frac{18}{30}$).

Which scenario is preferable for workers? Clearly, it would be the first, with the unchanged unemployment rate. But if the EPR is the single number that told you the story, your answer would have to be the second scenario, since the EPR fell by proportionately less:

Change in
Employment-Population Ratio

	Period	
	First	Second
Scenario I	63.3	59.4
Scenario II	63.3	60.0

Note: Numbers are percentages.

And the point is, those are the only ways the EPR can fall: the participation rate falls, the unemployment rate rises, or a combination of each. A decline in the EPR can tell us nothing about changing labor market conditions that isn't already conveyed by the labor force participation rate or unemployment rate. When you cite the EPR as "a single number that tells the story," you run the risk of getting the story wrong.

GENERAL GLUT'S MISLEADING TREND

For a good object lesson in calculating EPR, we need look no further than U.C. Berkeley economist Brad DeLong's web site.

To show that "the job market really is weak," DeLong quotes a blogger called "General Glut," on the EPR of men ages 25 to 64. DeLong's source observes:

I suggest focusing in on a group of workers who over time are almost always in need of work, who *do not wax and wane with* educational or *retirement opportunities,* nor with social trends to-ward greater workforce participation rates: men age 25–64.[2]

General Glut's need to assure us on that last point is well-taken. We said that a falling EPR could be caused by a decline in the labor force participation rate. But if the participation rate of men in this age group has indeed been steady as a rock, then in this exceptional case, we can rule out that possibility. The only possibility remaining is that a declining EPR would be due to a rising unemployment rate. Then the EPR really would be the only number we need to tell the story.

Except, General Glut had not done his homework. Notwithstanding his assurances that these men are "almost always in need of work,"[3] their participation rate has been falling every decade since the 1950s. If General Glut sincerely believes that participation by 55- to 64-year-old males does not "wax and wane with . . . retirement opportunities,"[4] then he has missed that part of the story also. The biggest decline in participation has come from men in this age group, almost surely because of the increase over time in their "retirement opportunities." More recently, their participation rate has inched back up, probably because their retirement opportunities have somewhat diminished. But by 2004, the participation rate of 55- to 64-year-old men still ran only 68.7%, compared to 90.5% for men ages 25 to 54.[5]

So when DeLong's source cited a declining EPR among men in this age group as proof of recent labor market weakness, we were given cause for suspicion. It turns out that our suspicions were justified. With the same logic, we could draw conclusions from the EPR data that General Glut himself would probably disavow. For example, we could show that the labor market was noticeably weaker in 2000 than in 1979, when the EPR was noticeably lower: 87.1% versus 85.2%, respectively.[6] But how could that be, when the unemployment rate for men in this age group was lower in 2000 than it was in 1979? The answer, of course, is that the labor force participation rate was also lower. Table 7.1 shows the details for those two years.

General Glut might prefer to have been a job market participant in 1979, but any practical person would choose the later period. Based

Table 7.1 Men 25 to 64

	1979 (%)	2000 (%)
Employment-population ratio	87.1	85.2
Labor force participation rate	90.1	87.7
Unemployment rate	3.3	2.8

Source: Bureau of Labor Statistics.

on the lower unemployment rate, he would incur a lower risk of being jobless. Since Krugman has himself rhapsodized about the "full employment" economy over this period, he could hardly disagree.

IS THE LABOR MARKET NO LONGER DETERIORATING?

Which brings us to DeLong and Krugman.

A few days after quoting General Glut at such length, DeLong himself cited a more recent chart of the EPR, which showed a flattening trend over the past year. DeLong interpreted this to mean that "At least the labor market situation is no longer deteriorating," adding, "That's good news."[7]

Krugman's own mention of the "single number that tells the story,"[8] appearing just 10 days earlier (July 6, 2004) said much the same thing. "By last August [2003]," he observed, the EPR "had fallen to 62.2 percent," and "in June [2004], the number was 62.3," which meant "the job situation . . . may have improved slightly," although "jobs are still very scarce, with little relief in sight."[9]

Table 7.2 10-Month Scorecard

	August 2003 (%)	June 2004 (%)
Employment-population ratio	62.2	62.3
Labor force participation rate	66.2	66.0
Unemployment rate	6.1	5.6

Source: Bureau of Labor Statistics.

Table 7.3   Hidden Unemployment Rates

	August 2003 (%)	June 2004 (%)
U-3	6.1	5.6
U-4	6.4	5.9
U-5	7.1	6.5
U-6	10.2	9.6

Source: Bureau of Labor Statistics.

But as we've seen, no judgments could be formed about the job situation based on the EPR alone, whether good or bad. In fact, the relevant data showed that "no longer deteriorating" and "improved slightly" could only be the judgments of those who really did put stock in the EPR as a stand-alone number. Based on the decline in the unemployment rate (see Table 7.2), the employment situation had improved noticeably.

But what about the falloff in the participation rate? All the hidden unemployment rates the BLS routinely tracks—discouraged worker (U-4), marginally attached (U-5), and involuntary part-time (U-6)—showed roughly proportionate declines (see Table 7.3).

We might also want to know how these alternative measures stood up against the year 1995, when the official unemployment rate was also 5.6% (see Table 7.4).

June 2004 was either the same or better. But if there was any reason to doubt the improvement in the labor market, these numbers could have

Table 7.4   Then versus Now

	1995 (%)	June 2004 (%)
U-3	5.6	5.6
U-4	5.9	5.9
U-5	6.7	6.5
U-6	10.1	9.6

Source: Bureau of Labor Statistics.

Table 7.5   What Could Have Been

	1995 (%)	June 2004 (%)
U–3	5.6	5.6
U–4	5.9	6.5

revealed it. For example, the decline in the labor force participation rate could have swelled the ranks of the discouraged by another million at least. U–4 would have been 6.5% and the comparison with 1995 would put the discouraged worker unemployment rate way out of sync (see Table 7.5).

The widening gap between U–4 and U–3 would have been strong evidence that something was amiss. It didn't happen that way: As Table 7.4 shows, U–4 was also 5.9% in June 2004.

May Average Hourly Earnings Rest in Peace

Testifying before the House Financial Services Committee on May 17, 2006, then-U.S. Treasury Secretary John Snow observed that "average hourly earnings are picking up. We learned from this month's jobs report that average hourly earnings have risen 3.8% over the past 12 months—their largest increase in nearly five years."[1] Representative Barney Frank then asked Snow whether average hourly earnings had been keeping up with inflation. After much embarrassing confusion on the Treasury Secretary's part, he was finally forced to concede that inflation had been rising faster. Snow's real mistake, however, was to cite average hourly earnings in the first place.

So far in this book, I have mainly extolled the employment measures developed over the years by the Bureau of Labor Statistics (BLS). I now indict several key BLS measures—very popular with the markets, the media, and the politicians—that have long since outlived their usefulness: the employee hours and earnings data that are released monthly with the

BLS jobs report as part of the Establishment Survey. Of the five broad indicators, three are calculated as averages per worker: average hourly earnings, weekly earnings, and weekly hours. The other two are totals for all workers: aggregate earnings and aggregate hours.

The employee hours and earnings data have two seductive attributes: *timeliness*—since the figures are part of each employment report, data released the first week of each month apply to the month just ended—and apparent *relevance*—the figures purport to speak for the wage-earners of this country. Virtually any news item on the monthly jobs report that runs to any length will cite the hours and earnings figures, and often quote some economist on their significance. Just before each employment report gets released, Wall Street analysts are asked to forecast four key numbers in the report: (1) the change in the unemployment rate, (2) the change in nonfarm payroll employment, (3) the change in average hourly earnings, and (4) the change in average weekly hours. The Index of Leading Economic Indicators includes average weekly hours in the manufacturing sector as one of those indicators.

But to appreciate the problems with the data, we may look no further than the issuing agency itself.

BUREAU OF LABOR STATISTICS PLANS TO DISCONTINUE EMPLOYEE HOURS AND EARNINGS DATA

As we'll see, by February 1994, the BLS announced it was planning to discontinue the entire series. It began posting a statement that repudiated the integrity of the data in such blunt terms that it was difficult to see why the BLS didn't immediately pull the plug on the whole series. One reason, I believe, is that the BLS does not want to provoke a firestorm of protest from the bond market, whose traders and analysts seem hooked on the figures. As matters stand, the BLS plans to discontinue the old series by "early 2010,"[2] by which point it will be able to provide users with a more broadly conceived hours and earnings series that should be more accurate.

Meanwhile, the figures the BLS does provide are unreliable, with the added irony that the earnings component usually understates wage gains. Sometimes releasing bad data can be worse than releasing none at all. And as it happens, the BLS already releases very high-quality data on wages and salaries that the Bureau of Economic Analysis (part of the Commerce Department) combines with comprehensive data on employee benefits. The figures are neither as timely nor as relevant as the other data, since they apply to all employees, not just wage earners. But they are light-years better when it comes to accuracy.

With the help of these figures, we can address another key question that will make up the core proposition of Chapter 9 (What Labor Is Paid): Has the comparatively low unemployment rate of the past few years been generally consistent with the trend in wages? Based on the very best data available, worker pay and the unemployment rate have been tracking each other remarkably well.

"NONSUPERVISORY"?

The hours and earnings data come from the same Establishment Survey that asks establishments to enter "the total number of persons on the payroll." The survey also asks private sector respondents a series of questions about the hours worked and pay received by the establishment's employees. However, based on a long-standing tradition it is now in the process of changing, the BLS does not ask for data on "the total number of persons on the payroll," but for the subtotal defined as "*production workers.*"

Or, more precisely, as the BLS explains in every employment report that accompanies the figures on hours and earnings, "Data relate to *production workers* in natural resources and mining and manufacturing, *construction workers* in construction, and *nonsupervisory workers* in the service-providing industries."[3]

In fact, "service-providing industries" now account for more than four-fifths of nonfarm private sector employment, up from about three-fifths in the mid-1960s. So when Krugman, for example, referred to "an average nonsupervisory worker's wage"[4] in an August 2005 column, or to "average hourly earnings of nonsupervisory workers"[5] in a column in December 2005, he quite appropriately used the term that stood for the vast majority of these workers.

Like so many others who cite such data, however, Krugman did not explain what *nonsupervisory* meant. No such luxury is afforded respondents at the service-providing establishments. Service-providing firms are asked to "enter the total number of employees who are nonsupervisory," which the "Instructions for Completing This Form" define as follows: " 'Nonsupervisory employees' includes every employee *except* those whose major responsibility is to supervise, plan, or direct the work of others" [italics in original].[6]

If two different people from the same establishment were asked that question, they might give widely different estimates. Those who do not "direct the work of others" can include lawyers, accountants, actuaries, scientists, and software engineers. But don't they "plan" the work of others, especially if they staff the company's planning department?

Even if an establishment can estimate its nonsupervisory workers, it isn't likely to keep separate records on the hours they work and the pay they receive—the two key questions respondents are next asked.

The definition of production or construction workers should be easier for manufacturing or construction firms to handle. In fact, the instructions that accompany these questionnaires do not define it, except to admonish that certain "working supervisors or group leaders who may be 'in charge' of some employees" would still be considered "production" (or "construction") workers, if their "supervisory functions are only incidental to their regular work."

The questionnaire also adds "individuals working in" such departments as "Accounting," "Advertising," or "Legal" cannot be considered "production workers." In a manufacturing or construction establishment, that sounds sensible enough. But what if that same establishment starts using outside firms to do its accounting, advertising, and legal work? When those service-providing establishments receive their survey questionnaire from the BLS, does it then spawn a completely new class of nonsupervisory workers?

Most solve the problem by not even bothering to fill out this part of the questionnaire. Of all the Establishment Survey questionnaires that are initially distributed, the full response rate is about 80%. But of that 80%, more than half leave the questions about nonsupervisory workers unanswered.[7]

Stuck with only partial results, but obliged to generate the hours and earnings data anyway, BLS statisticians resort to special methods. If users of the data knew how these methods work, they might use the data more reluctantly. For example, remember we said the Establishment Survey job tallies are eventually benchmarked to "universe counts" in the BLS's own Quarterly Census of Employment, drawn from the administrative records of unemployment insurance programs. That publication's full name is the *Quarterly Census of Employment and Wages,* since comprehensive wage and salary figures are also drawn from unemployment insurance data. But neither the employment nor wage data in the Quarterly Census are broken out for nonsupervisory workers, so no direct benchmarking is possible. But the hours and earnings data are still affected indirectly, with the ironic result that the benchmarking usually leads to revisions that are even greater (see the Box).

How Hours and Earnings Data Are Generated by the Establishment Survey

The following fictional example was inspired by BLS Supervisory Statistician and Branch Chief Kirk Mueller, who kindly reviewed it and wrote me that "the calculations are correct."

Hours and earnings data are supposed to apply to nonsupervisory and production workers in the private sector. Respondents are asked to estimate the number of these workers on the payroll, the number of hours they worked, and the total amount they were paid. But since the survey response rate is too low for the figures to be regarded as reliable, BLS statisticians use a roundabout method to generate these data.

To simplify, assume we have just two industries in the private sector (in practice, there are hundreds of industries and subindustries). For industry A and B, the BLS calculates three within-sample estimates based on the establishments that answered this part of the questionnaire. First, there is the share of the total that is accounted for by nonsupervisory or production workers, which we'll call the *nonsupervisory ratio*. And there are two averages: (1) average hours worked, calculated by dividing total hours worked by the number of nonsupervisory workers; and (2) average hourly earnings, calculated by dividing total pay by total hours worked.

Suppose the within-sample estimates look as follows:

Industry	Nonsupervisory Ratio	Average Hours Worked	Average Hourly Earnings ($)
A	0.7	30.0	15.00
B	0.8	25.0	20.00

(continued)

The key figure we need in each case is the total number of workers in each industry. For example, if it's 100,000 for industry A and 200,000 for industry B, then we can apply the nonsupervisory ratios and get an estimate for the number of nonsupervisory workers in each industry:

$$100,000 \times 0.7 = 70,000$$
$$200,000 \times 0.8 = 160,000$$

Once we have those figures, we can do all the other calculations. For example, we get aggregate hours (which is turned into an index) for this two-industry private sector by multiplying the number of nonsupervisory workers by the within-sample average hours worked for each industry:

$$30.0 \times 70,000 = 2.1 \text{ million}$$
$$25.0 \times 160,000 = 4.0 \text{ million}$$

Then we add the two together:

$$2.1 \text{ million} + 4.0 \text{ million} = 6.1 \text{ million hours}$$

We get *average weekly hours* for this two-industry private sector by dividing total hours by the total number of nonsupervisory workers:

$$\frac{6.1 \text{ million}}{230,000} = 26.5 \text{ hours}$$

We get aggregate earnings (which is turned into an index) by multiplying total hours by the within-sample average hourly earnings for each industry:

$$2.1 \text{ million} \times \$15.00 = \$31.5 \text{ million}$$
$$4.0 \text{ million} \times \$20.00 = \$80.0 \text{ million}$$

Then we add the two together:

$$\$31.5 \text{ million} + \$80 \text{ million} = \$111.5 \text{ million}$$

We get *average hourly earnings* by dividing aggregate earnings by aggregate hours:

$$\frac{\$111.5 \text{ million}}{6.1 \text{ million}} = \$18.28$$

Finally, we get *average weekly earnings* by multiplying average hourly earnings by average weekly hours:

$$\$18.28 \times 26.5 = \$484.42$$

How Benchmarking Causes Revisions

The earlier within-sample figures are never benchmarked because the *Quarterly Census of Employment and Wages* has no figures on nonsupervisory workers. But since the earlier calculations depend on the figures for total employment, the benchmarking of total employment can result in revisions that are even greater.

In the example, we said that industry A had 100,000 and industry B had 200,000 workers for a total of 300,000. And based on the within-sample ratios for each industry, nonsupervisory workers came to 230,000.

Now, say that when the figures are benchmarked, the total number of workers remains the same at 300,000. But industry A is revised up 20,000 to 120,000 and industry B revised down 20,000 to 180,000. These new values are then applied to the within-sample ratios:

$$120,000 \times 0.7 = 84,000$$
$$180,000 \times 0.8 = 144,000$$

Not only has the total number of nonsupervisory workers declined slightly (from 230,000 to 228,000), all the estimates for hours and earnings must be revised accordingly.

DOWNWARD BIAS IN THE DATA ON EARNINGS

As mentioned, the BLS's solution to the problem was officially announced in a press release first posted on its web site February 8, 2005. The entire "production and nonsupervisory workers hours and earnings series" would be discontinued, to be replaced with "data on the hours and regular earnings of *all* employees" (emphasis in original). On the reasons for the decision, the BLS remarks:

> The limited scope of the production and nonsupervisory worker series makes them of limited value in analyzing economic trends. *Just as important to this decision,* the production and nonsupervisory worker hours and payroll data have become increasingly difficult to collect, because *these categorizations are not meaningful to survey respondents.* Many survey respondents report that *it is not possible to tabulate their payroll records based on the production/nonsupervisory definitions.*[8]

If "survey respondents" don't find these "categorizations" to be "meaningful," how can we?

The BLS's devastating admission made me realize why the earnings data are probably understating the growth of wages. The service sector firms that still find such distinctions meaningful—that still think in terms of rigid hierarchies—would be less likely to push stock options and bonuses down to their lower-level employees. Those same firms would also be less likely to employ large numbers of people with professional degrees. So the establishments that are not responding to that part of the survey are disproportionately the better-paying firms. The lower-paying firms are speaking disproportionately for the whole. And this is not a static but a dynamic situation. Because the service sector continues to account for a growing share of total employment, the tendency for better-paying firms to be underrepresented in the data continues to worsen.

The percentage shares in Table 8.1 tend to confirm that suspicion. In any case, it's hard to believe the results can be entirely explained by widening inequality. I calculated total wages paid to nonsupervisory workers in private service-producing industries as reported by the Estab-

Table 8.1   Nonsupervisory Workers versus All
Workers—Service Providing Private Sector

	Share of	
	Payrolls	*Workforce*
1984–1985	63.3	84.0
1994–1995	61.7	83.9
2004–2005	54.9	83.4

Note: Numbers are percentages.
Sources: Bureau of Labor Statistics and Bureau of Economic
Analysis.

lishment Survey and then took these totals as a percentage of all wage and
salary data in the private service sector from the Quarterly Census
(which does not include benefits).

The results show, for example, that in 1984–1985, nonsupervisory workers in this sector received 63.3% of all wages and salaries
paid in this sector. By 2004/2005, however, their payroll share had
fallen to 54.9%, even though they accounted for nearly as great a share
of all employment in this sector.[9] Over the same period, service-
producing industries accounted for an ever-increasing share of all
employment in the private sector as a whole—a trend that is likely
to continue.

WORKER PAY AND THE UNEMPLOYMENT RATE

Has the trend in worker pay been reasonably consistent with the trend in
the unemployment rate? Representative Barney Frank and others have
been citing inflation-adjusted average hourly earnings to answer that
question and have responded in the negative. I've called that the wrong
data—and as we have seen, for more than one reason.

First, the numbers have effectively been repudiated by their own
source—the BLS.

Second, the same data could be used to prove that the first five years of the 1990s expansion were a snare and a delusion. (Krugman does not believe that—and neither do I.)

Third, the data probably suffer from a downward bias.

Finally, there is a very comprehensive data series for all labor compensation—wages, salaries, and benefits—that could be run against the unemployment rate, which deserves a chapter to itself.

Hourly Compensation and the Unemployment Rate

I f any chart in this book deserves to be hung and framed, it's Figure 9.1. If any correlation between two numerical series can demonstrate the power of measurement to shed laser-beam light on economic reality, this is the one. The brainchild of economist Jason Benderly, it tells the simple but compelling saga of price determination in that most vital of markets—the market for labor.

Figure 9.1 covers a half-century of the annual increases in labor compensation, from 1955 through 2005. To explain these fluctuations, Benderly uses a single measure of labor market tightness based on the unemployment rate. The findings can be summarized as follows: Contrary to what is commonly thought, *the rise in labor compensation over the past few years has been roughly consistent with comparable periods of labor market tightness over the past 50 years.*

Figure 9.1

A Half Century of Compensation Growth Explained

The Benderly Index of Labor Market Tightness, based on the unemployment rate for married males, has explained the growth of hourly compensation about as well over the past five years as it has over the past 50.

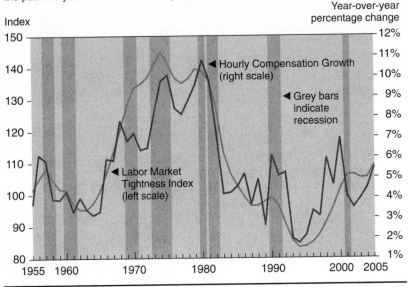

Source: Bureau of Labor Statistics.

We'll unravel the mysteries of the Benderly chart in this chapter; in Chapter 10, we'll make a related point about the connection between real compensation and productivity. First, let's look back on our story so far.

WHAT WE KNOW BY NOW

"It's not just employment-to-population ratios," wrote U.C. Berkeley economist Brad DeLong, "It's real wage growth. It's the relative amount of long-term unemployment. It's payroll employment. We have four of five indicators telling us that the state of the job market is not that good and only one—the unemployment rate—reading green."[1]

You should know by now that employment-population ratios (EPRs; Chapter 7) are really just a misleading combination of the labor force participation rate and the unemployment rate itself; that the Bureau of Labor Statistics (BLS) has already devised broader measures of unemployment to track undue declines in participation (Chapters 5 and 6);

and that these measures have been "reading" just as "green" as the unemployment rate.

You should also know by now that the "relative amount of long-term unemployment" had already been recognized as a creeping phenomenon of the 1990s (Chapter 4); and that, once you recognized it was mainly due to stronger attachment to the labor force (by women and by middle-aged baby boomers), whatever remained was reading neither red nor green.

As for "payroll employment," the *Wall Street Journal* editorial page could not wish away its poor long-term performance (Chapter 3). But by mid-2005, its disagreement with Household Survey employment concerned the past, not the present, since by then the two were tracking each other quite closely. So here, too, if the unemployment rate, which also comes from the Household Survey, was reading green, payroll employment could hardly be reading red.

Finally, "real wage growth" as measured by average hourly or weekly earnings is an unreliable indicator that probably understates compensation growth (Chapter 8). In this chapter, we turn to a far more accurate measure.

ALL COMPENSATION

In one mouthful: In Figure 9.1, we're looking at hourly compensation of all workers in the business sector, where compensation equals all wage-and-salary disbursements—including bonuses and exercised stock options—and all benefits, including pension contributions and healthcare.

If we can think of data as coming from a hierarchy of three different sources—an unrepresentative sample, a representative sample, and the sort of universe we associate with a census—then the superiority of this measure of hourly compensation data is overwhelming.

As I pointed out in Chapter 8, average hourly earnings come from an unrepresentative sample by the BLS's own admission. Or, at least, when the BLS admits that "many respondents" don't fill out that part of the Establishment Survey questionnaire because the concept of non-supervisory worker is not "meaningful" to them, the agency is warning us that its sample *could* suffer from major bias.[2] Once we consider the difference between firms that think of nonsupervisory as a meaningful concept and those that don't, we begin to appreciate why average hourly earnings and related measures tend to underestimate employee earnings. Firms that make a strict distinction between bosses and employees probably tend to pay those employees less than firms that have more trouble with such distinctions.

If we could break open the BLS's confidential books on which establishments answer that part of its questionnaire, we'd probably find, for example, that they do not include software firms that tend to distribute many stock options to their employees. This raises a further difficulty. Even if they did answer these questions, stock options probably would not be recorded because respondents are specifically instructed to omit all forms of irregular pay. Since the Establishment Survey also does not record conventional benefits such as pension contributions and healthcare, and since they are frequently given in lieu of regular pay, this introduces further potential for distortions in the Establishment Survey measures.

By including all forms of compensation, the data in Figure 9.1 avoids that pitfall. Just as important, the data originate from more than just a sample.

The wage-and-salary portion comes from the BLS's *Quarterly Census of Employment and Wages,* which is in turn drawn from the administrative records of the state unemployment insurance programs. These data are based on what amounts to a universe count. Also, their accuracy and completeness is not a matter of choice, but compelled by law. Companies must report, as a matter of law, all wage and salary disbursements because the premiums they pay into the program are based on those figures. And that covers all irregular payments to employees, including bonuses and exercised stock options.

One drawback to these figures is that we can make no distinctions between low-paid, well-paid, and superlatively paid workers. The other drawback is lack of timeliness. At any point, the last two quarters' worth of data are no more than educated guesses awaiting benchmark confirmation once the real data become available. Accordingly, Figure 9.1 goes through 2005, of which the first three quarters of wage-and-salary data have been benchmarked as of this writing—enough to get a fix on the Bush years.

The other compensation data—supplements and benefits generated by the Bureau of Economic Analysis—are also through 2005, although they are not as timely. For example, as of this writing, health benefits, the largest single component, are only benchmarked through 2003. But to pretend they aren't a part of employee compensation would be misleading. Their total share of private sector compensation is now more than 17%, nearly twice what it was in the 1960s.[3]

Start with the weakest part first: hours. Total compensation is divided by an estimate of total hours worked, the latter cobbled together from various flawed sources. One of those sources is the Establishment Survey's estimate of the hours worked by nonsupervisory employees, which we just pointed out the BLS itself practically disavows. Apart from that, an estimate must be made for hours worked by supervisory employees, which is keyed off information gleaned from the Household Survey.

Even if these sources weren't flawed, the inherent difficulty with this data is that much of it doesn't really exist. Bureau of Labor Statistics Assistant Commissioner Tom Nardone once illustrated the point by asking me, "How many hours did *you* work last week?" I didn't know. For millions of "knowledge workers," the fact that their work can follow them around 24 hours a day has led many to think total hours are being underestimated.[4] However, as one researcher in the BLS's productivity division also pointed out to me, the advent and ready availability of the Internet in offices across the land could mean that people are on balance working fewer hours than ever.

Where this nets out is anybody's guess. But we may treat total hours as, at best, a gross approximation, which the correlation seems to have survived.

On that score, the *r* squared is 0.76, which essentially means that 76% of the change in hourly compensation is explained by this indicator. Try adjusting the figures for inflation, and the correlation is nearly zero. Ultimately, of course, inflation-adjusted, or real, compensation is what really matters to those of who are on the receiving end of this income. Once you think about it, you realize that hourly compensation might by turn run faster or slower than the cost of living, but rarely track it directly.

Which isn't to say that prices have no influence at all. Benderly found that certain price measures (energy, industrial commodity, and non-oil import price) do influence compensation on a lagged basis. By including them as explanatory variables, you get an *r* squared that is a few points higher than 76%.

But the main explanatory variable is still Benderly's measure of labor market tightness. It's time we focused on it.

LABOR MARKET TIGHTNESS AND THE UNEMPLOYMENT RATE

Benderly has built an ingenious index of labor market tightness based on what economists used to call the nonaccelerating inflation rate of unemployment (NAIRU), but it isn't as intimidating as it sounds.

The NAIRU is supposed to be that rate of unemployment where the rate of increase in wages neither accelerates nor decelerates, but remains steady. (It could be called the "non*decelerating* inflation rate of unemployment," except the acronym doesn't work.) It's the Goldilocks unemployment rate—neither too hot nor too cold—where wage inflation does not change. The whole point about the NAIRU is that, above or below a certain level of unemployment, the percentage rate of increase in wages does not hold steady, but does tend to accelerate or decelerate.

When the unemployment rate is below the NAIRU, it doesn't have to drop further—although that, of course, would certainly help—for the *percentage increase in wages to keep rising.* Thus, for example, a 3.2% wage increase this year becomes a 3.6% next year and a 4.0% the year after that—and so on, without any limit, so long as the unemployment rate stays low enough. Again, it doesn't have to *go* any lower; it just has to stay low for this acceleration to persist.

But contrariwise, when the unemployment rate is above the NAIRU, it doesn't have to rise any further—although that, of course, would certainly hurt—for the *percentage increase in wages to keep slowing.* Thus, for example, a 3.2% wage increase this year becomes a 2.8% increase next year and a 2.2% the year after that—and so on, without any limit, so long as the unemployment rate stays high enough. Again, it doesn't have to *go* any higher; it just has to stay high for this deceleration to persist.

Notice, however, that we are still talking about a slowed rate of *increase* in hourly compensation. In principle, the deceleration could get to a point where compensation begins to decrease. But over the past 50 years, that possibility has not been put to the test. On a yearly basis, hourly compensation has always increased—although, of course, that hasn't always been true of *inflation-adjusted* compensation.

In the late-1990s, there was much discussion about whether the NAIRU, then commonly regarded as being 6%, was in need of downward revision. But while it was surely good news if the NAIRU was lower than originally thought, an unstable NAIRU meant it was hard to apply this measure over time.

Benderly has a strategy to get around this problem. He uses a NAIRU for a subgroup of the labor market with well-specified demographics. This subgroup consists of a certain kind of worker with strong labor force attachment—"married males" with "spouse present." If he could derive a stable NAIRU for this cohort, might it be used to stand for the whole? You could imagine so. To begin with, while the unemployment rate for married males has always been lower than the overall unemployment rate, the two have tracked each other fairly closely. And while married males account for a much lower share of the labor force than they used to, their strong labor force attachment must still give them an outsized role in the setting of wages.

In any case, Benderly's strategy of using the NAIRU for married males as a "proxy" for the whole seems to have worked. Based on data since 1955, which is as far back as the data on the married-male unemployment rate go, he finds that their NAIRU has been stable at 3.5%. Then comes the ingenious part.

We said that the deceleration of wage increases happens when the unemployment stays higher than the NAIRU, and the acceleration when it stays lower. The main point was that it doesn't have to go anywhere, just *stay* higher or lower, for the deceleration or acceleration to persist. And Benderly has found a way to capture this buildup with a stunning bit of arithmetical legerdemain.

In this math, there lies a new message about the NAIRU: It has a memory like an elephant. In 1995, the married male unemployment rate ran consistently lower than the NAIRU. In 2003, it ran consistently higher. Why, then, did hourly compensation rise faster in 2003 than in 1995 (4.0% versus 2.1%)? Because in the years leading up to 1995, the unemployment rate had generally been higher than the NAIRU, while in the years leading up to 2003, the unemployment had generally been lower. It turns out that if past trends have been persistent enough, the tightness or looseness of the labor market in the present will not be decisive. What will be decisive is the legacy of the past.

In other words, there is a kind of iron law of inertia that governs the way wage increases are figured. And as for quantifying that law, Benderly has found a formula of stunning simplicity.

Say the married male unemployment rate stays at 3.0%. It doesn't go any lower or higher, just stays there, one calendar quarter after the next. Since that's a full half-percentage point below the NAIRU of 3.5%, you'd expect the acceleration scenario to kick in. To capture it, Benderly keeps crediting that half-point difference to labor's account on a cumulative basis. Thus, for example, the first quarter it's up a half-point, the second quarter a full-point, the third quarter a point-and-a-half, and so on, for as long as the half-point difference persists. Now say the married male unemployment rate rises a bit, to 3.2%. Labor's account still gets credited by difference between the unemployment rate and the NAIRU, but, in this case, by less, or 0.3%.

What if the unemployment rate cuts above the NAIRU, say to 4.0%? Then the labor account starts to get debited by the difference—in this case, by a half-point—but the positive balances that might have accumulated from past quarters still remain to be drawn down.

The Labor Market Tightness Index (LMTI) you see in Figure 9.1 has been updated quarterly, but with four-quarter averages calculated for each calendar year. It begins with first quarter 1955 arbitrarily equal to the index number "100," plus or minus the difference between the married male unemployment rate and the NAIRU. Since the first quarter unemployment rate was 3.3%, the LMTI became 100.2. Since the second quarter unemployment rate was 2.9%, it gets another 0.6 added to it, for a second quarter LMTI of 100.8—and so on, with the four-quarter average for 1955 running 101.4 (see the Box).

Calculating the Index of Labor Market Tightness

In the table on page 109, we calculate the index of labor market tightness (LMTI) for the years 1955 through 1958, updating quarterly while calculating the four-quarter average (in bold) for each year.

For example, beginning with first quarter 1955, we subtract the married male unemployment rate of 3.3 from the married male nonaccelerating inflation rate of unemployment (NAIRU)—

always 3.5—and then add the difference of 0.2 to 100—for an LMTI of 100.2. For second quarter 1955, we subtract the married male unemployment rate of 2.9 from the married male NAIRU of 3.5 and then add the difference of 0.6 to the LMTI of the previous quarter of 100.2—for an LMTI of 100.8, and so on.

Notice that by first quarter 1958, the married male unemployment rate of 4.6 has gone above the NAIRU of 3.5; so to update the LMTI, we subtract the difference of 1.1.

(1) MM NAIRU	(2) Unemployment MM Rate	(1) – (2)	(3)	[(1) – (2)] + (3) LMTI
3.5	3.3	0.2	100.0	100.2
3.5	2.9	0.6	100.2	100.8
3.5	2.5	1.0	100.8	101.8
3.5	2.6	0.9	101.8	102.7
1955				**101.4**
3.5	2.5	1.0	102.7	103.7
3.5	2.6	0.9	103.7	104.6
3.5	2.7	0.8	104.6	105.4
3.5	2.7	0.8	105.4	106.2
1956				**105.0**
3.5	2.4	1.1	106.2	107.3
3.5	2.6	0.9	107.3	108.2
3.5	2.8	0.7	108.2	108.9
3.5	3.4	0.1	108.9	109.0
1957				**108.4**
3.5	4.6	−1.1	109.0	107.9
3.5	5.6	−2.1	107.9	105.8
3.5	5.5	−2.0	105.8	103.8
3.5	4.6	−1.1	103.8	102.7
1958				**105.1**

Notes: LMTI = Labor Market Tightness Index; MM = Married male; NAIRU = Nonaccelerating inflation rate of unemployment.

Notice the LMTI's long climb from the early-1960s through the mid-1970s to a record high in the fourth quarter of 1974 of 145.0. The accumulated legacy of positive balances did not begin to get whittled away until the 1980s, when the index began its long descent to a record low in 1994 of 83.3. So when the married male unemployment rate cut below the NAIRU in 1995, it was a long, slow climb.

By most standards, it works quite well. The percentage rate of increase in hourly compensation winds around the LMTI somewhat erratically, but it follows the LMTI's path pretty faithfully. It lagged behind most severely during the early-1970s, but that anomaly must have had a lot to do with the imposition of wage (and price) controls in August 1971, followed by wage guidelines through April 1974. It erred on the upside most severely in 1998 and 2000, but both these anomalies seem to have a lot to do with a concentration of stock options being exercised.

Otherwise, for an instructive lesson in the explanatory power of the Benderly's LMTI, compare 1997 with 2005, when the married male unemployment rates were identical, at 2.7%. Hourly compensation rose at a much faster rate in the recent period—at 5.5% in 2005 versus 3.1% in 1997. Before we blame the disparity on the economic policies of the respective presidents, we might better blame it on the recent period's much higher LMTI: 109.3 versus 87.6. The huge gap between the two could in turn be blamed not on the present, but on the legacy of the past. In 1997, the unemployment rate had spent most of the previous decade above its NAIRU, while by 2005, most of the previous decade had been spent below it. The law of inertia was working its will.

The most comparable year to 2005 was, in fact, 1957, when the LMTI ran just a point lower, at 108.2, and hourly compensation rose slightly faster, at 5.8%. The half-century gap in time is strong testimony to the explanatory power of this relationship.

Wages and Productivity

U p until now, it's remarkable how productivity has grown so well but *workers haven't benefited.*"[1] This statement was quoted in the May 7, 2006 *St. Louis-Post Dispatch* and attributed to the "chief U.S. economist at Global Insight in Lexington, Mass."

Similarly, a May 5, 2006 story in the *Chicago Tribune* observed that "Average workers are *losing ground* on an *inflation-adjusted basis,*"[2] adding that "demands [for greater pay] are *hard to find* in the *data on labor productivity.*"

The above pronouncements, though a bit extreme, are otherwise representative of a general view: Despite the leap in labor productivity over the past several years, the growth of wages has slowed to a crawl. The main finding of this chapter is that inflation-adjusted gains in pay *have* reflected gains in productivity, provided you look at the right data.

In Chapter 8, we saw that average hourly earnings tend to understate wage gains, and that hourly compensation as a measure is overwhelmingly preferable, both because it's more comprehensive in the forms of compensation it captures, and because it's far more reliable in terms of its data sources. In Chapter 9, we saw how yearly changes in hourly compensation that aren't inflation-adjusted could be explained by a measure of labor market tightness based on the unemployment rate. Now, we have a different challenge: to observe the relationship between the growth of real (i.e., inflation-adjusted) hourly compensation and the growth of productivity.

According to the textbooks, the two should roughly track each other over time. A look at the last 50 years reveals that they have tracked each other over long periods of time—and that the trend of the past five years is similar to past trends.

LABOR PRODUCTIVITY, LABOR COMPENSATION

The standard definition of *labor productivity* is the amount of output workers can produce in an hour. To get *output per worker hour,* you divide the value of total output by the total numbers of hours worked.

I've already shown that any estimate of hours worked is at best a gross approximation. But there is saving grace. To get hourly compensation, you likewise divide total compensation by the total number of hours worked. In this case, since both output per hour and hourly compensation are generated by the Bureau of Labor Statistics (BLS), we have an apples-to-apples comparison in terms of our denominator. Whatever errors might have crept into the estimates of total hours worked, at least they're the same apples.

But what about the numerators—total output versus total compensation? The broadest measure of output tracked by the BLS is defined as "business" output, mainly excluding the output of government and nonprofits. So our measure of compensation is also confined to workers in the business sector, tracking the cost in wages, salaries, and benefits of all workers employed in this sector.

Since both output and compensation are measured in dollars, any increase in these dollars must be adjusted for rising prices. Say the dollar value of all goods and services produced grows by 10%. If prices also rise by 10%, the entire increase is due to inflation. Real output does not grow at all. Similarly, a 10% rise in labor compensation becomes zero-growth in real terms if prices rise by 10%.

But on each side, which prices do we mean? Much of business output consists of goods and services businesses sell to each other. To inflation-adjust the dollar value of this output, the BLS uses prices that reflect that product mix. But this cannot be the right set of prices to inflation-adjust the dollars paid to workers. For them, the price-mix must reflect the goods and services consumers buy.

Maybe you see the apples-and-oranges problem. Employers have a stake in boosting the real value of business output, reflected in what they sell. Workers have a stake in boosting the real value of compensation, reflected in what they buy. But in this case, what workers buy is not exactly what employees sell.

To get as close as possible to an apples-to-apples comparison between real compensation growth and real output growth, we strike a compromise. We inflation-adjust compensation by the price index of personal consumption expenditures (PCE), which tracks the prices of goods and services consumers buy. Since the PCE is also a huge component of the price index normally applied to business output, we apply it to all of business output.

RESULTS

And what do we find?

First, to confirm that there really is a connection between the gains in productivity and our measure of real hourly compensation, Table 10.1 shows the calculations for four different periods since the early-1950s.

Each period has been recognized as part of a fairly well-defined era: the first (1953 to 1960), a period of strong productivity gains; the second (1960 to 1973), the era of productivity's growth's glory days; the third (1973 to 1990), the dark ages of slower growth; and the fourth (1990 to

Table 10.1 Productivity versus Compensation
(Average Annual Percent Gains)

Quarters	Productivity	Real Hourly Compensation
Q2 1953–Q2 1960	2.4	2.7
Q2 1960–Q4 1973	2.9	2.7
Q4 1973–Q3 1990	1	1
Q3 1990–Q1 2001	1.5	1.8

Note: Numbers are percentages.
Source: Bureau of Economic Analysis, "Table 2.3.4: Price Indexes for Personal Consumption Expenditures by Major Type of Product," http://www.bea.gov/bea/dn/nipaweb/TableView.asp#Mid; and Bureau of Labor Statistics, "Major Sector Productivity and Cost Index," http://www.bls.gov/lpc/home.htm.

2001), when growth began to make a comeback. All periods span from the beginning of a recession to the beginning of another recession ("business cycle peak to business cycle peak") to wash out the distorting effects of business cycles.

Notice that real hourly compensation grew somewhat faster than productivity in two of the periods (1953 to 1960 and 1990 to 2001), somewhat slower in another (1960 to 1973), and at the same rate in yet another (1973 to 1990). Some might place great significance on these variations. To my mind, the numbers are already such gross approximations, it's reassuring enough that they all match up so well.

But what about the recent period? The data we have picks up from first quarter 2001—the start of the last recession—through first quarter 2006, a span of exactly five years. Table 10.2 compares what has happened with all comparable periods in the first five years. Whenever another recession began before five years had elapsed, the period had to be omitted.[3]

Notice that the average annual increase in real compensation (2.0%), while strong, is not nearly as strong as the spectacular increase in productivity (3.3%). Now, notice that, in all comparable periods, productivity had also been rising faster than the increase in real hourly compensation through the first five years of an expansion. (We can't run this compar-

Table 10.2 Productivity versus Compensation in First 19 Quarters (Average Annual Percent Gains)

Quarters	Productivity	Real Hourly Compensation
Q2 1960–Q2 1965	3.3	2.5
Q4 1973–Q4 1978	1.8	1.5
Q3 1981–Q3 1986	1.3	1.1
Q3 1990–Q3 1995	0.8	0.4
Q1 2001–Q1 2006	3.3	2.0

Note: Numbers are percentages.
Source: Bureau of Economic Analysis, "Table 2.3.4: Price Indexes for Personal Consumption Expenditures by Major Type of Product," http://www.bea.gov/bea/dn/nipaweb /TableView.asp#Mid; and Bureau of Labor Statistics, "Major Sector Productivity and Cost Index," http://www.bls.gov/lpc/home.htm.

ison for the 1950s because no expansion lasted that long.) The pattern suggests that, in the early years of an expansion, increases in compensation tend to lag productivity. But as Table 10.1 indicates, over longer periods of time, the gap tends to close.

Notice that the last time productivity rose this fast, in the early 1960s, the gap was much narrower. We'll have to wait to see what happens this time. Meanwhile, it's clear workers have benefited from the rise in productivity, if we only look in the right place.

The Record Profit Boom That Never Happened

C apitalists are grabbing a rising share of national income at the expense of workers" read the blurb at the top of a February 10, 2005, feature story in the *Economist*. "Last year," the third sentence of the story declared, "America's after-tax profits rose to their highest as a proportion of GDP for 75 years."[1]

A related article in the same issue of the British newsweekly called the "record levels" on "corporate profits" an "extraordinarily positive economic trend" while only briefly expressing concern about a "profit growth built on the impoverishment of workers."[2] *New York Times* Senior Economics Reporter Louis Uchitelle had previously taken a darker view by warning that "the gorging on profits strains the recovery" (December 2003).[3] Two years later, Uchitelle noted that "corporate America" might "finally" be using its "record profits" to invest in plant and equipment (December 2005).[4] Meanwhile, *Times* Columnist Paul Krugman spoke of "the extremely lopsided nature of the economic recovery that officially began in late 2001," calling "the growth of corporate profits . . . spectacular."[5]

When both the *New York Times* and the *Economist* characterize corporate profits in this way, there is an understandable tendency to assume the facts are being characterized accurately. Corporations themselves like to call their profits "spectacular" when reporting to Wall Street but dismal when filing with the Internal Revenue Service (IRS). The main finding of this chapter is that the truth lies somewhere between these two extremes. For the corporate sector as a whole, profits have been neither at record highs or records lows, but somewhere between. One quick way to appreciate the plausibility of that statement is to recall the recent headlines on corporate behemoths in two related industries, oil and autos: Exxon Mobil and Royal Dutch Shell floating on black ink, General Motors (GM) and Ford drowning in red.

We'll focus mainly on the *Economist*'s version of the profits story, which spoke of a 75-year record on corporate after-tax profits as a "proportion of GDP." Strictly speaking, the statement is both accurate—and almost totally misleading. Before we assume it's sensible to measure corporate profits against total gross domestic product (GDP), bear in mind that a huge part of America's GDP is spoken for by other sectors, only one of which—unincorporated business—even generates profits. Otherwise, the output of state, local, and federal government, households, and nonprofits—the rest of gross domestic product—does not generate any profits.

It turns out that, when measured against the portion of GDP that is actually credited to the corporate sector, corporate after-tax profits are setting no records. How, then, could these after-tax profits be setting records as a share of total GDP? Mainly because corporate sector GDP has grown over the years as a share of total GDP, especially the share claimed by the highly profitable financial corporations. What if, instead of writing that "America's after-tax profits rose to their highest as a proportion of GDP for 75 years," the *Economist* had reported that "Russia's after-tax profits rose to their highest as a proportion of GDP for 75 years"? That would not have been surprising, because through most of those 75 years, Russia's GDP did not generate profits. But since not many readers were likely to be aware of the disproportionate growth of corporate GDP in the United States, the statement as given had journalistic "sizzle."

There is also a reinforcing tendency to believe that corporations must be pulling down record profits when the Republicans control Washington. But if politicians give special favors to certain corporations, it might even be at the expense of others. The corporate sector as a whole doesn't necessarily benefit. In any case, one of the findings of this chapter is that the profitability of corporate America seems to have little to do with the party in power.

There are, of course, various data sources on profits. In what follows, I stick exclusively to the profits data kept by the Bureau of Economic Analysis (BEA)—keeper of the National Income and Product Accounts, which include gross domestic product. The raw numbers themselves are periodically revised to reflect the corporate tax filings of the IRS; the last benchmarking to IRS data was done through 2002. Post-2002 data are largely taken from what companies tell Wall Street.

You might think that pre-2002 numbers suffer from a downward bias. But the tendency to minimize profits for tax purposes often has more to do with accounting methods than with outright misreporting. Or you might think that that post-2002 numbers suffer from an upward bias. But here, too, the tendency to exaggerate profits before Wall Street is often driven by creative accounting methods rather than outright mis-reporting.[6] The BEA's accounting methods in figuring profits suffer from no special bias, other than to get the numbers right.

WHICH GROSS DOMESTIC PRODUCT?

Ironically, in one of its articles on the profit boom, the *Economist* had observed that "Economists take it for granted that profits cannot grow by more than nominal GDP over the medium term."[7] But the two reasons then adduced for "why profits could defy this conventional wisdom" did not include the possibility that profits can grow faster than total GDP over any term if corporate GDP grows faster.

The use of total GDP as the base of comparison for corporate profits turns out to be similar to the deaths-from-cancer fallacy mentioned in Chapter 4. If the elderly are a rising share of the population, the death rate from cancer can increase for that reason alone, even if a lower share of the elderly die of cancer. Think of total GDP as the overall population, corporate sector GDP as the elderly—especially the financial corporate sector—and profits as the cancer deaths.

We'll start with the corporate sector as a whole before we break it down between its two key components: nonfinancial and financial. The facts based on corporate GDP make the "spectacular profit boom" sound more like a battle cry of Wall Street than the analysis of neutral observers:

- In 2001, the proportion of corporate sector GDP accounted for by pre-tax profits hit lows not seen since 1982. After-tax profits as a proportion of corporate GDP hit lows not seen since 1986.[8]
- The recovery in corporate profitability had indeed been spectacular relative to the lows of 2001. Otherwise, 2004 and 2005 hardly set records. In 2004, neither pre-tax nor after-tax profits as a share of GDP even matched the peak of 1997. In 2005, both pre-tax and after-tax profitability went slightly higher—but each fell short of peaks hit routinely from the mid-1940s through the mid-1960s.[9]

Now strip away the financial sector from the total, leaving the far larger nonfinancial sector (which includes the domestic output of GM and Exxon), and the previous story becomes somewhat grimmer. Take pre-tax profits of the nonfinancial corporate sector as a proportion of the GDP of that sector, and you find that 2001 hit lows not seen since 1934 in the depths of the Great Depression. After-tax profits of nonfinancial corporations compared more favorably with the past, hitting lows not seen since 1980.[10]

Similarly, the recovery in profitability of the nonfinancial corporations had indeed been "spectacular" relative to the lows of 2001. But neither 2004 or 2005 matched the highs of the Clinton years—and even those highs fell short of peaks hit routinely from the mid-1940s through the mid-1960s,[11] pre-tax or after-tax.

The performance of the financial corporate sector (banks, brokerages, insurance, and real estate) looked much better. But it was not setting any records either. When taken as a proportion of the financial corporate sector's own GDP, 2004 and 2005 highs on both pre-tax and after-tax profits fell short of the *average* level of performance from the mid-1940s through the early-1970s—and far short of the peaks.[12]

GROWTH OF THE FINANCIAL VERSUS NONFINANCIAL CORPORATE SECTORS

So much for historical comparisons that reach back to 1929—the year of the stock market crash—which ushered in the Great Depression. From now on, all comparisons will be limited to the more relevant 60 years since World War II.

Over the 60 years, corporate sector GDP as a whole rose from about 50% of the total in the mid-1940s to nearly 60% by the late-1970s and has hovered there ever since. But within the corporate sector, there has been a shift in favor of the financial companies. The nonfinancial corporate sector's share of total GDP rose from less than 50% in the mid-1940s to a peak of nearly 56% by the early-1980s. Since 2001, its GDP has accounted for 51% to 52% of the total. The difference has been made up by the financial corporate sector. Its share of total GDP has steadily increased over the years, from a little over 2% in the mid-1940s to 4% by the mid-1970s to nearly 8% by 2000—where it's been hovering ever since.[13]

So the shift in terms of GDP share, while significant, has not been huge. But the effect on profits has been magnified by the much greater profitability of the financial companies. In 2004, for example—the year of the 75-year record cited by the *Economist*—the nonfinancial corporations made $8.14 in after-tax profit for every $100 of nonfinancial corporate GDP, while the financial corporations made $23.68 in after-tax profit for every $100 of financial corporate GDP.

Again, those figures were hardly records. The $8.14 fell short of its recent 1997 high of $9.35 and its post–World War II peak in 1965 of $11.81. The financial sector's $23.86 looks less impressive against its own *average* from 1946 to 1973 of $25.38 and its own peak of $31.15 in1948.[14]

But the trick of math worked its will. Since the profitability of the financial versus the nonfinancial companies was roughly three times greater ($23.86 vs. $8.14), the shift in GDP share was enough to set a record in terms of total GDP.

As a further irony, in its only mention of the tilt toward the financial sector, the *Economist* expressed concern that "America . . . relies too much on financial firms as a source of profit growth."[15] But the only

Table 11.1   Financial Corporate Sector—Average Yearly
Profit per $100 of Own Sector's GDP

	Pre-Tax	After-Tax
2004–2005	35.11	23.17
1946–2005	35.01	19.63

Note: Numbers are in dollars.
Source: Bureau of Economic Analysis.

profits the nonfinancial firms could ever rely on had to come from their own growth. And relative to their own norms, their after-tax profitability has held up quite well.

Starting with the financial corporations (Table 11.1). Notice that in the most recent two years (2004 to 2005), pre-tax profitability was very close to its 60-year average (1946 to 2005). But since corporate tax burdens are lower than they used to be, recent after-tax profitability has been running higher than its 60-year average.

For the nonfinancial corporations (see Table 11.2), pre-tax profitability over the most recent two years has been running lower than its 60-year average. But because of declining corporate tax burdens, the nonfinancial corporations have been doing better than their 60-year average on an after-tax basis.

Over the past two years, after-tax profits accounted for a higher share of the nonfinancial corporate sector GDP than over the past 60. Nor has this sector's own GDP growth lagged far behind the growth of total GDP. Take the most unfavorable comparison with overall GDP

Table 11.2   Nonfinancial Corporate Sector—Average
Yearly Profit per $100 of Own Sector's GDP

	Pre-Tax	After-Tax
2004–2005	11.63	8.27
1946–2005	13.19	7.76

Note: Numbers are in dollars.
Source: Bureau of Economic Analysis.

growth—the period since 1981, when nonfinancial corporate GDP peaked as a share of the total. From 1981 to 2005, overall GDP grew at an average annual rate of 4.7%, while nonfinancial corporate GDP grew at an average annual rate of 4.2% (both GDP figures in nominal dollars).

THE IRONY OF COMPENSATION SHARES

One could, of course, still deplore the ascendancy of the financial industry that both permits capitalists to gorge on profits, and gives labor a smaller share of GDP as compensation.

In the nonfinancial corporate sector, by contrast, employee compensation showed no real signs of losing ground (see Table 11.3). In 2004 to 2005, the share of that sector's GDP that went to employees ran slightly higher than in 1994 to 1995, and almost as high as its 60-year average.

But the same figures for the financial corporate sector were not nearly as favorable (see Table 11.4). Employee compensation claimed a lower share of financial than of nonfinancial GDP, and its 2004 to 2005 share ran lower than in either of the two previous periods.

In the financial corporate sector, it seemed that capitalists *were* "grabbing a rising share of national income at the expense of workers,"[16] just as the *Economist* had reported. Nonfinancial companies were certainly allocating more to labor compensation as a share of their own

Table 11.3 Nonfinancial Corporate Sector—Yearly
Compensation per $100 of Own Sector's GDP

2004–2005	64.88
1994–1995	64.80
1946–2005	65.39

Note: Numbers are in dollars.
Source: Bureau of Economic Analysis.

Table 11.4   Financial Corporate Sector—Yearly
                  Compensation per $100 of Own Sector's GDP

2004–2005	52.94
1994–1995	56.80
1946–2005	57.75

Note: Numbers are in dollars.
Source: Bureau of Economic Analysis.

GDP, but the difference in shares did not necessarily mean the average worker stood to earn less from financial than from nonfinancial corporations. In fact, according to BLS data, financial employers still pay more than nonfinancial employers.[17] So to the extent that workers were earning a lower share, the news lacked drama.

End the Monthly Madness: The Change in Payroll Employment Data

Y ou won't want to miss anything in the next few minutes," says CNBC's *Squawk Box* host Mark Haines at 8:24 A.M. on January 9, 2004, adding: "We've got the employment report coming out next, live,"[1] as though the jobs monster was about to be uncaged in his very studio.

The show cuts to commercials, then cuts back to some chat among the guests. According to the Dow Jones Survey of forecasters, the consensus expects nonfarm payroll employment to increase by 150,000, and for the unemployment rate to hold steady. "I'm going to stay in the over, even though I was slammed last time," says guest host Larry Kudlow, meaning that he expects an increase of more than 150,000. "I'm taking the under," says Haines, explaining that "the huge productivity surge which . . . while normally it works to produce jobs, seems to be working against jobs"—a spin on the influence of productivity that's all his own. (Productivity growth can *only* work "against jobs"; when workers are more productive, fewer are needed.)

Suddenly the host exclaims, "We gotta go, we gotta get out of here, so we can overreact when the data comes out!"

With that cliffhanger, the show cuts to more commercials, then back to Haines, who invites us to "go live to Washington and Hampton Pearson," who rattles off the numbers in front of a door that reads Department of Labor. Later revisions render most of what Pearson says about payroll employment either wrong or misleading: "December increased by just 1,000 jobs [since revised to 122,000] . . . the biggest hit was in the retail sector which shed 38,000 [since revised to a gain of 3,500] . . . the November figures were revised downward [since they have been revised upward]."[2]

Reporter Pearson pronounced the December figures "overall . . . very disappointing." But he probably would not have done so had he known the revised figures that currently appear in the record books. Forecasters expected an employment increase of 150,000 and got 1,000. But the revised figures now show 122,000. There would also have been an upward—not a downward—revision to prior months.

Bond yields fell on the day, which usually occurs when an economic release is thought to signal a weak economy. The yield on the two-year Treasury note fell an unusually large 17 basis points to 1.68% on January 9, 2004. But that probably would not have happened if the revised figures were reported at the time.

Squawk Box is a morning show about the markets that devotes more time to the employment report, and to the economic data generally, than any other comparable broadcast. I've seen the show off and on for many years, and (full disclosure) even appeared once as a guest. If what I say in this chapter about the quality of the coverage seems harsh, it would be no less so about the show's competition on video, radio, or in print.

Every edition of *Squawk Box* that I have seen on the monthly employment report has nuggets of insight. And despite his occasional gaffes, host Mark Haines is a clever man capable of pricking his guests' pretensions when appropriate. He occasionally cuts off over-the-top enthusiast and frequent bull market cheerleader Larry Kudlow, wittily referring to him as "Lawrence of America." He can dismiss some of his guests' fly-by-night analyses with a contemptuous wave of his hand, as when CNBC's Senior Economics Reporter Steve Liesman trotted out a seven-data-point performance record on the employment data's response to hurricanes. (Haines' point was that nothing could be inferred from that skimpy record.)

But if Haines cut in whenever appropriate, the proceedings would grind to a halt every time. The need to milk the numbers for suspense and drama blows their importance way out of proportion. The excessive focus on the minutia of the report ensures that meaningless figures will keep getting mentioned, as when Liesman obsesses about differences of a hundredth of a percentage point in the unemployment rate. Yet the Bureau of Labor Statistics (BLS) keeps warning that a tenth-point difference is within the range of statistical error (as we'll discuss in Chapter 13). Kudlow can refer to a "220,000" increase in household survey employment, even though the BLS keeps warning that anything less than 400,000 is not meaningful.[3]

Sometimes what's reported is flat-out wrong. Whoever decided to devote a little airtime on November 5, 2004, to manufacturing jobs latched on to the wrong story. Rebecca Quick of the *Wall Street Journal* began her presentation by informing us that factory employment had "mostly followed" gains in overall employment until "the sector lost 18,000 jobs" the previous month. In fact, the tally for this sector was up a negligible 9,000 over the previous 12 months, a "gain" of 0.06%, compared to a 1.3% gain over the same period for employment generally. Quick next observed that unless manufacturing employment resumed this nonexistent uptrend in the about-to-be released October data, it would be a sign that "the economy is slowing as some fear."[4] Later, when the data were released, Quick's remarks were quickly—and prudently—forgotten. (If there was a story, it was that gains in factory employment were probably showing up in temporary-help services, which showed a 12-month increase of 240,000.)

That same morning of November 5, 2004, Haines let at least one blooper slide. Commentator Jack Bouroudjian exulted that, because the strong payroll gain was being released after the presidential election of three days ago, it was therefore not "political." "It's a real number!"[5] he exclaimed. As though the BLS *could* be accused of releasing fake numbers going into the election.

Even the normally level-headed Mark Zandi was somehow impressed that the job market had rallied in October—just before the presidential election instead of after—as though employers make decisions to hire in the same way investors speculate in stocks.[6]

Haines never skips the suspense-building ritual of polling his guests on whether they're taking "the over," "the under," or going "with the consensus" on the change in employment just before the number's release. It's bad enough (as former Bureau of Economic Analysis Chief Statistician Robert Parker has complained) that the consensus bet on the newly released figure can attract as much attention as the figures themselves. To collect bets on the consensus bet takes the absurdity to another level.

Maybe Haines would end the game if he stopped to ask how accurate the consensus forecast has been. Most of the time, the forecast does not even fall within a 50% range of the reported figure.

SKIP THE HEADLINE NUMBERS

Squawk Box is only symptomatic of a larger problem. The change in payroll employment could be, in principle, reported hourly, daily, weekly, monthly, quarterly, annually, or decennially. It was decided many decades ago to release monthly updates. But just because that decision was made doesn't mean it was prudent. At one point, it was seriously proposed that estimates of gross domestic product (GDP) be released monthly rather than quarterly. The markets could have had the excitement of dealing with 12 GDP figures per year rather than just four. We can be grateful that wiser heads prevailed in scotching that idea.

And we'd be similarly fortunate if all that data-noise from the one-month, three-month, and even six-month trend in payroll employment data were suddenly rendered silent.

What I'm actually proposing is a kind of compromise. The BLS should announce that each newly minted monthly figure and prior-month revisions will henceforth be treated as though they add one-twelfth to our knowledge. A dozen of these out-of-focus snapshots must be laid side by side before we can discern what might be going on. So it would continue to release its monthly report, but the headline figure would be the 12-month change.

Once you accept that, consider what the 12-month figure can do—
and has done over the years.

If a picture is worth a thousand words, Figures 12.1 through 12.4
should go for several million at least: the minimum quantity of spoken
and written verbiage that could be saved if the markets, the media, the
policymakers—and the folks at *Squawk Box*—would only take notice.
The charts use real-time (RT) data—the data known at the time—to
compare the 12-month change in payroll employment with the one-
month, three-month, and six-month change. But they could just as well
be tracking virtually any monthly series.

The lesson in these charts is simply this: If the trend in payroll employment is what matters—and as we'll see, it's all that does—the one-
month, three-month, and six-month measures add nothing to our
knowledge. What they are supposed to bring to the party, of course, is
greater timeliness. When the trend begins to turn, they are there first.
But all they really add is greater confusion. You can never tell the false
signals from the true. Even the 12-month measure has been volatile at

Figure 12.1

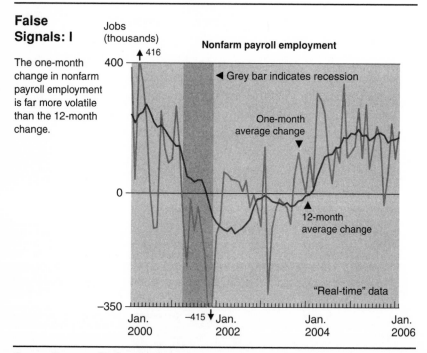

False Signals: I

The one-month change in nonfarm payroll employment is far more volatile than the 12-month change.

Jobs (thousands)

Nonfarm payroll employment

◀ Grey bar indicates recession

One-month average change ▼

12-month average change ▲

"Real-time" data

Source: Bureau of Labor Statistics.

Figure 12.2

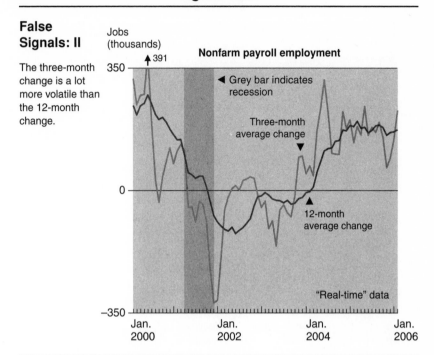

False Signals: II

The three-month change is a lot more volatile than the 12-month change.

Jobs (thousands)

Nonfarm payroll employment

◀ Grey bar indicates recession

Three-month average change ▼

12-month average change ▲

"Real-time" data

Source: Bureau of Labor Statistics.

times. But for the most part, when it does signal a change in trend, it doesn't reverse itself.

However, what can you say about the one-month number, except that if it were a stock price, momentum players would have gone broke long ago? Effective in May 2003, the BLS instituted an improvement in methodology that made the one-month change less volatile. While that has clearly helped, its pattern still looks like an electrocardiogram. Does the three-month number signal turning points faster than the 12-month? Not if you factor in its many false signals. In February 2001 and then in September 2002, it seemed to be on the rebound, only to plunge into negative territory again. It spiked in early 2004, only to reverse itself. The six-month measure over did the upside in summer 2004, before falling back again. More recently, the six-month has been tracking the 12-month fairly closely. But if it does veer in one direction or another, will we have any reason to believe it?

The charts are measured in terms of the standard metric: thousands of jobs. But for reasons I'll soon explain, I urge the BLS to start reporting

Figure 12.3

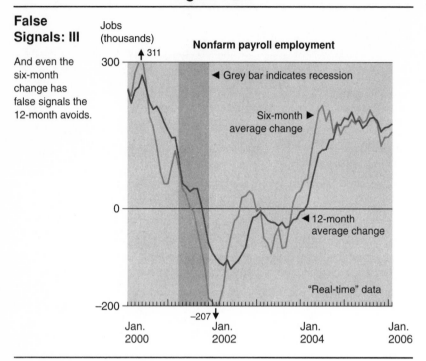

False Signals: III

And even the six-month change has false signals the 12-month avoids.

Jobs (thousands)

Nonfarm payroll employment

◀ Grey bar indicates recession

Six-month ▶ average change

◀ 12-month average change

"Real-time" data

Source: Bureau of Labor Statistics.

these figures as monthly year-over-year percentage changes. For example, instead of beginning the January 2006 press release with, "Nonfarm payroll employment increased by 193,000 in January," it would announce instead, "Nonfarm payroll employment in January ran 1.6% above a year ago." Of course, all the job data broken down by sector and industry (manufacturing, retailing, and so on) should be reported in the same way.

If the kick won't be as great, the hangover won't be as bad, either. The way these figures are currently reported has made numbers junkies of all who use them. And as I'll explain, it helps spread dangerous misconceptions about the dynamics of the job market.

THE *SQUAWK BOX* FALLACY

Others may object: The one-month may be volatile, but what number isn't? The markets are also volatile, but we still report the change in the

Figure 12.4

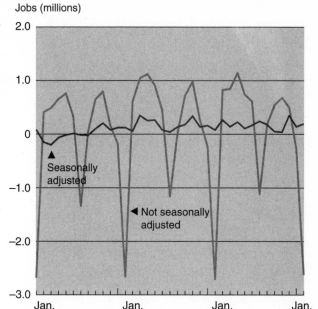

To Everything, a Season

The actual monthly swings in payroll employment generally dwarf the seasonally adjusted swings that are routinely reported.

Source: Bureau of Labor Statistics.

S&P 500. Don't the payroll employment numbers deserve to be reported because they are meant to reflect what actually happened that month?

The *Squawk Box* fallacy would have us treat each figure as though it has the same reality as a market close. But there are three reasons why we can't and shouldn't, and they're called *sampling error, revision,* and *seasonal adjustment.* Let's take each one in turn.

Sampling Error

The payroll survey is based on a very broad sample: 400,000 establishments in the private and government sector. But the monthly change is still subject to a huge sampling error of plus or minus 100,000. That means, for example, that when the number prints at a positive 70,000, you can't rule out that possibility that it was really a decline of 30,000.

Numbers on the industry level are subject to even wider sampling error in proportion to their size. In any given month, most of the sampling errors on the industry level are greater than the reported changes. When Haines and company cite these changes, the numbers are meaningless.

Similarly, when economic consultant Bernard Baumohl wrote in *The Secrets of Economic Indicators,* "the business community" was "healthy enough to add 30,000 workers,"[7] he forgot that that the sampling error in that case is plus or minus 90,000. For all we knew, the "business community" might have been *unhealthy* enough to shed 60,000 workers. With a 12-month trend, however, sampling error shrinks to negligible size.

Revision

Even if sampling error weren't a problem, there would be the problem of revision. Each number is always in danger of barely resembling its initial version. A January 2001 "jump" of 268,000 eventually became a decline of 53,000. The October 1998 employment report showed gains in September and October of 157,000 and 116,000,[8] which may have prompted the Federal Reserve to cut the short-term interest rate another quarter-point. Had the more solid-looking revised gains of 221,000 and 197,000 been known at the time, the Federal Reserve might have acted differently.

And even after the data go the full round of revisions, the monthly changes are still approximations. Each January, the tallies for the previous March are benchmarked to a "universe count" from the BLS's "Quarterly Census of Employment and Wages," which is in turn drawn from state unemployment insurance records. Since the tallies are benchmarked only as of every March, the historical data are never more than fairly complete counts of paycheck employment from March to March of each year. Everything in between is still an estimate.

In fairness to the BLS, its methods have improved over recent years, although the jury is still out on whether this will lead to fewer revisions. Meanwhile, 12-month trends will always hold up far better than monthly data.

Seasonal Adjustment

Now, get ready for the shocker. These figures are, by intention and design, almost light years away from what actually happened. The reason is that they've all been seasonally adjusted.

In fact, every monthly (and quarterly) number cited so far in this book has been "adjusted for normal seasonal variation." It seemed pointless to mention this fact until the process was fully explained. The logic of seasonal adjustment keys off the striking fact that virtually all economic data is subject to wide seasonal swings. For example, employment plunges in January, even in good years—and soars in April, even in bad. So the BLS assigns a positive or negative number to each calendar month based on the amount by which employment can usually be expected to rise or fall in that month. To be scored as a gain *after* seasonal adjustment, employment must do better—falling by less, rising by more—than its usual score. As a practical matter, the volatility of the seasonal swings is so great that the seasonally adjusted figures often look surreal by comparison.

For example, when the BLS reported in its January 2006 report that "Payroll employment increased by 193,000 in January,"[9] its data showed payroll employment actually plunging by 2.625 million. So even if the BLS had included the conventional modifier ("increased by a *seasonally adjusted* 193,000"), the statement would hardly do justice to what actually happened. A more accurate way of putting it would have been, "Payroll employment fell by 193,000 *less than is usual* for January," but that would hardly do justice to the magnitude involved. A full account might have read, "Employment fell 2.625 million in January; if it had fallen 193,000 more, that would have been typical for January—and we would have said that seasonally adjusted employment is unchanged. But since it fell 193,000 *less than is usual* for January, we are calling it a seasonally adjusted *increase* of 193,000."

The plunge in January is by far the largest because cutbacks occur in major industries like retailing, construction, and education simultaneously. But in most months (Figure 12.4), the actual, "not seasonally adjusted" change is greater than the seasonally adjusted by a few orders of magnitude. The biggest increases tend to be in April and October. For example, against an actual increase of 652,000 in April 2003, the BLS recorded a seasonally adjusted decrease of 68,000. What it really found is that the increase of 652,000 was 68,000[10] *less than is usual* for that month of the year.

None of the foregoing is meant to attack the legitimacy of seasonal adjustment. On the contrary, so long as you insist on tracking periods that run less than 12 months, it's a necessary process. The only point here is that, far from reflecting what actually happened, seasonally adjusted figures are specifically designed to distort it: Their purpose is to capture the underlying trend.

Table 12.1   Total Nonfarm Payroll Employment

	(1) January 2006	(2) January 2005	[(1)(2)]/12
SA	134,564	132,471	174
NSA	132,419	130,368	171

Note: Numbers are in thousands.
Source: Bureau of Labor Statistics.

But if 12-month trends are all we need, then we can do without formal seasonal adjustment. That's because monthly year-over-year changes bring built-in seasonal adjustment—in much the same way that Wall Street measures quarterly earnings against the same quarter a year ago. In fact, over any 12-month cycle, the seasonally adjusted and the not seasonally adjusted figures are designed to net out to virtually the same number.

To see that this is so, subtract the seasonally adjusted and the not seasonally adjusted totals and match them up (Table 12.1). For example, the difference in these totals is greatest in January. But the differences in the 12-month trend are barely worth a rounding error.

In each case, subtract the January 2005 total from the January 2006 and divide by 12: You get an average monthly increase either of 174,000 or of 171,000.

Or in each case, divide the January 2006 total by the January 2005 total, and you get an increase of 1.6% in both cases.

END THE CREATIONIST FALLACY

Did the 12-month increase in payroll employment through January 2006 average 174,000 jobs per month, or was payroll employment up 1.6% from the year before? While both figures are correct, I much prefer the second way of putting it, for three good reasons.

First, percentage changes are the only appropriate way to make historical comparisons. A rise of 178,000 in 2005 is not the same as a rise of 178,000 in 1995. Since there were more jobs in 2005 than in 1995, the increase must be put in percentage terms. Similarly, we don't say that GDP rose by $42 billion; we say it increased by 3.5%.

Second, the use of percentages discourages false accuracy. If economists show their sense of humor by putting decimals in their forecasts,
the BLS does it by putting its employment gains in thousands. In the
above example, the percentage increase came to 1.66%, but only the
worst numbers junkies would choose to put it that way.

Third, and most important, it would deter the practice of what I call
the *creationist fallacy*—the worst kind of surreal reporting of all:

The American economy *created* 337,000 new jobs.[11]

Employers *created* 207,000 jobs.[12]

The Labor Department said Friday that businesses added 112,000
jobs . . . half the number . . . that many economists were expecting the economy to *create*.[13]

Even if these numbers weren't seasonally adjusted, they'd be egre-
giously misleading. All these acts of creation were supposed to have taken
place over a single month. But according to the BLS's *Quarterly Census of
Employment and Wages* (QCEW), the private sector normally creates about
14 million to 16 million jobs per year, which comes to an average of more
than a million a month.[14] If something like 2 million jobs are added in a
year, that's only a net figure—the difference between the number of jobs
created and destroyed. That's what monthly figures like "112,000" and
"207,000" really mean. And yet the media keeps confusing these much
smaller numbers with the number of jobs actually created.

Why does this matter? Because if we're conditioned to think it's a
good month when 207,000 jobs are "created," we fall prey to people like
Lou Dobbs and his precursor, Ross Perot, who would scare us about foreigners taking our jobs away (see Chapter 17 for more on this debate). If
corporation Y announces 10,000 layoffs, 20 such announcements per
month will just offset the number of jobs *created*. If "3.4 million white-
collar service jobs" will be shifted to low-wage countries by 2015, it
sounds like a serious threat. But to anyone who knows the private sector
must create more than 12 million jobs a year just to stand still, it sounds
like the least of our problems.

If the BLS reported only 12-month percentage changes, creationism
might be quashed. And if it did not seasonally adjust figures, another
kind of surreal reporting would have to be abandoned:

"U.S. workers enjoyed another bumper month in January as the rapid pace of job growth continued."[15]

In January, employment always falls by more than 2 million.

"The American job creation machine went into reverse in April as companies shed employees across much of the weak economy."[16]

In April, employment always rises by more than half a million.

I don't expect any of this to happen. Timeliness is next to godliness in both the markets and the media—never mind the quality of what is being reported. If the statistical agencies tried denying them their quota of freshly harvested data, the outcry would be overwhelming. (There is, of course, the argument that if the Federal Reserve cares about short-term data, the bond market must also; for doubts about this, see Chapter 13.)

But it does mean that most media coverage of the headline change in payroll employment data should be ignored—and not just of payroll employment. Everything I've said in this chapter applies to virtually all monthly data, including retail sales, industrial production, the trade deficit, new home sales, and the Consumer Price Index.

End the Monthly Madness: The Unemployment Rate

The monthly employment report has the power to move the bond market. But does it move the market in the right direction? The evidence suggests that if anything, the employment report gives off more false signals than true. As a case in point, this chapter will examine the recent run-up in short-term interest rates that began with the first Federal Reserve tightening in late-June 2004. While the jobs data should have been of great help in informing the bond market about the developing situation, the record shows it was no help at all. The problem may lie in the market's excessive preoccupation with volatile monthly swings—which is one reason I've proposed the monthly change in payroll employment be replaced by a 12-month change.

But what about the other headline figure in the employment report—the unemployment rate? Partly because the unemployment rate is a ratio (between the number of unemployed and the number in the labor force), it tends to be less volatile. So in that case, a six-month trend will do.

But first let's look at certain forms of monthly madness a six-month trend might prevent, and then we'll put the two headline trends to-gether—the 12-month percentage change in payroll employment, the six-month average on the unemployment rate—and see how they might have informed the bond market more than misinformed it during the recent period of tightening.

As an addendum to this chapter, I'll tell the untold story of President Richard Nixon and the "Unemployment-gate" scandal of 1971, which involved the purging of a few Jewish employees who were perceived as troublemakers from the Bureau of Labor Statistics (BLS). Given the passions involved, it may seem naive to suggest that the outcome could have been different if the BLS had been reporting the unemployment rate as a six-month average instead of a one-month figure. But the volatility of the monthly figures was certainly a factor.

REPORTING STATISTICAL INSIGNIFICANCE

The following quotes from real news stories have one thing in com-mon—numerical nonevents:

> The unemployment rate . . . rose to 5.7 from 5.6 percent.[1] (April 2, 2004)

> The unemployment rate declined to 6.1 percent from 6.2 per-cent in July.[2] (September 6, 2003)

> The unemployment rate fell to 5.6%, a two-year low, in January from 5.7% in December, the Labor Department said Friday.[3] (February 9, 2004)

In no case did the BLS (part of the Labor Department) say any such thing. In all cases, the BLS had called the unemployment rate "about" or "essentially unchanged."[4]

The BLS uses such handy modifiers whenever the rate of joblessness prints a tenth-of-a-percentage point lower or higher than the previous month. As the BLS explains, any monthly change of less than 0.2%, up or down is within the range of statistical error—too close to call when your nationwide sample consists of only 60,000 households. For example, when the unemployment rate falls from 5.7% to 5.6%, there is a fair chance that other samples of 60,000 would have shown an *increase* to 5.8%.

Even that 0.2% range of error is a minimum estimate, referring only to sampling error. As the BLS is the first admit, the figures are also prone to "nonsampling error," which "can occur for many reasons," the agency explains, "including the failure to sample a segment of the population, inability to obtain information for all respondents in the sample, inability or unwillingness of respondents to provide correct information on a timely basis, mistakes made by respondents, and errors made in the collection or processing of the data."[5]

At a National Press Club forum on "improving the release and reporting of data," BLS Commissioner Kathleen P. Utgoff objected to the media's habit of covering a statistically insignificant change as actually having happened—or even worse, as the "first significant decline since X" or "largest increase since Y."[6]

Then-*Washington Post* reporter John Berry brushed Utgoff's objections aside as incompatible with the way news reporting works. "I can't put in a story that you regard 0.1 percent as statistically insignificant," Berry said. "If I did, the editor would take it out. Very detailed stuff is never going to be reported."[7]

But Utgoff wasn't suggesting that "very detailed stuff" be reported. The month before, Berry had rendered a 0.1% "decline" as "the unemployment rate dipping to its lowest level since last spring."[8] Going into even less detail, the BLS had called it "essentially unchanged."[9] Berry could have written those same two words.

For Utgoff, the lesson should have been plain: The only way to get the media not to report a 0.1% change is to keep it from them. One good way to keep it from them is to report a six-month trend instead.

DECONSTRUCTING THE DENOMINATOR

Here's an irony: While most 0.1% declines are erroneously reported as meaningful, most declines of 0.2% have been dismissed as dubious, simply because most of these declines have been accompanied by a decline in the labor force. But most monthly changes in the two components of the labor force—the employed and the unemployed—are not statistically significant either.

This can often lead to numerical nonevents of a more subtle kind. For a typical example, take the following item about the December 2003 decline in the unemployment rate from *New York Times* reporter Louis Uchitelle:

> Rather than hunt for scarce work, tens of thousands of people disappeared from the labor force. . . . The unemployment rate dropped to 5.7% from 5.9% . . . , but that was mainly because so many people chose not to look for work, a requirement to be counted as unemployed. Normally, a falling jobless rate means that the unemployed are seeking and finding jobs. But in December, 309,000 working-age men and women who would normally be job hunting either left the labor force or did not bother to enter it in search of work, the Bureau reported.[10]

The numbers did show a 309,000 decline in the labor force, with the unemployed falling by 255,000 and the employed by 54,000. Declines in the labor force are generally short-lived—every calendar year since 1951 has witnessed an increase so the reported figures did seem disconcerting, making it look as though: (1) 255,000 unemployed people gave up looking, thus dropping out of the labor force; (2) another 54,000 employed people lost their jobs, and instead of looking for work, also left the labor force; and (3) once these 309,000 people (or others like them) came back for another try, that initial fall in the unemployment rate would only reverse itself.

But let's say that, instead of falling by 54,000, the number of employed had risen by 236,000; and that this 236,000 rise in the employed had been perfectly matched by a 236,000 fall in the unemployed. The 236,000 formerly unemployed would have shown up as employed; the labor force would have stayed flat; and the unemployment rate would also have declined to 5.7% from 5.9%.

I chose those figures for a reason: Based on BLS figures on sampling error, they reflect what could have happened. According to the December 2003 employment report, the sampling error "for the monthly change in employment" was "plus or minus 290,000."[11] So for all we know, the reported 54,000 decline in the employed could have been an *increase* of 236,000.

According to that same report, the sampling error "for the monthly change in *un*employment was plus or minus 270,000."[12] So for all we know, the reported 255,000 decline in the unemployed could have been slightly overstated. The real decline could have been 236,000.

But for a statistical error, then, *Times* reporter Uchitelle would have accepted the decline in the unemployment rate as real.

A LEADING INDICATOR?

One final story about short-term obsession with the unemployment rate.

"The unemployment rate," writes former *Time* magazine reporter Bernard Baumohl in *The Secrets of Economic Indicators,* "can serve as a leading indicator . . . by warning of an impending downturn in economic activity."[13] This book has been published by the prestigious Wharton Business School where manuscripts "meet Wharton's standard by addressing important topics with ideas and insights that are . . . empirically based . . . and implementable in real decision settings."[14]

Baumohl credits the unemployment rate with signaling the last two recessions: "In the 1990–1991 recession," he writes, "the jobless rate began to climb three months before business activity turned down. And when the 2001 recession started, the unemployment rate bottomed out a year earlier."[15]

The author neglects to mention that by this standard, the unemployment rate was fairly screaming recession on three other occasions (July 1992, April 1995, and June 2003) when none was near.

SMOOTHING OUT THE UNEMPLOYMENT RATE

Figures 13.1 and 13.2 show what I would do with the unemployment rate: Turn it into a six-month moving average (*moving* because it keeps updating the most recent average for the past six months).

Notice that, as of March 2006, the six-month average has been in a steady downtrend since March 2004. But those who followed the

Figure 13.1

False Signals: I

The one-month reading on the unemployment rate is more volatile than the six-month moving average.

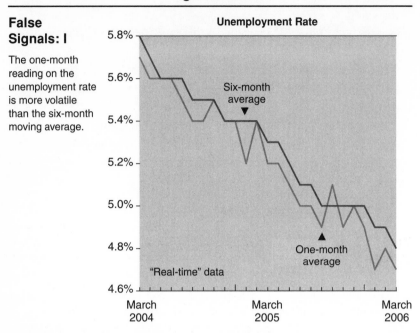

Source: Bureau of Labor Statistics.

Figure 13.2

False Signals: II

The three-month average on the unemployment rate is more volatile than the six-month average.

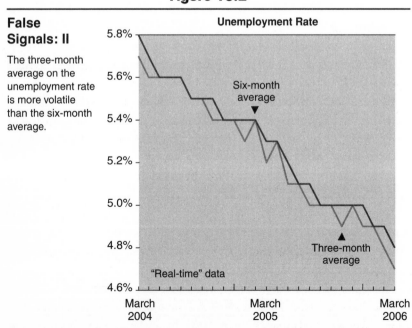

Source: Bureau of Labor Statistics.

one-month change would have been distracted by at least three false signals of an uptrend on the way down (see Figure 13.1).

Similarly, those who followed the three-month average would have been distracted by false signals on the way down (see Figure 13.2).

Finally, just as the payroll employment figures are seasonally adjusted—and therefore should not be taken literally—the same is true of the unemployment rate. It hits seasonal lows in the spring and fall but seasonal highs in the winter and summer.

THE EMPLOYMENT REPORT AND THE BOND MARKET

I began this chapter by saying that there is evidence that the employment report misinforms the bond market more than it informs it.

First, how well does the consensus forecast perform? If it's good at predicting the reported change in payroll employment, it must do a good job of getting bond prices to discount the change before it's reported. If it's bad at predicting the reported change, it may throw bond prices off.

In fact, as I pointed out in Chapter 12, it performs terribly.

I took all the consensus forecasts from January 1998 through March 2006—99 observations in all—and asked: How often has it gotten within 25%, give or take, of the reported figure? That would mean, for example, that if the reported figure were 200,000, the consensus would pass the test if it were anywhere between 150,000 and 250,000—a broad enough target, you'd think.

The consensus failed to hit within the defined range nearly three times out of four.

So I lowered the standard. Getting within 50%, give or take, of the reported figure merely requires that you fall between 100 and 300 if the reported figure is 200. The consensus still failed to do that half the time (see Table 13.1).

But perhaps it got better over the recent period? No, it got slightly worse. Since January 2003, consensus failed to be accurate within 50% more than half the time (see Table 13.2).

Table 13.1 Consensus Scorecard
(January 1998 to March 2006)

Within Plus or Minus	Out of 99 Cases
25%	28
50%	50

Source: "Market News Survey of U.S. Economic Forecasts: Employment," Market News International and
Bureau of Labor Statistics, Monthly Situation Report,
Table B-1: Employees on nonfarm payrolls by industry
sector and selected industry detail. http://www.bls.gov
/schedule/archives/empsit_nr.htm.

But if the consensus throws the bond market off the scent of the
nonfarm payroll number, there is still a second chance to get it right.
Once the number is announced at 8:30 A.M., bond prices can react
accordingly.

But do they react the right way? The recent run-up in short-term
interest rates does not inspire confidence.

From June 30, 2004, to March 28, 2006, the Federal Reserve hiked
the interest rate on federal funds by a quarter-percentage point (25 basis
points) 15 times in a row. The yield on the two-year Treasury note rose
in response, from 2.64% on July 2, 2004 (the day before the release of

Table 13.2 Consensus Scorecard
(January 2003 to March 2006)

Within Plus or Minus	Out of 39 Cases
25%	10
50%	16

Source: "Market News Survey of U.S. Economic Forecasts: Employment" and Bureau of Labor Statistics.

the June 2004 employment report), to 4.89% by April 7, 2006 (the day the March employment report was released).

That makes 22 employment reports released over this period. How much credit can they be given for alerting the bond market to this 225 basis point rise in the two-year interest rate? No credit can be given at all.

Since the yield on the two-year Treasury note rose by nearly a half-basis point per day over this 22 month period, the 22 trading days on which these employment reports were released should have risen by the same average to be merely "neutral." In fact, the yield rose 11 times, fell in 9, and was flat the other two times, for a net increase of 11 basis points (see Table 13.3). Over 22 days, that comes to the same average increase of a half-basis point per day.

Maybe the yield showed a substantial increase the day before the report, already discounting a strong jobs figure? On the contrary, it did no better, rising by about the same average of a half-basis point per day (see Table 13.4).

Is this too brief a period to prove anything decisive? I suppose so. But you have to wonder if the roar of the noisy data didn't drown out the quieter sound of the underlying trend. The March 2006 report showed that, over these 22 months, nonfarm payroll employment had risen by an average of 160,000 per month. While that was not strong by the standards of

Table 13.3 Employment Report Scorecard Showing Change in Two-Year Note Yield from Day before to Day of Report (June 2004 to March 2006)

	Days	Total Points
Rose	11	82
Fell	9	−71
No change	2	0
Grand total	**22**	**11**

Source: Federal Reserve, "Two Year Treasury Interest Rates," statistical release, http://www.federalreserve.gov/releases/h15/data/Business_day/H15_TCMNOM_Y2.txt.

Table 13.4 Employment Report Scorecard Showing Change in Two-Year Note Yield from Two Days before to Day before Report (June 2004 to March 2006)

	Days	Total Points
Rose	13	40
Fell	7	−30
No change	2	0
Grand total	**22**	**10**

Source: "Market News Survey of U.S. Economic Forecasts: Employment" and Bureau of Labor Statistics.

the 1990s, it was enough to bring the unemployment down by nearly a full point—to a six-month average of 4.8% by March 2006.[16]

Had you tracked the payroll change as a 12-month percentage change and the unemployment rate as a six-month average each release would have generally confirmed that the labor markets were getting increasingly tighter and that interest rates were bound to rise as a result.

COPING

Do I think the BLS will heed my call for radical change? No. Investors want up-to-the-minute news. And journalists, economists, and government statisticians—not to mention television reporters—won't exactly welcome stripping the jobs report down to such bare essentials since that would put their own jobs at risk.

But that needn't stop you from kicking the habit, or not acquiring the habit if you're not already so afflicted.

ADDENDUM: NIXON, UNEMPLOYMENT-GATE, AND HAROLD GOLDSTEIN

"There are no copies of this memo. Please do not circulate it. Please destroy it."[17]

What was contained in this "High Priority-Eyes Only" memo of December 8, 1971, from White House Special Counsel Charles Colson to White House Chief of Staff H. R. "Bob" Haldeman? The memo contained a discussion of the way the BLS seasonally adjusted the unemployment rate.

It all started earlier that year, when the Nixon administration began to get very obsessed with monthly readings on the unemployment rate. Indeed, President Nixon himself got so worked up he ordered an investigation of the Jewish influence at the BLS, which culminated in actions taken against three Jews at the agency soon thereafter. Historians, take note. Certain threads of this story have been tied together as never before.

On March 22, 1971, President Nixon's Labor Secretary James D. Hodgson made the surprise announcement that the BLS would no longer be allowed to hold press briefings when it released its monthly figures. The decision was reached, said Hodgson, to "avoid the awkwardness of subjecting BLS staff to questions with policy implications."[18]

But muzzling Harold Goldstein was the real objective, as anyone familiar with the press briefings knew. Assistant Commissioner Goldstein had managed to offend the White House three months in a row with his persistent and skeptical remarks about whether the unemployment rate was really declining.

So Goldstein's press conferences were halted. But soon after Hodgson announced the blackout, Senator William Proxmire responded with an announcement of his own. As Chairman of the Joint Economic Committee of the Congress, he had written a letter to both Goldstein and BLS Commissioner Geoffrey Moore to request their appearance at a public hearing on the morning the employment figures were released.

That kept Goldstein in the spotlight, which proved his undoing.

Appearing before the Joint Economic Committee on Friday, July 2, 1971, to comment on the June figures, the employment maven finally angered the president himself. June showed a plunge in the unemployment rate to 5.6% from 6.2%, which Hodgson greeted as "a real improvement."[19] But Goldstein couldn't say "how much of the total drop in unemployment is real and how much is the result of statistical factors."[20] (He was later vindicated.)

These remarks "evoked dismay and anger within the Administration," according to an official account, "and the Department of Labor was privately told of President's Nixon's anger concerning the incident."[21]

The transcript of a conversation Nixon had with Chief of Staff
H.R. "Bob" Haldeman the following morning quotes the president
muttering the name, "Goldstein." He then tells Haldeman about a conversation he had with Special Counsel Charles Colson—"a clever bas-
tard" for having his office "call the Bureau of Statistics." The president
quotes himself asking Colson, "Were they all Jews?" and then quotes
Colson's response: "Yes. Every one of them is a Jew."[22]

Then, "I want to look at any sensitive areas where Jews are involved,
Bob. See, the Jews are all through the government"[23]

Monday, July 5, the president ordered Haldeman to have Special Assistant Fred Malek tally up the number of Jews in top-level positions at
the BLS.[24] Malek had to be prodded to do the deed, but finally submit-
ted a Jew count of 13 (while listing no names) in a memo to Haldeman
on July 27.[25]

At the top level, BLS Commissioner Geoffrey Moore was not Jewish, but his two lieutenants, Chief Economist Peter Henle and Chief Statistician Leon Greenberg, were Jewish. The agency announced on
September 29 that the positions of chief economist and chief statistician
had been eliminated; both incumbents left the BLS. It was also announced that Harold Goldstein was being transferred to another job.[26]
Two years later, he left government service altogether.

Even after the bloodletting, Colson continued his investigation. In
that "High Priority-Eyes Only" memo to Haldeman, he wrote: "Let's
not be in a position next September of kicking ourselves for allowing
phony unemployment figures to be murdering us politically."[27]

Colson believed that the BLS was, at that very moment, deciding
how it would seasonally adjust the unemployment rate in such a way as
to make it look unfavorable just before the November election. It was
therefore necessary to oust BLS Commissioner Geoffrey Moore immediately, since Moore was too passive to foil the plan. Colson even had a
replacement for Moore lined up—"a man who understands the problem
[and] who is prepared to go in tomorrow."[28]

Colson's urgent warning apparently went unheeded. Geoffrey
Moore was forced out, but not until after the election.

Economist Joel Popkin recalls another relevant story. Nixon's Labor
Secretary James D. Hodgson required that all BLS press releases be final-
ized in his office before being issued.[29] Popkin, who was then an assistant
commissioner in charge of writing the monthly press release on the Con-

sumer Price Index, recalls responding to this subtle intimidation by resorting to a classic strategy.

In the hope of distracting Hodgson from striking out anything substantive, Popkin would consciously include words in his write-up to which he expected Hodgson to object. This strategy of the red herrings worked so well, that at times Hodgson even let the offending words go by. Then, Popkin himself would suggest they be struck.[30]

Greenspan Idolatry

When Alan Greenspan succeeded Paul Volcker as Federal Reserve chairman in 1987, he stood in the shadow of a charismatic predecessor. When Ben Bernanke succeeded Greenspan in January 2006, he had an even harder act to follow. Greenspan has been the object of such idolatry you'd call it a cult if it didn't have such a mass following.

"For 17 years, Mr. Greenspan, who is now 78 years old, has *deftly steered the American economy*"[1] wrote *Wall Street Journal* reporter Greg Ip in a front-page, two-part retrospective on "Greenspan's Legacy" that unfortunately contributed to the chairman's hagiography.

This is hardly the place for a full assessment of Greenspan's tenure at the Federal Reserve, but in an effort to lighten Bernanke's burdens, I will expose three myths about the Greenspan record in this chapter. The first concerns his inflation-whipping gamble of 1994 to 1995. The second is his visionary leadership through the boom of the late-1990s—probably his major claim to greatness. And finally, I deal with the popular image of him as a fabulous forecaster.

There is plenty of legitimate controversy about Alan Greenspan; I try to avoid it here. Nothing that follows should require a great deal of imagination, except perhaps from Greenspan's idolaters.

THE SLOWDOWN THAT DIDN'T HAVE TO HAPPEN

Let's start with that first triumph: Mr. Greenspan's bold monetary moves of late-1994 through 1995 to curb inflation. After boosting the interest rate target on federal funds from 3% to 3.75% in three quarter-point steps, and then from 3.75% to 4.75% in two half-point steps, *Wall Street Journal* reporter Greg Ip writes that Chairman Greenspan:

> made a dramatic proposal to the Federal Open Market Committee [FOMC], the body that votes on interest rates: Jack up the Fed's key short-term interest rate by three-quarters of a percentage point in one shot, something he had never recommended before. Mr. Greenspan believed such a move would demonstrate the Fed's resolve and finally stamp out inflation worries.[2]

Other FOMC members preferred to continue raising the federal funds target in smaller increments. But "Mr. Greenspan held firm," writes Ip, hiking the federal funds rate by three-quarters of a point, to 5.5% on November 15, 2004, followed by another half-point hike to 6% 11 weeks later on February 1.

In Ip's view, "Mr. Greenspan's gamble paid off." But with the benefit of hindsight, we can see that the "gamble" exacted heavy costs in return for elusive benefits. By boosting the Federal Reserve's short-term interest rate too fast and too far, he slowed economic growth to a crawl. From an annual rate of 4.8% in fourth quarter 1994, growth in real gross domestic product (GDP) plunged to 1.1% in the first quarter and then to 0.7% in second quarter 1995. The unemployment rate, which had been falling through 1994, rose through the first half of 1995.

If curbing inflation was the objective, the cost in terms of lost income and lost jobs was hardly worth it, though, in fairness, Greenspan probably can't be faulted for not realizing he was fighting yesterday's

battle. The irony is that Greenspan himself would soon realize that disinflationary forces were already in place that made his hawkish action an
overreaction. Not that he should have become dovish. The economy *was*
booming in 1994, and Greenspan was right to believe that more moderate growth would be more sustainable. But instead of doing violence to
the economy by ramping up rates, he should have continued nudging
federal funds rate up in smaller increments, as his colleagues at the Federal Reserve had advocated.

In fact, Mr. Greenspan himself might have realized he had overre-
acted. In any case, just three weeks after the February 1, 1995, tightening to 6.0%, the chairman made a public statement that "amounted to a
monetary easing"—according to then-Federal Reserve Governor Alan
Blinder—since long-term interest rates fell in response. And starting in
July, he began to ease the federal funds rate in three consecutive quarter-
point steps from 6.0% to 5.25% by February 1996.

Now try *Wall Street Journal* reporter Greg Ip's assessment:

> Mr. Greenspan's gamble paid off. Investors concluded that the
> Fed's actions would contain inflation. Long-term interest rates
> stabilized shortly after the November increase and fell steadily
> after February's. The stock market rallied. The economy slowed
> sharply in the first half of 1995 but didn't lapse into recession.
> By the second half of the year it was growing briskly again. In-
> flation remained at 3%. Mr. Greenspan had achieved the "soft
> landing," central banking's holy grail. It set the stage for six
> more years of growth and the longest U.S. economic expansion
> on record.[3]

Ip's account is more interesting for what it leaves out than for what it
says. To begin with, his reference to long-term interest rates falling
"steadily after February's" hike in rates makes no mention of the key
event widely credited with having touched off most of that fall: not the
tightening action on February 1, but the dovish tone of Mr. Greenspan's
testimony before the Senate Banking Committee on February 22.
"Greenspan Sees an End to Rate Increases—Fed Chief Hints Restraint
despite Some Inflation, Cheering Wall Street,"[4] read the February 23,
1995, *Wall Street Journal* headline. According to former Federal Reserve

Governor Alan Blinder, "In fact, the [Fed chairman's] statement itself amounted to a *monetary easing,* since it fueled a bond-market rally long before the Fed started cutting interest rates."[5]

Which brings us to Ip's other statement: "By the second half of the year [the economy] was growing briskly again . . . [which] set the stage for six more years of growth."[6] We don't need to know the full reason why the economy started "growing briskly again" to be appalled by Ip's omissions. He not only omits Greenspan's aforementioned monetary easing statement in February of that year, Ip also doesn't tell us that the chairman began easing the federal funds rate by early July. If Mr. Greenspan's initial lurch to 6% by February 1995 "set the stage for six more years of growth," how about those stage-setting quarter-point cuts that left federal funds at 5.25% a mere 12 months later?

Finally, consider Ip's brisk assessment of the costs and benefits: "The economy slowed sharply in the first half of 1995 but didn't lapse into recession. . . . Inflation remained at 3%." But would inflation really have gone that much higher if the economy had not slowed sharply? Ip himself inadvertently answers no when he deals with Greenspan's quick changeover from inflation-fighter to productivity seer. By September 1996, Ip writes that Greenspan's "fellow Fed officials worried that economic growth was so robust it would push up inflation." But not the chairman. He had come to realize that robust growth would not push up inflation because of faster productivity growth:

> He knew it had taken decades [writes Ip] for the innovation of electricity to boost productivity. Now, he thought, the advent of computers was finally having a similar delayed effect. Mr. Greenspan was so sure of his insight that he was ready to bet the fortunes of the U.S. economy.[7]

But Greenspan himself had only recently worried that robust growth would push up inflation, having only recently persuaded "fellow Fed officials" to take a very different "gamble" with the U.S. economy that "paid off." Ip somehow ignores this irony. But it's doubtful that the chairman had.

In his congressional testimony of February 1995, Greenspan had deemed it "still too soon to judge" whether "our dominance in computer software" had boosted "long-term productivity growth . . . closer to the more vibrant pace that characterized the early post–World War II period."[8] One and a half years later, he'd apparently decided it was no longer "too soon to judge." Since trends can be judged only after the fact, he must have realized that productivity's power to undermine inflation had been just as strong in 1995 as in 1996—even if his hagiographers didn't.

THE TRIUMPH OF THE 1990S BOOM

The boom of the late-1990s has been viewed as one of the chairman's unquestionable triumphs. Instead of raising interest rates, goes the story, Mr. Greenspan had the vision to keep rates flat. But many of the excesses of the boom led directly to the bust that followed. Let's grant Mr. Greenspan's argument that he could not have directly pricked the stock market bubble without risking recession. But one of his key themes has been that economic growth must be kept moderate to be sustainable. Had he gently tilted against the boom starting in 1996, growth from 1996 through 2000 would have been slower, but from 2000 on, it might have been more sustainable.

Greenspan's hagiographers do not even consider this issue. Ip writes:

> At a meeting to vote on interest rates, Mr. Greenspan . . . argued that rates should be held flat. . . . Following his analysis of the productivity data, he believed companies could now make and sell more without having to hire more employees, reducing the threat of inflation. . . . His colleagues, with misgivings, went along.

In Ip's version, his insight about faster productivity, on which "he was ready to bet the fortunes of the U.S. economy," again proved triumphantly right. On that point, Ip invokes the authority of Nobel laureate economist Robert Solow:

> By not raising rates, the Fed chairman allowed the economy to continue growing and unemployment to drop to its lowest level in a generation, even as inflation edged downward. Other cen-

tral banks "would have clamped down," says Nobel Prize-winning economist Robert Solow, "[Mr. Greenspan] refused to be slave to a doctrine. He kept saying, 'Let's look around us and see what's happening, and act accordingly.'"[9]

By not raising rates, the Federal Reserve chairman also helped unleash the "irrational exuberance" (his words) that led to the post-2000 bust. Nor were his policy choices in 1996 limited to "clamp[ing] down" or holding rates flat. Instead, Greenspan could have done exactly what his colleagues had originally advocated, and which he himself faithfully observed in 2004 and 2005: taken the edge off the boom by slowly nudging up rates in quarter-point steps. The abrupt cut in rates in fall 1998 in the wake of the Asian crisis would still have happened. But it would have been from a much higher plateau. Economic performance from 1996 through 2000 might not have been as stellar. But overall performance from 1996 through 2004 might have turned out better. The excesses that helped create the bust—including the stock market bubble—might have been reined in.

So the chairman's ostensible decision to "let-'er-rip" through the late-1990s may well have been unfortunate or at least not quite the triumph it's been made out to be. These comments are surely obvious enough to be accepted with little argument. What's less obvious is why they aren't more commonly held.

One reason, I believe, is that the economy's performance through 2000 looks so dramatic that it fires people's imaginations. Perhaps a more modest performance would have been more long lasting, but such truths can be tedious to contemplate.

There might also be special reasons why people create an arbitrary wall in this case between the boom and its aftermath. And while none are very rational, they are all quite potent. They include (1) the idea that the record-breaking 10-year expansion, which ended March 2001, had somehow died a natural death; (2) the vision of 2001 ushering in the "new millennium"—reinforced by (3) the Bush era replacing the era of Clinton; and by (4) 9/11.

But while 9/11 certainly hurt the economy, and the Bush era certainly altered it, there is still no reason to assume a better outcome wouldn't have been possible had Mr. Greenspan acted differently. The other barrier to such thinking, of course, is the human need to crown philosopher kings.

A MASTER FORECASTER?

"Mr. Greenspan . . . ," wrote Ip, "has deftly steered the American economy by relying on two strengths: an unparalleled grasp of the most intricate data and a willingness to break with convention when traditional economic rules stop working."[10]

One looks vainly at his forecasting record for evidence of this.

I referred above to the chairman's *ostensible* decision to let the economy perform the way it did, because it really wasn't his decision at all. The boom did not just owe its life to Mr. Greenspan's prescience about rising productivity. His poor forecasting record also played a key role. Had he known the boom was coming, he would very likely have raised rates to slow it down. The only reason he didn't act was that he kept expecting the boom to moderate on its own.

First understand that no Federal Reserve chairman can operate without some idea of what the future will bring. As Greenspan himself has said more than once, "Because monetary policy works with a lag, we need to be forward-looking, taking actions to forestall imbalances that may not be visible for many months."[11]

According to Ip, the chairman pinned all on the expectation that faster productivity growth could relieve inflationary pressures. But Ip unintentionally does him an injustice. Mr. Greenspan fully understood that while productivity could make a difference, it was no panacea. Among other concerns, there was the risk that tight labor markets could bring accelerated wage gains (see the Box). For example, in his July 1997 testimony before Congress, no amount of faith in the disinflationary effects of higher productivity could prevent him from voicing concern about the recent decline in the unemployment rate:

> The key point is that continuously digging ever deeper into the available work age population is not a sustainable trajectory for job creation. The unemployment rate has a downside limit. . . . *If the pace of job creation continues,* the *pressures on wages and other costs* of hiring . . . *could escalate more rapidly.*[12]

Alan Greenspan and the Quit Rate

Federal Reserve Chairman Alan Greenspan has suffered various bouts of numerical obsession during his illustrious career. The one that will be recounted here dates to 1997: the time he expressed concern about a one-month estimate in one of the tiniest numbers of all—the unemployed who had become jobless by quitting their jobs.

These "job leavers" typically account for a little over 10% of the unemployed and about 0.6% of the labor force. But the chairman pared even that figure down to job leavers out of work less than five weeks (data he must have gotten on special order from the BLS)—which he apparently preferred to consume in morsels of a thousandth of a decimal place. Thus, the February 26, 1997, *Wall Street Journal* reported this "quit-rate" figure at "only 0.243%" in 1996, down from "a relatively high '0.306%'" in 1989, while adding that it "rose sharply" the month before to "0.294%."[a]

Why did the Federal Reserve chairman prefer to see this quit rate stay low? Because workers brazen enough to quit a job before lining up another one were just the sort to feel secure enough to hold out for higher wages when they did work. So the decline in the quit rate since 1989 was a source of satisfaction just as its January increase was a source of concern. (The chairman wasn't categorically opposed to higher wages—just very sensitive to the risk of inflation.)

As Greenspan explained to the Senate Banking Committee February 26, 1997 (the same day the *Journal* story appeared), "heightened job insecurity" was the "most significant explanation" of the "suppressed wage cost growth" of recent years. But

---

[a] Zachary G. Pascal and Michael M Phillips, "Fewer Workers Worry About Losing Job," *Wall Street Journal* (February 26, 1997).

(continued)

since "people were somewhat more willing to quit their jobs to seek other employment in January . . . the labor markets bear especially careful watching."[b]

It isn't clear whether the chairman knew that part of that decline since 1989 was yet another statistical illusion caused by the redesigned survey of 1994. The pre-1994 question that determined the quit count—"At the time you started looking for work, was it because you lost or quit a job or was there some other reason?"— had been split in two. Respondents were first asked, "Before you started looking for work, what were you doing: working, going to school, or something else?" Only if "working" was the answer would the field interviewer then ask, "Did you lose or quit that job, or was it a temporary job that ended?"

From this seemingly innocuous change, the share of the unemployed who had quit fell 13%.

As for the January increase in the quit rate that Greenspan cited, real-time data showed that temporary spikes this time of year had happened before. Sure enough, the February 1997 employment report released just nine days after Greenspan's remarks showed that most of January's increase had been reversed.

Bureau of Labor Statistics Division Chief Tom Nardone had the best postmortem on Greenspan's short-lived obsession with this figure: "I never understood how a 0.05 percentage point swing in job leavers could tell us very much about the changing attitudes of 125 million workers. But then, I'm not the Fed chairman."[c]

This is a true story: Greenspan's staff once asked a money market economist for his near-term outlook on bond prices. When this economist jokingly replied it depended on the weather, the questioner remarked in all seriousness, "Just keep that from the chairman, or he'll have us researching global warming."

---

[b] Federal Reserve, *Semi-Annual Monetary Policy Report,* testimony of Chairman Alan Greenspan before the Committee on Banking, Housing, and Urban Affairs, U.S. Senate (February 26, 1997), http://www.federalreserve.gov/boarddocs/hh/1997/february/testimony.htm.
[c] Interview with Bureau of Labor Statistics Division Chief Tom Nardone on February 18, 1997.

Had Greenspan expected "the pace of job creation" to continue, purchase of a little "inflation insurance" in the form of a higher federal funds rate would surely have been his next topic. But as he made clear in this same July 1997 testimony, he mistakenly believed the pace of job creation had already slowed:

> Fortunately, the very rapid growth of demand over the winter has eased recently. . . . Monetary policymakers, balancing these various forces, *forecast a continuation of less rapid growth* in coming quarters. . . . This pace of expansion *is expected to keep the unemployment rate close to its current low level.*[13]

That same forecast about the "pace of expansion" was Mr. Greenspan's refrain for four straight years from 1996 through 1999, and it never failed to be wrong. So after tweaking federal funds up a quarter-point in March 1997 to 5.5%, he stood pat until fall 1998, when he quickly eased three-quarters of a point in the wake of the Asian crisis to 4.75%. Not until June 1999 did he begin to hike rates steadily to 6.5% by May 2000—by which point it was too late: The stock market was already in free-fall with the economy contracting.

Had he been more prescient about the economy from the beginning, then that emergency easing in fall 1998 would have been from a much higher level—say, 6.5% or more—and recent economic history might have been very different.

My counterfactual should also be fairly obvious—except that it undermines Mr. Greenspan's image as flawless forecaster. According to a celebratory article in the *Financial Times:*

> Mr. Greenspan has studied the U.S. business cycle since the late-1940s. At the Fed he has shown a mastery of data, drawing not only on governmental statistics and data series developed by the Fed but also on company reports and anecdotal evidence.[14]

The article then quotes Carnegie Mellon professor (and "historian of the Fed") Allan Meltzer as follows:

> "He [Mr. Greenspan] takes in information from a wide variety of sources and distils it rather accurately. I don't know of any other Fed chairman who has paid so much attention to the daily,

weekly, monthly events, in thinking about what they mean, and *mostly getting it right.*"[15]

"Mostly getting it right" surely includes mostly getting the economic outlook right. And there his track record can be fairly easily checked.

In February and July of each year, the Federal Reserve Board releases its "Monetary Policy Report to the Congress," which accompanies the Federal Reserve chairman's semiannual testimony before committees of the House and Senate. The report includes forecasts of key economic indicators, including growth of real (i.e., inflation-adjusted) GDP, measured as the percentage change in fourth quarter GDP from the fourth quarter of the previous year. The forecasts are put in "ranges" and in more narrow measures of "central tendency." In most cases, the range must be wider than the Federal Reserve chairman's, since it might take into account higher or lower forecasts from other members of the FOMC. So if we judge Mr. Greenspan's performance record according to the range, we are being quite lenient.

How did we do? Well, judge for yourself.

In Table 14.1, we list the forecast range released in the February "Report to the Congress" from 1994 through 2005. Alongside each, we

Table 14.1   February Forecast by Federal Reserve Board Q4/Q4 Percentage Growth of Gross Domestic Product

February Report	Forecast Range (%)	Actual (%)
1994	2½ to 3¾	4.1
1995	**2 to 3¼**	**2.0**
1996	1½ to 2½	4.4
1997	2 to 2½	4.3
1998	1¾ to 3	4.5
1999	2 to 3½	4.7
2000	3¼ to 4¼	2.2
2001	2 to 2¾	0.2
2002	2 to 3½	1.9
2003	3 to 3¾	4.0
2004	4 to 5½	3.8
2005	3½ to 4	3.2

Source: "Monetary Policy Report to the Congress."

list the actual fourth quarter year-over-year growth of GDP in that year. Wherever actual growth fell within the forecast range, we make the generous assumption that Mr. Greenspan got it right that year, marking the figures in bold.

Now notice the figures are in bold in only one year: 1995. Also notice that from 1996 through 1999, Mr. Greenspan consistently underestimated GDP growth by a wide margin.

But that was in February, with the fourth quarter still at least eight months away. By the time July came around, the Federal Reserve chairman probably did much better.

In a sense, he did (see Table 14.2). From being proved right once in 12 years, he was now right twice—in 1995 and in 2005. While he still consistently underestimated GDP growth from 1996 through 1999, his margin of error was generally lower.

We can also ask whether the Federal Reserve chairman compiled a better record than the consensus of private forecasters routinely polled by blue chip economic indicators. Since Mr. Greenspan had some power to affect the outcome—and might have had unique access to facts—you'd expect him to have the edge. But on GDP growth, the performance

Table 14.2 July Forecast by Federal Reserve Board Q4/Q4
Percentage Growth of Gross Domestic Product

July Report	Forecast Range (%)	Actual (%)
1994	3 to 3½	4.1
1995	**1⅜ to 3**	**2.0**
1996	2½ to 3	4.4
1997	3 to 3½	4.3
1998	2¾ to 3¼	4.5
1999	3¼ to 4	4.7
2000	3¾ to 5	2.2
2001	1 to 2	0.2
2002	3 to 4	1.9
2003	2¼ to 3	4.0
2004	4 to 4¾	3.8
2005	**3 to 3¾**	**3.2**

Source: "Monetary Policy Report to the Congress."

records are strikingly similar. The consensus was also right in 1995 and 2005, and about as wrong in other years.

THE SECRETS?

Former Federal Reserve Governor Alan Blinder has been quoted as saying, "When Greenspan's replacement . . . walks into that office and opens the drawer for the secrets, he's going to find it's empty. The secrets are in Greenspan's head."[16]

Greenspan may or may not share them at some point in the future, but the media should be a bit more discerning in crowning philosopher kings. Hagiography in reporting is unbecoming.

Best-Selling Myths: Freakonomics

W hat a shame about that title," observed the British weekly, the *Economist*. *"Freakonomics* is bound to dampen the spirits of any intelligent reader, suggesting an airport-ready, dumbed-down romp. . . . But . . . Steven Levitt . . . shows . . . what plain old-fashioned economics can do in the hands of a boundlessly curious and superbly skilled practitioner."[1]

On the other side of the Atlantic, the *New York Times* called *Freakonomics* "a splendid book, full of unlikely but arresting historical details."[2] "Mr. Levitt's . . . genius," observed the *Wall Street Journal*, "is to take a seemingly meaningless set of numbers, ferret out the telltale pattern and recognize what it means."[3] The *New Republic* agreed, remarking that "Levitt stands out . . . because of his remarkable ingenuity, creativity, and sheer doggedness in investigating empirical questions about which no one seems to know much at all."[4]

Co-authored by journalist Stephen Dubner and by University of Chicago economist and John Bates Clark Medal award-winner Steven

Levitt, *Freakonomics* has been a runaway bestseller. In this chapter, I concentrate on two major topics in the book: the supposed effect of abortion on plummeting crime rates that helped make the book famous, and the value of services rendered by real estate agents, which was heavily promoted by Stephen Dubner in his *New York Times Magazine* article about Levitt.

What these topics have in common is that in each case, the holes in Levitt's research are truly of the emperor-has-no-clothes variety. Otherwise, the abortion thesis is not even about economics. But the better we understand the real causes of falling crime, the more likely it is that crime will keep falling. And the sooner we recognize that Levitt's thesis only confuses the issue, the better.

As for his indictment of real estate agents: They can probably take care of themselves. The issue has larger significance as an insight into the mind-set of the "asymmetric information" theorists of academe.

I focus mainly on the academic papers Levitt did on these topics rather than on the write-ups in *Freakonomics,* which "kind of got dumbed down for the layperson,"[5] as Levitt observed when I interviewed him. (This occurred by telephone on June 9, 2005; the interview was taped, as Levitt was duly informed, and quotes are drawn from the transcript.)

ABORTION AND CRIME

"We offer evidence that legalized abortion has contributed significantly to recent crime reductions."[6] That's the very first sentence in "The Impact of Legalized Abortion on Crime," a paper by John J. Donahue III and Steven D. Levitt that appeared in the *Quarterly Journal of Economics* in May 2001.

And that's the sentence that turns out to be untrue. Donahue and Levitt offer no persuasive evidence that legalized abortion contributed to recent crime *reductions,* significantly or otherwise. They offer no persuasive evidence, regardless of whether those crime reductions are measured in absolute terms (number of crimes committed) or, more appropriately, in terms of crime rates (crimes as a share of the population).

Since we are dealing with an empirical research study in a respected scholarly journal, the authors must have done a lot of empirical research. And they did—except not the research that would have made their evidence persuasive. They show that the legalization of abortion coincided with a decline in birth rates among women whose offspring would be prone to commit crimes. They also show that the decline in crime began about 18 years after the legalization of abortion, when these offspring would have been starting their high-crime years.

But all that evidence is just circumstantial—unpersuasive for a simple reason: It does not show that there was an actual decrease in births of crime-prone offspring, only that there might have been. But if there were, say, a 10% increase in the number of women who fit that demographic profile, and a 5% decline in birth rates among these women, there still would have been an increase in births of crime-prone offspring. Only if the decline in birth rates had been enough to bring a noticeable decrease in births of crime-prone offspring could you make a persuasive case that the legalization of abortion had contributed to the decline in crime. The way to resolve the question is to directly examine the number of births of the crime-prone population itself. And that's what Donahue and Levitt fail to do.

What the data on births actually reveal is that the crime-prone population did increase as a share of the overall population. So there would have been no reason to expect crime rates to decline—and thus no plausible evidence that abortion was a factor.

"Our goal," the authors make clear, "is to understand why crime has fallen sharply in the 1990s, and to explore the contribution to this decline that may have come from the legalization of abortion in the 1970s."[7] Accordingly, they find that "Legalized abortion appears to account for as much as 50% of the recent drop in crime."[8]

A more accurate statement would have read, "0%."

"The simplest way in which legalized abortion reduces crime," Donahue and Levitt write, "is through smaller cohort sizes. When those smaller cohorts reach the high-crime late adolescent years, there are simply fewer people to commit crime." And what is "far more interesting" from their perspective is that "abortion has a disproportionate effect on the births of those who are most at risk of engaging in criminal behavior."[9]

But that's just the point: Not only did cohorts *not* get "smaller," when they reached their "high-crime adolescent years," there were simply *more* "people to commit crime." And abortion did not prevent an increase in births of those "most at risk of engaging in criminal behavior": *Births of the crime-prone population increased.*

The authors did a great deal of research—except they did not look directly at the relevant data. In their use of sophisticated "multivariate" analysis, they content themselves with such variables as "abortion rates"—abortions per live births. The correlation they get with rates of crime apparently convinces them that causation has been established. All it really demonstrates is that our economists have been snookered by their own heavy-duty statistical techniques.

If you insisted on making some claim for abortion as a factor, you could say that, but for abortion, crime rates might have gone even higher since abortion slowed the increase in the crime-prone population. When I spoke with Levitt by telephone, and presented him with this evidence, that is what he did say (I quote from the transcript of our conversation):

> I guess it's semantics. It doesn't matter to me if you want to say that abortion has made crime *15 to 20% lower than it otherwise would have been* and *otherwise it would have been higher.* Then we are on the same page. That's *all* I'm really saying.[10]

But it wasn't "semantics" at all. Crime was already sky-high by the early-1990s. The important question is what lowered it so dramatically—not what might have prevented it from going higher. The answer to this question could have profound effects on social policy in the United States and is of interest to any urban police chief, mayor, or city resident, especially if he or she can't afford a doorman. How do we replicate or perpetuate one of the most positive social trends in recent memory? To that question, Levitt contributes nothing.

CRIME RATES VERSUS BIRTH RATES VERSUS BIRTHS

First, consider the main phenomenon we're trying to explain: the sudden plunge in the rate of violent crime through the 1990s (see Table 15.1).

Notice, for example, that by 1999, the rate of violent crime was more than 30% lower than its 1991 to 1992 peak. It had dropped more than 20% from the level of 1989. As we'll see, there was no observable decline in the crime-prone population over the same period.

Table 15.1   Violent Crimes per 100,000
of the U.S. Population

Year	Violent Crimes
1989	663
1990	732
1991	758
1992	758
1993	747
1994	714
1995	685
1996	637
1997	611
1998	567
1999	523

Source: Federal Bureau of Investigation, http://www.fbi.gov.

Donahue and Levitt provide a fairly conventional profile of the demographics of the crime-prone population. For example, they write that "fertility declines for black women" from legalized abortion were "three times greater than for whites"—a key finding, since "homicide rates of black youths are roughly nine times higher than those of white youths."[11] Apart from race, the two other demographic factors that put one "most at risk of engaging in criminal behavior" are, not surprisingly, "teenage motherhood" and "unmarried motherhood."

The authors also write that "the *peak ages* for violent crime are roughly *18 to 24,* and crime starts turning down around 1992, roughly the time at which the first cohort born following [the Supreme Court's Decision in] *Roe v. Wade* would hit its criminal prime."[12] Later they write:

The timing of the break in the national crime rate is consistent with a legalized abortion story. In 1991 the first cohort affected by *Roe v. Wade* would have been roughly seventeen years old, just beginning to enter the highest crime adolescent years. In the [five] early-legalizing states . . . , the first cohort affected by legalized abortion would have been twenty years of age, roughly the peak of the age-crime profile.[13]

Accordingly, it should have been easy enough to use those figures and work backward. For example, 24-year-olds in 1991 would have been born in 1967; 20-year olds would have been born in 1971; and 17-year-olds in 1974. Abortion was legalized in five states in 1970 and in all states—by *Roe v. Wade*—in 1973. So by 1991, the population of 17- to 24-year-olds would have been affected. By taking the number born in those years to black, teenage, unmarried mothers, it should have been possible to link a decline in births to the decline in the crime-prone population. At the other end, fewer crime-prone people in the 1990s would have been associated with the decline in crime.

But Donahue and Levitt never directly cite the actual data on births. They mention that abortion brought a decline in birth *rates*—births as a share of women capable of giving birth. But as noted, that should not be confused with declines in the actual number of births as a share of the population as a whole. If 5% fewer teenagers had out-of-wedlock children in the 1979 than in 1969, there would still be more babies born if there were 10% more teenagers in 1979 to begin with. And that, in turn, depended on events *Roe v. Wade* could not influence—birth rates in the 1950s and 1960s.

Their thesis does not hold up if you take actual births for virtually any definition of the crime-prone population that reflects Donahue and Levitt's—for example, out-of-wedlock births to teenagers or to teenaged blacks. Assembling the numbers in Table 15.2 was a more pedestrian arithmetical exercise than any they engaged in. But it has the virtue of addressing the issue head-on. It also cast Donahue and Levitt's thesis in the most favorable light possible, since it does show some decline by the late-1990s.

I simply took the number of out-of wedlock births to black teenagers and carried them forward by those peak crime ages of 17 to 24 to the years 1989 through 1999. For example, to estimate the number of those who would have been 17 to 24 in 1989, I took the number born in:

- 1965, who would have been 24 in 1989; and
- 1966, who would have been 23 in 1989;

and so on, up to those born in:

- 1971, who would have been 18 in 1989; and
- 1972, who would have been 17 in 1989.

Similarly, to estimate the number of those who would have been 17 to 24 in 1999, I took the number born in:

- 1975, who would have been 24 in 1999; and
- 1976, who would have been 23 in 1999;

and so on, up to those born in:

- 1981, who would have been 18 in 1999; and
- 1982, who would have been 17 in 1999.

I did the same exercise for every year in between and got the results in Table 15.2.

Table 15.2 Offspring of Black Unmarried Teenagers Who Would Have Been Ages 17 to 24

Year	Offspring (in Thousands)
1989	803
1990	855
1991	902
1992	946
1993	980
1994	1,013
1995	1,030
1996	1,044
1997	1,049
1998	1,049
1999	1,048

Source: National Center for Health Statistics, "Vital Statistics of the United States: Natality," vol. 1, years 1965–1982 (Hyattsville, MD: U.S. Department of Health and Human Services), http://www.cdc.gov /nchs/products/pubs/pubd/vsus/1963/1963.htm.

In 1989, the vast majority of those ages 17 to 24 were born prelegalization. By 1995 or 1996, the majority of those ages 17 to 24 would have been affected by postlegalization—but, as Table 15.2 shows, not by enough to bring a decrease in the actual number of births.

Since the cohorts are the hard-core crime-prone population by the authors' own definition, then insofar as demographics were concerned, you would have predicted an *increase* in the number of crimes. But, of course, we are mainly talking about crime rates—crimes as a share of the population. So I took the figures in Table 15.2 and recalculated them as a percentage of the population in each of these years (see Table 15.3).

Based on this data, one might have expected a flat-to-rising trend in the rate of violent crime. Nothing would have prepared you for the

Table 15.3   Offspring of Black Unmarried Teenagers Who Would Have Been Ages 17 to 24 per 100,000 of the U.S. Population

Year	Offspring
1989	326
1990	343
1991	357
1992	369
1993	377
1994	385
1995	387
1996	388
1997	385
1998	380
1999	376

Source: National Center for Health Statistics, "Vital Statistics of the United States: Natality," vol. 1, years 1965–1982 (Hyattsville, MD: U.S. Department of Health and Human Services), http://www.cdc.gov/nchs/products/pubs/pubd /vsus/1963/1963.htm.

plunge that actually did take place. The data on those born out of wed-lock to black teenagers are most favorable to Donahue and Levitt's the-sis. Take virtually any other relevant data, and you get figures that would have predicted an *increase* in crime rates. For example, I projected the number who would have been ages 17 to 24 based on out-of-wedlock births to teenagers in general. As a share of the population, I got the re-sults shown in Table 15.4.

"Obviously, recent abortions," Donahue and Levitt explain, "will not have any direct impact on crime today since infants commit little crime." But "the continual decrease in crime between 1991 and 1999 is . . . consistent with the hypothesized effects of abortion. With each passing year, the fraction of the criminal population that was born postlegalization increases."[14]

But as we've seen, once you look at the data on "the fraction of the criminal population" that was actually "born postlegalization," the "hypothesized effects of abortion" turn out to be very different from

Table 15.4 Offspring of Unmarried Teenagers Who Would Have Been Ages 17 to 24 per 100,000 of the U.S. Population

Year	Offspring
1989	138
1990	143
1991	147
1992	155
1993	158
1994	171
1995	170
1996	176
1997	179
1998	177
1999	180

Source: National Center for Health Statistics, "Vital Statistics of the United States: Natality," vol. 1, years 1965–1982 (Hyattsville, MD: U.S. Department of Health and Human Services), http://www.cdc.gov /nchs/products/pubs/pubd /vsus/1963/1963.htm.

abortion's real effects. Legalized abortion brought a decline in birth rates of crime-prone cohorts, but not by enough to cause an appreciable decrease in the number of births as a share of the overall population once these people were of an age to commit crimes.

Even if we go beyond the 1990s, we find little future for the abortion-cuts-crime thesis. Based on births to black, unmarried teenagers through the early 1990s and on Census Bureau projections for the total population, we were able to project the share of this crime-prone population through 2010. We found that after a slight dip in 2004 and 2005—which still put it higher than 1989 and 1990—the share is due to rise back to levels comparable to 1991 and 1992 by 2010.[15]

DID LEVITT RECANT?

That still leaves the door open to a be-thankful-it-wasn't-worse argument. If it hadn't been for legalized abortion, the crime-prone population would have risen even faster. Legalized abortion either prevented crime from rising or at least slowed its rate of increase. But that does not tell us why crime rates fell. There is no shortage of plausible explanations, starting with tougher sentencing leading to many more criminals being locked up and therefore unable to commit crimes. By claiming half the credit for abortion instead of none, Donahue and Levitt minimize these other factors, especially the effect of innovative policing techniques, which they dismiss almost completely.

I do give Levitt credit, however, for having conceded my point—although he didn't at first. In our phone conversation, when I mentioned the data that showed an increase in the number of babies born to unmarried teenagers, his immediate response was to play the "wantedness" card. Since legalization made abortion available to these teenagers, and since they didn't opt for it, they must have "wanted" their children in a way that pregnant teenagers prelegalization did not. Their offspring were therefore not crime-prone in the way that such offspring used to be.

Levitt, in fact, had already beaten a hasty retreat behind this tautological fortress in his published writings on the subject. Recall that he and Donahue had written in their 2001 paper that "legalized abortion reduces crime . . . through smaller cohort sizes" and by having "a disproportionate effect on the births of those who are most at risk of engaging in criminal behavior."[16] In a later popularization of his views in the *Journal of Economic Perspectives* (2004), his "underlying theory" suddenly consisted of "two premises: (1) unwanted children are at greater risk for crime, and (2) legalized abortion leads to a reduction in the number of unwanted births."[17]

No one can doubt the definitional truth of either of these premises: Unwanted births are certainly aborted more often than wanted; and if for no other reason than criminals are disproportionately born to unmarried teenagers, unwanted children are hardly at *smaller* risk for crime. But precisely because we are talking about unmarried teenagers, that extra margin of "wantedness" may soon wear thin.

To Levitt's credit, I didn't even have to make this point. Instead, he suddenly remarked (I quote again his key admission):

> I guess it's semantics. It doesn't matter to me if you want to say that abortion has made crime *15 to 20% lower than it otherwise would have been* and *otherwise it would have been higher.* Then we are on the same page. That's *all* I'm really saying.[18]

"Otherwise it would have been higher." I didn't press the point that it wasn't semantics at all. While I'm glad he and I are finally "on the same page," too bad it's only in this book and not in his.

Freakonomics itself retains both earlier and later versions of Levitt's argument, and on virtually the same page. "What sort of woman was most likely to take advantage of *Roe v. Wade*?"[19] the authors ask. Their answer:

> Very often she was unmarried or in her teens or poor, and sometimes all three. . . . Growing up in a single-parent home roughly doubles a child's propensity to commit crime. So does having a teenage mother. Another study has shown that low maternal education is the single most powerful factor leading to criminality.[20]

Except for the substitution of poor for black, these demographic factors are very similar to those mentioned in the Donahue and Levitt paper. Here, too, we might expect data on actual births—say, to unmarried teenagers.

In fact, we do get the statement that "conceptions rose by nearly 30%, but births actually *fell* by 6%, indicating that many women were using abortion as a method of birth control"[21] [emphasis in original]. But this seems to mean that (1) for every 1,000 conceptions previously, there were now 1300, or 30% more, and (2) of these 1,300 conceptions, there were now 78 fewer births, or 6% fewer—which still nets out to more births. In any case, this could not mean there were literally fewer births for the crime-prone population, since the data show otherwise.

But elsewhere in the book, births are forgotten, and unwantedness again becomes the touchstone. Levitt and Dubner write:

> In the early 1990s, just as the first cohort of children born after *Roe v. Wade* was hitting its late teen years—the years during which young men enter their criminal prime—the rate of crime began to fall. What this cohort was missing, of course, were the children who stood the greatest chance of becoming criminals. And the crime rate continued to fall as an entire generation came of age minus the children whose mothers had not wanted to bring a child into the world. Legalized abortion led to less unwantedness; unwantedness leads to high crime; legalized abortion, therefore, led to less crime.[22]

But remember that they are mainly talking about decisions by teenagers—generally in materially deprived circumstances already—to bear or not to bear a child out of wedlock. The idea that these decisions can be made with any real foresight about the child's future strains credulity.

Of course, those who think abortion itself should be illegal might not like Levitt's thesis for that reason. Others (like me), who are pro-choice, have a different concern: It might discourage further research into the real causes of falling crime.

ASYMMETRIC INFORMATION AND REAL ESTATE AGENTS

Asymmetric information refers to the imbalance of knowledge between buyers and sellers, experts and amateurs—in this case, real estate agents and their clients. If Levitt fell victim to his own sophisticated statistical techniques in dealing with abortion and crime, he was done in by simple lack of data in his broadside against real estate agents: a form of asymmetric information of his own.

Nothing in what follows should be interpreted to mean that real estate brokers need to continue earning their 5% to 6% commission. My analysis is agnostic on that issue, but the industry is currently being challenged by Internet-based discount brokers. If such discount brokers end up dominating the industry, they'll effectively prove that buyers and sellers can be serviced for much less.

But Levitt's thesis addressed a very different issue: the nature of the services real estate agents provide. Let's start by summarizing his findings.

According to Levitt, people who sell their homes are manipulated by real estate agents into accepting a price that is less than the market will bear. The agent, after all, has every incentive to get the deal done quickly, at a price low enough to attract ready buyers. His or her commission is only a small percentage of the sale price anyway. So between two alternatives—(1) getting a house sold for $200,000 now or (2) spending time and effort selling the house for $208,000 in 10 days—the agent will always prefer the lower-priced deal.

The seller of the home would be better advised to wait the 10 days in return for $8,000 more, but he or she agrees to sell for less only because the agent scares him or her into thinking that if he or she doesn't accept the low bid, he or she could end up selling for *much* less. The "[real estate] agent's main weapon [is] the conversion of information into fear,"[23] write Dubner and Levitt in a chapter called, "How is the Ku Klux Klan Like a Group of Real Estate Agents?"

If we are to believe Levitt's thesis, however, there is already a rather strange implication. The successful attempt by real estate agents to get homeowners to sell for less necessarily means that buyers of homes end up paying less. But once we realize that buyers are also represented by real estate agents, we can only wonder why the game gets systematically tipped in their favor. Don't the agents who represent buyers also have incentives that are adverse to the interests of their clients?

The agent representing the buyer will also want to get the deal done quickly, at a price *high* enough to attract ready sellers. His or her commission is also a small percentage of the sale price. So between two alternatives—(1) getting a house bought for $208,000 now or (2) spending time and effort buying for $200,000 ten days from now—the agent will always prefer the *higher-priced* deal. In that case, too, the buyer of the home would be better advised to wait the 10 days to pay $8,000 less. If the seller of the home can be manipulated through fear, why can't the buyer be as well?

Why does Levitt draw this distinctly asymmetric conclusion? As we'll see, it is because of the asymmetric nature of his research.

This section of *Freakonomics* draws on a paper called "Market Distortions When Agents Are Better Informed: The Value of Information in Real Estate"[24] that Levitt co-authored with University of Chicago colleague Chad Syverson. "The [seller's] agent has strong incentives to sell a house quickly," Levitt and Syverson state at the outset, "even at a substantially lower price, and thus may encourage clients to accept sub-optimally low offers too quickly."[25] Based on their data, that's what the authors claim they found. But they could have written with equal logic: "The *buyer's* agent has strong incentives to get a house bought quickly, even at a substantially *higher* price, and thus may encourage clients to *make excessively high* offers too quickly."[26] Since they had no data to test that possibility, they completely ignore it.

Lay those two statements side by side, however, and you begin to see the problem with the authors' whole formulation. In the real world, buyers may well have strong feelings about what they want to pay and sellers about what they want to charge. Depending on how agents read those feelings, their desire to get the deal done quickly could lead to any number of outcomes. Under certain circumstances, for example, seller's agents may recognize the need to negotiate a *high* price for the deal to get done at all.

AGENTS DISTORT INFORMATION?

Levitt and Syverson base their findings on a "data set with roughly 98,000 home sales" in Cook County, Illinois, of which "about . . . 3,330 sales . . . involve a real estate agent selling his or her own home."[27]

But of the 98,000 home sales, there must have been something like 3,330 cases in which real estate agents were *buying* homes for themselves. In fact, most of this buying was probably being done by the very same real estate agents who were selling. But since the data isn't available, Levitt and Syverson don't mention it.

Based on their data, Levitt and Syverson find:

Agent-owned homes sell for about 3.7% (or roughly $7,700 at the median sales price) more than comparable houses and stay on the market about 10% longer (an extra 9.5 days), even after controlling for a wide variety of house and neighborhood characteristics.[28]

The $7,700 differential, they conclude, can only be due to "agents distorting information to mislead clients,"[29] to their "encourag[ing] clients to accept sub-optimally low offers too quickly."[30] In drawing this conclusion, Levitt and Syverson specifically reject two other explanations that are far less sinister.

First, they reject the possibility that "realtor homes are more attractive to buyers on unobservable dimensions (e.g., realtors know better what features the market values or invest more in maintenance of their houses)."[31] As the authors go on to inform us, "Real estate agents tend to live in homes that are larger, newer, and have greater numbers of amenities like master baths and fireplaces, even compared to other homes on the same block"[32]—which would already suggest that they go to greater lengths to add features with market values.

Second—and especially if they did make improvements—agents have a unique incentive to spend time and effort trying to capture their investment. When they represent a client, they normally get 1.5 cents on every dollar of purchase. When they represent themselves, they get 100 cents. That they spend less time and effort selling a client's property does not necessarily mean they shirked their responsibility to do the best they can for their client. It may simply reflect what the authors themselves call "the typical principal-agent story."

"The possibility remains," the authors commendably admit, "that realtor-owned properties might be correlated with unobservable characteristics of the housing."[33] Why can't this be a key factor? Because, they explain, while it would account for the "higher house price . . . the longer time on the market is puzzling."[34]

But "puzzling" to whom? That it would take a longer time to find prospects who can be convinced they are getting better value sounds plausible, not puzzling. Indeed, Levitt and Syverson elsewhere report that 22% of all homes failed to sell at all,[35] and that this happened more frequently among agent-owned houses. To the authors, this only "reinforces the fact that agent-owned homes take longer to sell."[36] Well, of course, but a greater failure rate is hardly the mark of professionals working for themselves. Might it also reflect the failure to earn a premium for improvements that were made in vain?

On the issue of working for yourself, Levitt and Syverson outdo themselves for microeconomic metaphysics. In their view, it simply isn't credible that real estate agents are putting in more time and effort selling their own home simply because they have a greater financial incentive (100 cents on the dollar versus 1.5 cents). As they explain, "If agents exert less effort in selling their clients' houses (the typical principal-agent story), agents would sell their houses for higher prices, but *should sell their own homes more quickly,* contrary to the evidence."[37]

This sort of magic thinking doesn't even work on its own terms. The magical part is the assumption of a ready trade-off between time and effort. According to the math, if clients' houses took an average of 95 days to sell, then agents will merely increase their effort to (1) sell for a higher price in (2) fewer than 95 days. But in the real world, it may be that no amount of extra effort can shorten the time it takes to sell a home for a higher price.

Even in Levitt and Syverson's magical world, however, where there is always a trade-off between time and effort, how are these economists to know the terms of trade? Perhaps real estate agents did increase their effort by 10% to *shorten* the time to 104.5 days. But perhaps shortening it any further—and still fetching a higher price—required *doubling* their effort, which might not have been the most cost-efficient use of their own time. So perhaps the agents did choose the optimum trade-off between effort and time, given their own cost constraints.

Far from dismissing the alternative explanations for the $7,700 premium, our economists only succeed in making them sound more plausible. It might simply be a combination of the fact that (1) real estate agents really are selling a more valuable commodity that (2) requires more time and effort to get a buyer for, reinforced by (3) the 100% return they get on the $7,700 premium rather than the 1.5% they would get if the home belonged to a client.

THE BUYER'S AGENT

The authors give three other reasons for believing the premium reflects "agent-induced distortions" that are no more persuasive than the others. In fact, the third reason boomerangs on them even more than the others do.

First, they find that both the agent's price premium and time on the market were greater where the houses sold were more unique or hetero-geneous.[38] In their view, this is further evidence of "agent-induced distortions" because "greater heterogeneity is likely to increase the agent's informational advantage" by making it harder for the average homeowner to find "directly comparable prior home sales."[39] But just as obviously, these would be precisely the neighborhoods where agent-homeowners would be likely to make their most aggressive improvements that would take the longest to market.

Second, they report that premiums and time on the market were greater in the period from 1992 through 1995 than from 2000 through 2002. In their view, the difference is explained by "the rise of the Internet [which] has made it much easier for sellers to directly observe the characteristics of other houses on the market and to find recent transaction prices, reducing the informational advantage of realtors."[40]

But if heterogeneous markets are where realtors are able to do most of their mischief, we can only wonder how effective Internet listings could really be, since they are more suited to homogeneous markets. In any case, before we accept such reasoning, we have a right to wonder if another kind of heterogeneity was operating: Home prices rose two to three times faster from 2000 through 2002 than from 1992 to 1995.[41] Spreads may have narrowed in the later period for that very reason.

The final factor that Levitt and Syverson cite for believing that "agent-induced distortions" are at work only succeeds in highlighting the asymmetric hole in the authors' data. It has to do with different outcomes when the buyer of the house is not represented by a real estate agent of his own.

One of their findings is that "when the agent is selling his or her own home . . . , the absence of a buyer's agent is associated with a . . . 1.9% increase in the sale price,"[42] which they interpret to mean he or she does better for himself or herself when every dollar of the higher sale price belongs to him or her.

But if a buyer pays 1.9% more when *not* represented by an agent, what happens when he or she is? By implication, he or she then pays 1.9% less. Now restate the above finding by substituting "presence" for "absence" and "decrease" for "increase." It would then read as follows: "When the agent is selling his or her own home . . . , the *presence* of a buyer's agent is associated with a 1.9% *decrease* in the sale price."

While there is no substantive difference between this way of putting things and the authors', it does highlight an anomaly. For if sellers' agents systematically misinform their clients, why would buyers' agents negotiate a *lower* sale price in the very toughest of circumstances? These are circumstances in which the seller is another professional who stands to make 100 cents on every dollar added to the sale price. The buyer's agent, by contrast, not only has a mere 1.5% stake in the price. Since his or her commission is determined by multiplying 1.5% by the sale price, the lower it is, the less he or she gets.

And yet we are to believe that under these circumstances, the buyer's agent manages to knock a few thousand off the sale price. (At an average price of $200,000, 1.9% less comes to $3,800.) The reason might lie in the grudging words of the authors themselves: "Agents are often better informed than the clients who hire them."[43] While the incentives of buyers and their agents are not perfectly aligned (buyers' realtors prefer to have deals go through, even if buyers overpay), *buyers' agents are nonetheless acting on behalf of buyers* and *may credibly contradict statements by the selling agents about the current state of the market.*[44]

Now, rerun *this* statement, playing the same game we played earlier: Substitute *seller's* for *buyer's,* and vice versa, while reversing all the other terms, where appropriate. It then would read:

> A *seller's agent* is likely to be better informed than the clients he or she represents. While the incentives of *sellers* and their agents are not perfectly aligned (*sellers' realtors* prefer to have deals go through, even if *sellers undercharge*), *sellers' agents are nonetheless acting on behalf of sellers* and *may credibly contradict statements by the buying agents about the current state of the market.*

If Levitt and Syverson believe that first statement about the motivations of agents representing buyers, why not the second, about the motivations of agents representing sellers? Especially since the same people represent either side?

On each side, "acting on behalf of" clients does not always mean driving the hardest bargain. Agents are not exactly acting on their client's behalf if "deals" do *not* "go through"—and they apparently don't in one out of five cases. But as I mentioned earlier, depending on the clients' feelings—and how agents read those feelings—deals may not go through *unless* agents negotiate harder for their clients.

That last point may help explain the anomaly of why the presence of a buyer's agent "has a negligible impact on the sale price when a selling agent is representing a client,"[45] but why a buyer's agent can nonetheless negotiate a 1.9% decrease in far tougher circumstances—when an "agent is selling his or her own home."[46]

In the latter case, the focus of the negotiations may be the value of the improvements the agent made on "his or her own home." But in the former case, the main dynamic may simply be that the seller of the home drives a harder bargain than the buyer. Later on, I'll explain why. But assuming it is true, then with or without a buyer's agent, the price would tend to be the same—although it may be that more deals go through when buyers' agents are involved.

Levitt must surely be right, however, that "incentives" of clients and "their agents" can never be perfectly aligned.[47]

When I spoke with him, he predicted that "what the Internet is going to do is . . . divide the realtors' job, which has been bundled in the past" between providing information on what a home can be sold for and providing "labor services [with] the goal of selling a house." Those "labor services," continued Levitt, "would be billed on an hourly basis."[48]

That might sound to some as the worst alignment of incentives imaginable, resulting in hundreds of hours billed with no sale to show for it.

HELPING THE DEAL GO THROUGH

Levitt might have benefited from the reminiscences of a real estate broker named Joe Stratford, who makes it clear that clients are rarely the hapless ciphers Levitt makes them out to be. "My clients were careful buyers, the Sloans,"[49] Stratford ruefully observes at one point, adding:

> I made a living in real estate by keeping track of what a buyer wanted . . . but you couldn't get ahead of the Sloans. What they wanted to know about every house they looked at . . . defied preparation. . . . The one thing that made me think the Sloans would eventually go for something was their conviction that something valuable or even precious was out there. The more I assured them we were on top of every available property, the more worried they got that we were missing one.[50]
>
> Making a low offer wouldn't solve these problems, it would only convince the Sloans that they were settling for less than they wanted.[51]

Actually, that's from a novel, Pulitzer-Prize winner Jane Smiley's highly entertaining *Good Faith,* which her made-up character Stratford narrates. Levitt told me he hadn't read the novel, but if he had, it could have helped him realize that deal makers might need more than just hourly pay to get them to do their job. In one tense scene where a deal is about to fall through, a temperamental seller demands to know, "What do I pay you for, Stratford?" to which Joe Stratford observes, "He paid me for exactly what I was about to do . . . helping the deal go through."[52]

On the difficulties of helping deals go through, *Freakonomics* makes the point that sellers "may have an enormous emotional attachment"[53] to their homes, which implies they may drive a harder bargain than buyers. To that, we might add that the mental accounting of "mortgage thinking" could motivate buyers to drive an easier bargain: To a seller, an extra $1,000 on the price is counted dollar for dollar, but to a buyer, it might feel like a few dollars extra per month on the mortgage.

So if Levitt and Syverson actually did have data on the sale prices of agent-bought homes, they might find that these professionals paid almost as much as the amateurs did. The finding would be consistent with the view that sellers as a group drive a harder bargain than buyers; that to get the deal done under these circumstances, real estate agents tend to get more accommodation from buyers than they do from sellers; and that the extra time and effort real estate agents commit when they purchase a home for themselves nets them a discount that might be real but not very large.

The greater premium earned by agent-sellers might then be explained by the factors already mentioned (tendency for realtors to enhance the value of their home; financial incentive to put in more time and effort).

As for the degree to which agents are willfully misinforming their clients, I'm sure it's very real. I just wouldn't trust Levitt to tell me by how much.

ASYMMETRIC INFORMATION THEORY RECONSIDERED

There is a larger point involved that is beyond the scope of this chapter and of this book. But it deserves to be made: The whole theory of asymmetric information is based on a stunted view of human ingenuity.

Levitt's view of real estate agents is a case in point. In the chapter bearing the provocative title, "How Is the Ku Klux Klan Like a Group of Real-Estate Agents?" *Freakonomics* authors Levitt and Dubner recount the following "true story, related by John Donahue"—Levitt's collaborator on abortion and crime:

> The agent does not want to come out and call you a fool. So she merely implies it—perhaps by telling you about the much bigger, nicer, newer house down the block that has sat unsold for six months. Here is the agent's main weapon: the conversion of information into fear. Consider this true story, related by John Donahue, a law professor who in 2001 was teaching at Stanford University: "I was just about to buy a house on the Stanford campus," he recalls, "and the seller's agent kept telling me what a good deal I was getting because the market was about to zoom. As soon as I signed the purchase contract, he asked me if I would need an agent to sell my previous Stanford house. I told him that I would probably try to sell without an agent, and he replied, 'John, that might work under normal conditions, but with the market tanking now, you really need the help of a broker.'"
>
> *Within five minutes,* a zooming market had tanked. Such are the marvels that can be conjured by an agent in search of the next deal.[54]

Levitt and Dubner leave it at that—leaving us to wonder if this "true story" could really be true. After the agent made that last remark about the "market tanking"—to a Stanford law professor, no less—did he get Donahue's business anyway? Levitt and Dubner don't say. "The agent does not want to come right out and call you a fool,"[55] they have just observed. But then, why didn't Donahue respond with, "What do you take me for?"

Here is another case study of asymmetric information, also taken from *Freakonomics:*

> Information is so powerful that the *assumption* of information, even if the information does not actually exist, can have a sobering effect [italics in original]. Consider the case of a one-day-old car.

The day that a car is driven off the lot is the worst day in its life, for it instantly loses as much as a quarter of its value. This might seem absurd, but we know it to be true. A new car that was bought for $20,000 cannot be sold for more than perhaps $15,000. Why? Because the only person who might logically want to resell a brand-new car is someone who found the car to be a lemon. So even if the car isn't a lemon, a potential buyer assumes that it is. He assumes that the seller has some information about the car that he, the buyer, does not have—and the seller is punished for this assumed information.[56]

Look, you just bought a brand-new car for $20,000. You need to sell it right away, presumably because of the bizarre happenstance that you just suffered a major and unforeseen financial reversal that requires you to recoup your money fast. You won't get the full $20,000. But do you really have to settle for only $15,000? Here's an idea: What if you urged prospective buyers to take the car to a service station of their choice, at your expense, to get it evaluated (with documentation on where and when you bought the car)?

Put yourself on the buyer's side of this transaction. You're in the market for a new car. But why pay $20,000 when you can get the same car for $18,000?

The irony this highlights about situations of asymmetric information is fairly obvious, but so far as I know, never mentioned: Often, those who have the superior information (you, in this case) are at a *disadvantage* until you can find some credible way to better inform the other side.

With a little ingenuity, usually, you can. Levitt might not offer to pay you $18,000 for the car, but his brand of "plain old-fashioned economics" is hopefully not yours.

Best-Selling Myths: Nickel and Dimed

The official poverty level," writes Barbara Ehrenreich in her best-selling book, *Nickel and Dimed,* "is still calculated by the archaic method of taking the bare-bones cost of food for a family of a given size and multiplying this number by three." The problem with this method, as she points out, is that "food is relatively inflation proof, at least compared with rent."[1]

She's right. Since the cost of most other necessities has risen faster than the cost of food, it wouldn't make sense to keep updating the poverty threshold by applying the same multiple to food. "We might as well abolish poverty altogether, at least on paper," Ehrenreich observes, "by defining a subsistence budget as some multiple of average expenditures on comic books or dental floss."[2]

Quite valid, if only it were true. Had Ehrenreich read the very source she cites on the bottom of page 200 in her book, she would have learned that the poverty threshold isn't calculated that way. It was

originally formulated in the 1960s as a multiple of the cost of food. But
ever since 1969, it's been raised in line with the overall consumer price
index that reflects the rising cost of all goods and services bought by
wage earners, including rent, gasoline, and healthcare—a method that
directly addresses her concerns.

While not the most egregious error in *Nickel and Dimed,* it provides
a few clues about the author's methodology. For one thing, while Ehrenreich clearly spoke with qualified people, she appears to have asked none
to vet the technical material in her book. Anyone from the frequently
cited Economic Policy Institute could have spotted this error right away.
Nor did she bother to check her broad, impressionistic conclusion that
low-wage work leads nowhere against research that directly contradicts it.

Originally a bestseller in both hard- and soft-cover editions, *Nickel
and Dimed: On (Not) Getting By in America* has achieved a second life as a
staple on college reading lists. An Internet search reveals that it's assigned
in sociology courses at institutions that include Berkeley, Duke, Cornell,
Emory, and the University of North Carolina at Chapel Hill, and even
in economics courses at schools that include Bucknell, Vanderbilt, and
UMass Boston. I would have no problem with any of this, so long as
Nickel and Dimed was also taught as a case study in econospinning.

Both the strengths and weaknesses of this book remind me of
George Orwell. Like the Orwell of such classics as *Down and Out in Paris
and London* and *Road to Wigan Pier,* Ehrenrich offers a journalistic account of one middle-class person's experiences with low-wage work, and
Nickel and Dimed is an engaging and eye-opening read. Ehrenreich
vividly portrays the hassles, privations, and indignities she experiences as
a waitress, a hotel aide, a cleaning woman, a nursing-home aide, and a
Wal-Mart sales clerk. Her observations are often moving and memo-
rable, as when she calls low-wage workers "the major philanthropists of
our society." She writes, "They neglect their own children so that the
children of others will be cared for; they live in substandard housing so
that other homes will be shiny and perfect."[3]

As a work of analysis, however, *Nickel and Dimed* suffers from the
usual blinders that tend to mar such personalized accounts. First, there is
too much about the inner life of the first-person narrator and not enough
about the feelings of those who are stuck with this life. For example,
when working as a Wal-Mart sales clerk, Ehrenreich speaks of "hating
the customers for . . . their size," adding, "I don't mean just bellies and
butts, but huge bulges in completely exotic locations, like the backs of

the necks and the knees,"[4] we acknowledge her all-too-human reaction. But when she declares, *"those of us who work in ladies'* . . . live with the fear of being crushed by some wide-body as she hurtles through the narrow passage from Faded Glory to woman size, lost in fantasies involving svelte Kathie Lee sheaths,"[5] we wonder if Ehrenreich is projecting her own fears and fantasies on the women who work there.

In any case, she offers no confirmation that those fears and fantasies are shared by any of her coworkers. A more serious omission occurs when she concedes that "most of my fellow workers are better cushioned than I am; they live with spouses or grown children or they have other jobs in addition to this one."[6] We get brief examples of the second jobs, but nothing further is said about the living arrangements that make "most" others "better cushioned."

This omission indicates that the author is less concerned with well-rounded reportage than with moral bullying: cutting off the escape hatches her readers might seek from their own culpability. ("Guilt . . .," she later writes, "guilt doesn't go anywhere near far enough; the appropriate emotion is shame.")[7]

Which brings us back to the main problem with *Nickel and Dimed*.

EHRENREICH'S ECONOMICS

Ever hear of the *killer anecdote*? In economic journalism, it's that real-life story you tell that renders unforgettable the thesis you wish to prove.

The trouble with most economic journalism, however, is that it often confuses anecdote with evidence. *Nickel and Dimed* is a classic case in point. Ehrenreich's core thesis is that low-wage workers find themselves "sinking ever deeper into poverty and debt."[8] Now, to prove this, you need what is generally referred to as a "longitudinal study" of the same workers over time.

One such study is discussed in a 2000 paper called "Wage Progression Among Less-Skilled Workers" by Northwestern University labor economists Tricia Gladden and Christopher Taber. Gladden and Taber used data from the National Longitudinal Study of Youth to track the pay of high school dropouts and graduates over 10-year periods. Over the decade and a half that they covered (1978 to 1993), labor markets were generally slack and jobs far harder to get than in the late-1990s. But they still found, for example, that among African American women, the average annual wage increase, in return for continuous work, ran 5% over the rate of inflation.

As Taber explained to me, since these workers were essentially progressing up an income ladder, that 5% is independent of whatever gains get bestowed on any particular rung of the ladder.[9] So add the 3% real annual gains that a tighter labor market has recently been bringing and you find that a person making $10 an hour or less can more than double her real income in 10 years.

Accordingly, Gladden and Taber draw the trite inference that "we should encourage low-skilled workers to work."[10]

Studies like this are left out of Ehrenreich's personal account. A simple search of wage-and-age data on the Bureau of Labor Statistics (BLS) web site would have shown her that wage data broken out by sex, race, or ethnicity (female, non-white, Hispanic, or Asian) consistently show that older workers earn more than younger workers or that lower-wage tiers tend to consist disproportionately of younger workers. Might the reason be that older workers have more experience?

Before we consider, on its own terms, Ehrenreich's analysis of how the wages of low-paid workers are determined, compare her mind-set on the different ways *prices* are determined. As mentioned, she regards food as "relatively inflation-proof," pointing out (when indicting the imaginary way the poverty threshold is calculated) that "in 1999, food took up only 16% of the family budget," down from "24%" in the "early 1960s."[11]

She already has first-hand knowledge of clothing by working as a sales clerk at Wal-Mart: "Within each brand-name area," she observes, "there are of course dozens of items, even dozens of each *kind* of item [her italics]. This summer, for example, pants may be capri, classic, carpenter, clam-digger, boot, or flood . . ."[12] all of it affordable by "the multiethnic array of our shoppers—Middle Eastern, Asian, African American, Russian, former Yugoslavian, old fashioned Minnesota white."[13]

But while the cheapness of food and clothing goes unexplained, "The problem of rents is easy for a noneconomist, even a sparsely educated low-wage worker, to grasp: It's the market, stupid. When the rich and the poor compete for housing on the open market, the poor don't stand a chance. The rich can always outbid them."[14]

Try rewriting that last sentence by substituting "housing" with "food and clothing": "When the rich and the poor compete for food and clothing on the open market, the poor don't stand a chance. The rich can always outbid them."

Why don't the rich buy up all those brand-name pants and all that cereal, bread, and cheese to fill up their McMansions? The answer is probably easier for a "sparsely educated" mind to grasp than for over-educated ones like Ehrenreich's: It's the markets, stupid.

Some might object that rents are a special case because land is finite. But once we realize that *shelter* can overcome that limitation through the building of high-rises, we might begin to wonder if zoning restrictions, real estate taxes, and federal mortgage interest subsidies—*nonmarket* influences—are the real cause of the "problem of rents." Even a "noneconomist" like Ehrenreich is able to grasp, as she comments, two pages later, that "housing subsidies for homeowners—who tend to be far more affluent than renters—have remained at their usual munificent levels."[15]

Yet, in the very next paragraph, she declares that "if rents are *exquisitely sensitive to market forces, wages* clearly are not."[16]

On that last point, as noted, her basic message is loud and clear. Working for chump change is a sucker's game—not the sort of activity calculated to better one's lot in life. She writes:

> I grew up hearing over and over, to the point of tedium, that "hard work" is the secret of success: "Work hard and you'll get ahead" or "It's hard work that got us where we are." No one ever said that you could work hard—harder even than you ever thought possible—and still find yourself sinking ever deeper into poverty and debt.[17]

Lest there be any doubt that she means this observation to be taken seriously, it occurs in a final chapter called "Evaluation," replete with the citation of studies and statistics. The *New York Times* certainly got the point, observing in a celebratory note on her book that the author set out "to test the vaunted ideal of work as a ticket out of poverty: the ticket, she discovered, turns to be an unplanned round trip."[18]

But Ehrenreich certainly doesn't discover this from her own brief experiences as a low-wage worker. And in her brief snapshots of coworkers, she compiles no information on their "sinking ever deeper into poverty and debt." In fact, while poverty comes up often, debt is barely mentioned. Whatever evidence she has for this discovery is in the final chapter.

There we read that one of the key problems with workers earning more is that "employers resist wage increases with every trick they can think of and every ounce of strength they can summon."[19] This insight gets buttressed with a killer anecdote that dies a natural death:

> I had an opportunity [she writes] to query one of my own employers on this subject in Maine. You may remember the time when Ted, my boss at the Maids, drove me about forty minutes to a house where I was needed to reinforce a short-handed team. In the course of complaining about his hard lot in life, he avowed that he could double his business overnight if only he could find enough reliable workers. As politely as possible, I asked him why he didn't just raise the pay. The question seemed to slide right off him. We offer "mothers' hours," he told me, meaning that the work was supposedly over at three—as if to say, "With a benefit like that, how could anybody complain about wages?"[20]

The problem with stories like this is that they prove nothing. Maybe Ted didn't realize that, even if paying higher wages reduces profit earned per worker, overall profit can jump by employing twice as many (since "he could double his business overnight")—a variant on the old principle of making it up in volume. More likely, Ted was mainly interested in telling her about "his hard lot in life," and that, whatever his reason for not taking her suggestion, he preferred to talk up the virtues of the wage he paid to one of his wage earners rather than treat her as a profits consultant.

Ehrenreich's formulation about employers resisting higher wages could just as easily be rendered as "retailers resist price cuts with every trick they can think of and every ounce of strength they can summon." Capitalists should be just as reluctant to cut prices as they should be to raise wages. The fact that they routinely do the former should help make it more plausible that they also do the latter.

In fact, Ehrenreich is forced to deal with the *actual fact* that wages have risen. But after duly reporting certain relevant figures, she then declares, "Obviously we have one of those debates over whether the glass is half empty or half full: the increases that seemed to have mollified many economists do not seem so impressive to me."[21] That's one debate you can have, but you can also ask, just how is it possible for the glass to be even half empty if employers use all their strength and wiles to keep it drained?

Ehrenreich manages to duck that question altogether:

> When I persisted in my carping to the economists, they generally backed down a bit, conceding that *while wages at the bottom are going up,* they're not going up very briskly. Lawrence Mishel at the Economic Policy Institute, who had at the beginning of our conversation taken the half-full perspective, heightened the mystery when he observed that productivity—to which wages are theoretically tied—has been rising at such a healthy clip that "workers should be getting much more."[22]

We're then off to the races with the reasons they're not "getting much more," which soon get so dense and detailed, she all but forgets that they did, after all, get more:

> In evading and warding off wage increases, employers are of course behaving in an economically rational fashion; their business isn't to make employees more comfortable and secure but to maximize the bottom line. So why don't employees behave in an equally rational fashion, demanding higher wages of their employers or seeking out better-paying jobs?

We might render the above statement as:

> In evading and warding off *price cuts,* retailers are of course behaving in an economically rational fashion; their business isn't to make *customers* more comfortable and secure but to maximize the bottom line. So why don't *customers* behave in an equally rational fashion, demanding *lower prices of the stores they patronize or taking their business elsewhere?*

Ehrenreich answers her own question by setting up the usual straw man about low-wage workers falling short of being "economic man." They're not as mobile as she imagines "economic man" to be, nor as well informed. "For the laws of economics to work," she opines, "the 'players' need to be well informed about their options."[23] Since most retail customers—and certainly most workers—are at best only partially "informed about their options," she must wonder that prices ever fall or wages ever rise.

Meanwhile, Lawrence Mishel's own Economic Policy Institute was reporting at the time that "most workers . . . were promoted, changed employers or experienced other job changes that were often accompanied by a pay increase."[24]

Ironically, while Ehrenreich memorably points out that "unskilled" jobs often require great skill,[25] and while she mentions in passing that the supervisors she encounters are "former cooks" and "former clerks,"[26] it doesn't occur to her that for most people who actually do apply themselves, the glass may well be half full.

Toward the end of her book, Ehrenreich reports that she "never met an actual slacker," but was "on the contrary . . . amazed and sometimes saddened by the pride people took in jobs that rewarded them so meagerly."[27] I happen to think the system cheats these people of their rewards in various direct and indirect ways: zoning restrictions that crowd them out of decent housing, a payroll tax that falls on their very first dollar of wages, a school system that denies their children any kind of meaningful choice. I could go on, but such matters are well beyond the blinders Ehrenreich so determinedly wears. Otherwise, given the opportunities that work in America offers, the pride they take in their work deserves our deepest respect.

Dobbs and Jobs

From the December 8, 2005, broadcast of the CNN show, *Lou Dobbs Tonight:*

> DOBBS: Still ahead . . . , *Communist China* planning a *massive new assault on American consumers.* . . . [later] Our trade deficit with China alone is expected to top a record $200 billion this year. But that's apparently not enough for the Chinese government. . . . China is *aggressively* trying to sell even more cheap Chinese products in this country, under their own brands straight to you, the American consumer. Bill Tucker reports.
>
> TUCKER: China brought 100 of its companies to New York City. . . . Their presence paid for by the *Communist Chinese* government. . . . But some of the products on display would threaten some American products still made here, like floor clocks . . . or Steinway pianos . . . which cost a great deal more than the products being offered at this show.

DOBBS: Basically, what China is saying . . . is, let's cut out the middleman. . . . Who needs Wal-Mart if we can have a Chinese discounter, right?

TUCKER: I think that sums it up exactly, Lou.[1]

Tucker might have added that this "massive new assault on American consumers" pales beside the massacre regularly inflicted by Wal-Mart, which happens to be the main outlet for Chinese imports anyway. From a December 14, 2005, broadcast:

DOBBS: Our nation's record trade deficits with *Communist China* and the rest of the world have surged, again. . . . The trade deficit with *Communist China* alone tops an astounding $200 billion this year, nearly a quarter of a trillion dollars. Kitty Pilgrim reports.

PILGRIM: Congress is blaming the skyrocketing trade deficit on failed trade policy and *Communist China*. . . . Senators sent out press releases as fast as instant messages: "Behind those deficits are massive numbers of American jobs lost to foreign countries."[2]

Use of the outdated term *Communist* for China certainly doesn't enlighten us on how the trade deficit might be dealt with and can only serve to stir up visceral hatred, especially when the "Communist Chinese" state is "planning a massive new assault." On the substantive issues, Dobbs quotes a talking head who warns that the trade deficit can lead to a "dramatic drop" in the value of the dollar, but who then exhorts the need for a dramatic drop in the dollar's exchange value against China's currency. In a final exchange with reporter Pilgrim:

DOBBS: It's a trade crisis at a time when this Treasury Department of this administration—the U.S. Treasury—doesn't have the guts to refer to . . . the Chinese currency pegged to the dollar [at] about a 40% . . . undervaluation. . . . If the U.S. Treasury doesn't have that kind of guts, that kind of intellectual honesty, what in the world are we going to do in trade negotiations?

PILGRIM: I think that was the single biggest issue that people brought up today, that we have be so much tougher on the currency issue, it's absolutely critical right at this moment and it's just not happening.

DOBBS: Tough is great, I'd just like to see some honesty.[3]

The next item in this broadcast concerned the World Trade Organization (WTO) meeting in Hong Kong:

DOBBS: Tonight, there are new fears the World Trade Organization is growing so strong that it is threatening this nation's democratic process, our very sovereignty . . . Lisa Sylvester reports.

SYLVESTER: Wal-Mart is lobbying the World Trade Organization to lift government limits on the size, height, and number of stores that can be established in the country, a move that could make it easier for the giant retailer to expand into smaller communities over the objections of its residents.

LIZ FIGUEROA, CALIFORNIA STATE SENATOR: Why even have a city council? Why even have state governments if WTO agreements are superseding our judgment?

SYLVESTER: And another group, the National Retail Federation, says that *markets* [her voice rising a scorn-filled half-octave] should decide issues such as the size of a store or location, not city, state, and local governments. But lawmakers say taxpayers in a local community would then have no say over zoning issues. And that would allow a big-box retailer to plant itself in the middle of any main street—Lou?

DOBBS: It must be exceedingly difficult for companies and those economists and those political partisans, when democracy—*participatory democracy* in this country and the concerns of middle-class Americans, and of a broad community, obstruct their mission in life, this is outrageous *by any definition*.

SYLVESTER: You know, Lou, this is a perfect example [of] how trade agreements are so much more than just about trade . . . where things that are decided by trade negotiators can have a real impact on local communities.

DOBBS: A real impact on all of us. And particularly those who are losing their jobs in this country.[4]

Dobbs's use of the 1960s slogan "participatory democracy" is particularly ironic. The whole idea behind that slogan was that representative democracy is not responsive to people's needs, usually because it's held hostage to one or another special interest group. If Dobbs and Sylvester had followed the implications of that thought about participatory democracy, we can imagine the following conversation:

> SYLVESTER: You know, Lou, this is a perfect example of how partici-patory democracy can foil those big-box retailers once and for all. How about getting local citizens to stop patronizing those stores?
>
> DOBBS: You mean getting tough on those retailers by organizing an old-fashioned boycott?
>
> SYLVESTER: That's it, Lou!
>
> DOBBS: *Tough is great, I'd just like to see some honesty.* Maybe citizens in local communities are voting with their feet and their dollars, while special interest groups are using zoning laws to keep out the competition. And if markets should decide the size of a store or location, instead of city, state, and local governments, then doesn't State Senator Figeroa sound like *she* comes from Com-munist China?
>
> SYLVESTER: Now, Lou, on this show, such thoughts are *outrageous by any definition.*

MAIN ARGUMENT

Lou Dobbs's lessons in whacky economics could be dismissed as merely funny if it weren't for the depressing fact that they seem to have helped his ratings. Happily, his 2004 book, *Exporting America: Why Corporate Greed Is Shipping American Jobs Overseas,* did not make any of the best-seller lists. But ever since he began doing a regular segment called "Ex-porting America" in early-2003, his nightly audience has jumped to nearly a half-million households.[5]

Since consistency is not Dobbs's strong suit, his ideas are not easy to summarize coherently. But if there is a message that runs through his railings against China, Wal-Mart, trade deficits, illegal immigration, and the outsourcing of services to foreign-based workers, it's that foreigners are taking America's jobs while giving nothing in return—indeed, less than nothing, at least when those foreigners are Chinese "planning a massive new assault on American consumers."

Consumers are no more assaulted when they buy goods at bargain prices than when they buy Dobbs's book or watch his television show. These are all capitalist acts between consenting adults that no one has a right to interfere with forcibly, except by force of persuasion. Dobbs has made it clear, however, that forcible interference is exactly what he would resort to if persuasion doesn't work. What he would interfere with, he also makes clear: Whenever foreign labor is used to produce what American workers could produce, the practice should be stopped.

He also seems to think this practice is somehow new. That he's wrong is hardly reassuring.

As he told an interviewer:

> The principal issue I have with outsourcing is that American companies . . . are killing jobs in this country and sending them overseas to provide the same goods and services back to the U.S. economy. . . . That's what's unique and different, and that's what has to be stopped. As far as ways to do it, we could do it with regulation. One would hope that before that, corporate America would find a conscience. But failing that, regulation is entirely necessary, I'm all for it, and my apologies to the Libertarians.[6]

We could ask Dobbs questions like: If a good was ever manufactured in the United States—shoes and clothing, for example—would he now require that it be manufactured domestically to restore life to the jobs originally killed? What manufactured imports would be exempt? And even if an importer could prove that a certain good was never manufactured in the United States, what difference would that make, since it always could be? That does exempt raw materials that have to be mined abroad, but does it really exempt farm goods?

For example, even though it's far more costly to grow sugar in the continental United States than to import it, the U.S. government forces the taxpayer to subsidize the domestic sugar industry. Should we lift the subsidies, thereby (to quote Dobbs) "killing jobs in this country and sending them overseas to provide the same goods . . . back to the U.S. economy,"[7] or should we—with "apologies to the Libertarians"—extend the same policy to a domestic coffee and cocoa industry as well?

Anyone who thinks these questions might raise a constructive dialogue with Dobbs should scan the list of more than 800 companies at the
back of his book, introduced as follows:

> Here is a list of companies we have confirmed are "Exporting
> America" as of this writing. These are U.S. companies *either*
> sending American jobs overseas *or choosing to employ cheap overseas
> labor instead of American workers.*[8]

The list includes Alcoa, American Express, AT&T, Boeing, Cater-
pillar, ExxonMobil, Coca-Cola, Ford, GM, Home Depot, IBM, Kraft
Foods, Microsoft, National Semiconductor, Pratt & Whitney, Procter &
Gamble, Whirlpool, and Zenith, among other household names—which
raises an ironic question: If so much of the gross domestic product has
been exporting America, how bad an idea could it really be?

The main argument of this chapter is that the use of foreign labor
through imports, illegal immigration, and outsourcing has bestowed
great benefits on the vast majority of U.S. residents. In any case, those
who would dictate to others about their right to engage in such transac-
tions bear a heavy burden of proof. Perhaps the best way to think about
this issue is to imagine that the United States is 50 different nations, instead of 50 different states of one nation. The free movement of goods,
services, labor, and capital across state lines would no longer be taken for
granted. ("Should Michigan be allowed to export cars to New York?
Should Nebraskans be allowed to take jobs from Texans?") Those "level
playing fields" of crank-trade theory would have new applications.
("Californians can't afford to lift their trade-barriers until Floridians
lift theirs.")

Dobbs could publish a book called *Exporting New Jersey.* And the
growth and development of the U.S. economy would be nowhere near
what it has been.

To refute Dobbs, we don't need to resolve more complicated issues
such as the potentially destabilizing effect of America's burgeoning trade
deficit, or the recent controversy on Capitol Hill over what to do about
the millions of illegal immigrants living and working here. Anyone
grappling with that last question must first acknowledge that perhaps as
many as 10 million jobs are done by these by "undocumented" residents,
and that, even if it were possible to deport them all, such a draconian act

would badly dislocate the U.S. economy, apart from being horrifically cruel to the deportees. In any case, Dobbs has mainly been concerned with the trade deficit's effect on employment.

REAL JOB DESTRUCTION

The old, tired idea that the United States has only a finite number of jobs—to be guarded zealously against raids from cheap foreign labor, or from rising productivity, or from changes in consumer buying habits—is probably best dealt with by considering the U.S. economy's real capacity for job creation and destruction.

Dobbs rues the day he supported the North American Free Trade Agreement (NAFTA) of 1994 because he believes it brought the loss of "at least 750,000 jobs."[9] In a February 2005 interview, he claimed that "an estimated 400,000–500,000 jobs a year [are] being exported to cheap overseas labor markets."[10] Now lay those figures alongside Bureau of Labor Statistics's (BLS) figures for the total number of private sector jobs destroyed each year. Since 1994, annual job losses have run between *12 and 16 million.*[11] Based on those figures, a loss of 500,000 per year is only *3% to 4% of the problem.*

The reason the private sector adds jobs at all is that in most years, job creation runs even higher. When Dobbs's intellectual precursor, Ross Perot, famously predicted in 1993 that NAFTA would "cause a giant sucking sound as jobs go south," he didn't realize it would barely be heard above the roar of the great American job-destruction machine already indigenous to the country. When Dobbs speaks of 500,000 jobs a year lost to foreign labor, he doesn't seem to realize that could be the least of our problems: Unless average job creation runs at least a million jobs per month, private sector employment will shrink.

As jobs are destroyed, new jobs are created because consumers' wants are, for all practical purposes, infinite.

If the loss of manufacturing jobs is impoverishing the U.S. economy now, the past 45 years must have been a steady march toward destitution, since that's how long manufacturing employment has been shrinking as a share of total employment.

As for the trade deficit, we may divide American history between 29 years of nearly uninterrupted trade surpluses from the late-1940s through the mid-1970s, followed by 29 years of consecutive trade deficits since then.[12] From the standpoint of either the long trend in the unemployment rate or the rate of increase in employment, the era of deficits did at least as well as the era of surpluses.

In his book, Dobbs declares, "The United States has not run a trade surplus with Europe since 1992. For more than a decade, the EU has sold the United States far more in goods and services than it bought."[13] Yes, and which economy has performed better? Both productivity and employment have grown faster in the United States. The U.S. unemployment rate ran 5% in 2005, compared with 10% in France and Germany.[14]

As for objecting to the U.S. deficit with China, it boils to the perverse complaint that more residents of China produce goods for sale in the United States than vice versa. Only Dobbs could fail to see the advantages in such an arrangement. Even if U.S. exports to China balanced with imports, this imbalance of labor would persist.

The reason would be higher productivity. Since U.S. workers are better educated and better equipped than their Chinese counterparts, they are more productive. So balanced trade would still mean more Chinese working for Americans than vice versa. And if they are less productive, how can they compete? They charge that much less for their labor. How is it that Dobbs fails to see the advantages in *that* arrangement?

OUTSOURCING

We now turn to the latest version of this old story. With Internet cables girding the globe, the services of skilled domestic workers have been increasingly outsourced to skilled workers abroad. This should be an especially welcome development, since it drives down the cost of this high-priced labor, making such services more affordable to the vast majority of Americans who aren't paid as well.

But since, by Dobbs's logic, it's yet another "assault on American consumers," its effect on the jobs of the high-paid workforce is the only reality for him. Bureau of Labor Statistics figures show, however, that he needn't worry. When skilled labor is freed from tasks that can be outsourced, it becomes available to perform others. Not surprisingly, skilled work in general continues to account for an increasing share of all employment.

We can tell by comparing high-paid employment in 2005 versus 2000—the year that was supposed to have ushered in the great wave of outsourcing, and a high plateau to begin with, since it also happens to be the peak year of the previous economic boom.

First, the bad news—or rather, news of how outsourcing freed skilled labor to perform other tasks: High-paid employment in computer-related fields (excluding "support specialists," "data-based administrators," and "network analysts") fell from 2.5 million in 2000 to 2.4 million in 2005 while their unemployment rate rose from 1.6% to 1.9%.[15] That 2005 employment level is still more than twice the level of 1995,[16] and that unemployment rate remains enviable by any standard. But those who see stagnation in these professions certainly have grounds.

Also, engineering employment fell 400,000 over this period, to 2.5 million, while the unemployment rate in these fields rose to more than 2%.[17] Even if outsourcing wasn't responsible, those who see shrinkage in these professions also have grounds for concern and complaint.

But all signs indicate that skilled workers as a group found other employment commensurate with their abilities. While computer and engineering professions shed 500,000 workers, the combined total of lawyers, physicians, college professors, and scientists in hard or soft disciplines gained 600,000 members.[18] Professional occupations in general rose by 2.2 million, while managerial jobs gained 1 million.[19] Managers and professionals increased their share of total employment over this period, a trend that has been in place for many years.[20]

The call to circle the wagons around high-paid labor is not only morally repellent but also distinctly premature.

DOBBS'S DISHONESTY

In his February 2004 study, "Occupation Employment Projections to 2012," BLS economist Daniel Hecker made the following prediction: Professions would grow the fastest and add the most number of jobs, while service jobs on the "opposite ends of the educational and earnings spectrum" would make the second greatest contribution.[21] But since managerial employment would still grow faster than average, managers and professionals together would continue to account for a greater share of total employment. (Hecker updated these same predictions in "Occupation Employment Projections to 2014," published November 2005.)

Now see how Dobbs wrote up Hecker's study in *Exporting America: Why Corporate Greed Is Shipping American Jobs Overseas:*

> As for creation of high-value jobs, the numbers speak for themselves, and they are not encouraging. When the BLS released its ten-year projections for American job growth in February 2004, seven of the ten biggest areas of job growth were in menial or low-paying service jobs. Here's the BLS projection:[22]
>
> 1. Waiters and waitresses
> 2. Janitors and cleaners
> 3. Food preparation
> 4. Nursing aides, orderlies, and attendants
> 5. Cashiers
> 6. Customer service representatives
> 7. Retail salespersons
> 8. Registered nurses
> 9. General and operations managers
> 10. Postsecondary teachers

Notice that only the lowest three on the list—"registered nurses, general and operations managers, and postsecondary teachers"—qualify as relatively high-paid work.

An unsuspecting reader would not know that Dobbs had misrepresented this BLS study. The CNN newsman could hardly have missed the following statement on its second page: "Employment in *professional and related occupations* is projected to grow the fastest and add more workers (6.5 million) than any other major group."[23] [Italics in original.] To access the data he'd lifted, Dobbs had to ignore "Table 3: Fastest Growing Occupations"[24] to focus instead on "Table 4: Occupations with the Largest Job Growth," buried toward the back.[25]

But as BLS economist Daniel Hecker makes clear, the term *largest* keys off the fact that these occupations are already quite large. For example, since there are already many cashiers, this category of employment is ranked sixth in terms of "largest job growth" even though its projected *rate* of growth is below average. But even so, the seven low-skilled jobs on this list account for a projected increase of 3.1 million, hardly rivaling the projected increase of 6.5 million in professional occupations.[26]

Now, for the most blatant distortion, even this rather misleading list of "largest" was rearranged by Dobbs to put two of the high-paying categories near the bottom. Table 17.1 shows his list versus the actual ranking as it appears in the original. Notice that BLS economist Hecker put registered nurses and postsecondary teachers at the top, while Dobbs put them near the bottom.

To be fair, he seemed to take full responsibility for the distortion when I pointed it out to him in a telephone interview:

DOBBS (LOUDLY): This not an interview! This is an attack!
ME: No, Lou, it's an informed interview.

To which I might have added, echoing the man himself, "Tough is great, I'd just like to see some honesty."[27]

Table 17.1 Bureau of Labor Statistics versus Dobbs Rankings on Occupations with Largest Job Growth

BLS Ranking[a]	Occupations with Largest Job Growth	Dobbs Ranking[b]
1	Registered nurses	8
2	Postsecondary teachers	10
3	Retail salespersons	7
4	Customer service representatives	6
5	Food preparation	3
6	Cashiers	5
7	Janitors and cleaners	2
8	General and operations managers	9
9	Waiters and waitresses	1
10	Nursing aides, orderlies, and attendants	4

[a] Bureau of Labor Statistics.
[b] Lou Dobbs, *Exporting America: Why Corporate Greed Is Exporting American Jobs Oversees,* p. 105.

AFTERWORD

Whenever I deliver a talk or write an article, I'm always frustrated by how much I have to leave out. So I thought I'd write a book, leaving out nothing that mattered. As I mentioned in the Preface, now that I've written a book, I can hardly believe how much I've left out.

Much of what had to be omitted falls under two topics that turned out to be so vast, they would have required a book in themselves. The first has to do with solutions to the healthcare crisis, the second with income inequality.

So I'm devoting the Afterword to some of the most egregious instances of economic reporting on these two topics. For the sake of brevity, I focus more on the reporting itself, without delving too deeply into the issues being covered.

HEALTHCARE

Chapter 1, on the soaring cost of eldercare, might have been followed by a chapter on the dialogue about solutions. But once I began to read the staggering amount of material on the subject, I realized that only a book-length treatment would be adequate. One reason I'm sorry for the omission is that I didn't get to dissect another article in the *New Yorker,* this one by staff writer (and best-selling author) Malcolm Gladwell, called "The Moral Hazard Myth."

As Chapter 1 showed, by far the biggest part of soaring eldercare costs is healthcare. In this article, Gladwell contributes to the dialogue about solutions by trying to dismiss as "myth" one of the standard objections to a government-run healthcare system: If all its goods and services are offered as "free," people will consume them wastefully.

"Moral hazard [he writes] is the term economists use to describe the fact that insurance can change the behavior of the person being insured. If your office gives you and your co-workers all the free Pepsi you want—if your employer, in effect, offers universal Pepsi insurance—you'll drink more Pepsi than you would have otherwise."[1]

Gladwell is right; under the circumstances, you *would* drink more Pepsi than otherwise. But the trouble is, he also uses the Pepsi example to help set up the argument that no such wasteful consumption would occur if your office gave you all the free healthcare you wanted. The bait and switch makes it necessary to appreciate the differences between healthcare and Pepsi even more than the similarities. One key difference is that wasteful consumption of healthcare does not have to mean consuming "more" of it, if by more we mean spending extra time and effort going to doctors, hospitals, and pharmacies. Sometimes more can simply mean more expensive. The priciest drug on the market can be just as easily obtained in a cheap generic version; fancy doctors can remove our moles just as speedily as nurse-practitioners can.

This brings up another key difference between healthcare and Pepsi that is almost the crux of Gladwell's argument: Most of us enjoy drinking a little Pepsi, but when it comes to spending even a little bit of time in a doctor's office or in a hospital—well, most of us would rather drink a lot of Pepsi.

"We go to the doctor grudgingly," observes Gladwell, "only because we're sick."[2] Actually, it's even worse than that: We also go to the doctor grudgingly to *avoid* getting sick. The potential for wasteful consumption of *preventive* care is a topic I'll have more to say about in a moment. Meanwhile, Gladwell quotes a Princeton professor on an even better alternative to healthcare *or* Pepsi: golf.

"Moral hazard is overblown," Princeton economist Uwe Reinhardt says [writes Gladwell]. "You always hear that the demand for health care is unlimited. This is just not true. People who are very well insured, who are very rich, do you see them check into the hospital because it's free? Do people really like to go to the doctor? Do they check into the hospital instead of playing golf?"[3]

Professor Reinhardt is surely right that most of us dislike going to doctors or checking into hospitals. He's also right that the demand for healthcare is not unlimited; for that matter, neither is the demand for golf or Pepsi. But there is still a danger that the demand for "free" healthcare will make an unlimited claim on gross domestic product (GDP). What if the hospital we grudgingly check into because we're ill, costs three times as much as the competing institution in the next town with no difference in reputation? Are we going to spend time price shopping when we could be playing nine holes?

Or what if that hospital actually does boast staff and facilities that normally attend to the needs of presidents and princes? Isn't it better that *our* routine procedure be performed by the very best even if it means turning away others with life-threatening ailments?

One reason I didn't devote a separate chapter to this topic is precisely because such questions require a book to themselves. The only point here is that the "moral hazard" of free healthcare is much greater than that of free Pepsi, not less.

Gladwell's discussion of preventive care is, if anything, even more surreal. First, when he writes, as quoted, that "we go to the doctor grudgingly, *only* because we're sick," he neatly forecloses the possibility that preventive care might be consumed wastefully. But assume we've already gone grudgingly to the doctor's for a physical. Would we resist the temptation to commission tests of marginal benefit (blood tests, gene tests) when they're all free?

Preventive care even brings up the possibility that some folks would nongrudgingly spend more time and effort consuming it if it were free. To quote a comprehensive study called *Lives at Risk* in which the authors compare healthcare systems throughout the world:

> The Cooper Clinic in Dallas now offers an extensive check-up (with a full body scan) for about $1,500 or more. Its clients include Ross Perot, Larry King, and other high profile individuals. Yet if everyone in America took advantage of this opportunity, we would increase our nation's annual health care bill by a third.[4]

I think the authors exaggerate. But are Ross Perot and Larry King the only ones who would sacrifice golf if the Cooper Clinic in Dallas waived its fee?

In Gladwell's own discussion of preventive care, he makes exactly the opposite argument. In his view, even wealthy folks like him wouldn't go in for preventive care unless it *did* cost nothing:

> How should the average consumer [he asks rhetorically], be expected to know beforehand what care is frivolous and what care

is useful? I just went to the dermatologist to get moles checked for skin *cancer.* If I had had to pay a hundred percent, or even fifty percent, of the cost of the visit, I might not have gone. Would that have been a wise decision? *I have no idea.* But if one of those moles really is *cancerous,* that simple, inexpensive visit could save the health care system tens of thousands of dollars (not to mention saving me a great deal of *heartbreak*).[5] [italics mine]

Gladwell seems to have a talent for choosing poor examples. *Heartbreak* is a powerful word, but *cancer* and *cancerous* are truly scary words. Imagine a private company—call it Cancer 'R Us—runs an ad campaign featuring the heartbreak of people like Gladwell who could have gotten their cancer treated early if they'd only gone in for the surprisingly affordable periodic checkup that Cancer 'R Us offers at its conveniently located outlets throughout the five boroughs. By cynically playing on our fears in this way, such a company could probably manipulate us into buying more preventive care than we really need at full price. I'm not saying whether private ventures like Cancer 'R Us should be allowed. Again, that's too big a topic. I'm just saying that people—probably including Gladwell himself—are not as stupid as author Gladwell would have us believe.

Gladwell comes close to being his own best parody. But before we leave him, let's imagine, for the moment, that the government offered free auto-repair insurance. Using the same logic, he might be capable of writing [words not in italics are all his]:

How should the average consumer be expected to know beforehand what *auto* care is frivolous and what *auto* care is useful? I just *took my car to the service station to get its brakes checked.* If I had had to pay a hundred percent, or even fifty percent, of the cost of the visit, I might not have gone. Would that have been a wise decision? I have no idea. But if *the car's brakes really were faulty,* that simple, inexpensive visit could save *the auto care and* health care systems tens of thousands of dollars (not to mention me a great deal of heartbreak).

By the way, *The Tipping Point* author Gladwell's recent bestseller is called, *Blink: The Power of Thinking without Thinking.* Perhaps his next book will be, *Blank: The Power of Not Actually Thinking at All*—which actually is the title of a funny forthcoming parody by "Noah Tall," author of *The Tippling Point* and "a member of NAMES, the dyslexic branch of MENSA."

Also recall that in Chapter 1, we left Krugman proposing his own radical solution to healthcare, which would include going "the next step" to "honest-to-God socialized medicine," similar to the Veteran's Health Administration (VHA), which "runs its own hospitals and clinics."[6] In a *New York Times* column devoted to the VHA, he declares that "the true future of American health care" can be found in "our very own Veteran's Health Administration, whose success story is one of the best-kept secrets in the American policy debate."[7]

But neither he nor the lengthy article, "The Best Care Anywhere," he cites on the VHA in the *Washington Monthly*,[8] even so much as mention a March 2005 Congressional Budget Office paper, "The Potential Cost of Meeting Demand for Veterans' Health Care," which projects a near-doubling in per capita costs between 2005 and 2025.[9] Krugman, by contrast, assures us at one point that "the veteran's system has managed to avoid much of the huge cost surge that has plagued the rest of U.S. medicine."[10] While the statement is hard to pin down, it turns out the Congressional Budget Office (CBO) paper does show that from 1999 to 2005, at least, enrollment in the system rose proportionately faster than the increase in its budget.[11]

Curious about this, I asked an informed source, who told me the following, on the condition of anonymity. A new enrollment system was installed in 1999 that expanded eligibility. A new enrollee may not end up being an actual user of VA healthcare services, and even then, not all users are alike. Many new enrollees were only seeking a portion of their healthcare from the system, and many were healthier than previous users, thus the per capita cost to the VA for these veterans was less. So per capita costs declined over this period, but that will have little bearing on future costs.

Ironically, the only negative note Krugman strikes is misplaced. "I don't want to idealize the veterans health system,"[12] he writes. "In fact, there's reason to be concerned about its future: Will it be given the resources it needs to cope with the flood of wounded and traumatized veterans from Iraq?"[13]

We don't know where he gets this from, but certainly not from the CBO paper. Congressional Budget Office analysts specifically state that the soaring post-2005 per capita costs they do project "do not include the small increase in the size of the population arising from the increase in activation of members of the Reserves and National Guard since September 11, 2001, nor do they include the increase in combat-disabled veterans arising from current conflicts in Iraq and Afghanistan."[14] They add, however, that "those omissions would probably affect the population projections by only 1 percent to 2 percent and the number of disabled veterans by a similarly small percentage."[15]

Meanwhile, Philip Longman's *Washington Monthly* article tantalizes us with statements like: "Most [VHA physicians] could make more money doing something else, so their commitment to their profession most often derives from a higher-than-usual dose of idealism."[16] If the system were to vastly expand its staff of physicians, might that cost have to rise? Or, like the children at Lake Woebegone, are all physicians above average in terms of their idealism?

While Krugman writes that "the V.H.A. bargains effectively on drug prices,"[17] Longman states that it gets "deep drug discounts."[18] If the system were suddenly to buy most of the drugs sold in the United States, might those "deep discounts" have to be at least partially rescinded?

Alternatively, Krugman declares approvingly, "the government doesn't just pay the bills in this system—it runs the hospitals and clinics."[19] Which raises the fair question, why shouldn't the government likewise be running the drug industry?

In forthcoming articles, Krugman and Longman should take up such questions.

COMPUTERS, GROSS DOMESTIC PRODUCT, AND PRODUCTIVITY

There might have been a chapter on a major myth about the way GDP and productivity are calculated. For example, in a September 2003 *U.S. News & World Report,* Mortimer B. Zuckerman complained that second quarter GDP growth would have been much lower than reported if it hadn't been for the "bizarre way government statistics are compiled."[20]

The September 4, 2003, issue of the *Financial Times* has Dresdner Bank's former chief economist, Kurt Richebacher making a similar point.[21] The *Financial Times* might have known that Richebacher's numbers were wrong and simply refused to print them as facts. Since Zuckerman happens to be the editor and publisher of *U.S. News,* he decides what gets printed. Both writers thought the contribution to measured output from investment in computers was being overstated. They were both wrong, simply because they weren't familiar with the new method of calculating a broad measure like GDP, which was first introduced by the Bureau of Economic Analysis (BEA) in 1996.[22]

For the private sector generally, each component of GDP is weighted by its price. Thus, loaves of bread get a lower weighting than personal computers, which in turn get a lower weighting than cars. But the question had always been, how often do these weights get updated? For example, in 2006, do you weight each item based on relative prices in say, 1993, or in 2006 itself?

Until it made the change in 1996, the BEA used to apply price weights based on a period of a year or two. At that point, for example, GDP in all years was calculated according to relative prices in the year 1992. But since I've already mentioned computers, maybe you're beginning to see the problem with this "fixed weight" method. The price of a personal computer was falling every year, at the same time that output was soaring. But if, say, GDP in 2002 were weighted according to relative prices in 1992, that would mean the output of computers in 2002 would be weighted according to 1992 prices. And the impact of computers on GDP would start to look grotesque.

The solution was to update the weights more frequently. That way, the weight received by computers would not be held hostage to its own past. And with its ingenious "chain-weighting" method, the BEA decided to go the full distance with that radical idea. Since 1996, GDP in any given year has been weighted according to the prices prevailing in that same year. Thus, for example, GDP in 2003 was weighted according to 2003 prices, in 1993 according to 1993 prices, and so on.

Since, as mentioned, productivity is measured as output per worker hour of the "business sector," the same stricture applies: For each year, the components of business output, including computers, are each measured according to the relative prices prevailing in that year.

Richebacher and Zuckerman didn't know about the change. So they believed mistakenly that computers were having precisely the kind of grotesque effect that BEA had already taken steps to prevent. I didn't devote a separate chapter to this issue, however, because Zuckerman's was the last example of this error that I could find. So maybe the media has learned its lesson.

INCOME DISTRIBUTION

My chapters on *Nickel and Dimed* and on wages in general could have used a chapter on income distribution. This, too, was planned—except it also proved to be a topic so large, it deserved a book to itself.

Any such book would require a properly nuanced discussion of developments over the past half-century. Widening income inequality has also been accompanied by greater equality of opportunity for previously excluded minorities (and in the case of women, majorities); by the liberalization of immigration restrictions, which offered historic opportunities to millions of new immigrants from Asia and Latin America; and by a decline in poverty generally.

Contrast those trends with a cover story by Krugman on income inequality, titled, "For Richer" in the *New York Times Magazine,* whose broad theme is the descent from the "middle-class society" of 50 years ago to the class-ridden society of today:

> The America I grew up in [Krugman writes]—the America of the 1950's and 1960's—was a middle-class society, both in reality and in feel. The vast income and wealth inequalities of the Gilded Age had disappeared. Yes, of course, there was poverty of the under class—but the conventional wisdom of the time viewed that as a social rather than an economic problem. Yes, of course, some wealthy businessmen and heirs to large fortunes lived far better than the average American.[23]

I quote the reference to the wealthy just to show the poor had indeed been kissed off. In 1960, the poverty rate was 22.2 %, compared to 11.7 % in 2001, the most recent figures available when Krugman's article appeared (12.5 % in 2005).[24] Did people of the "under-class"—who probably *thought* they had an "economic problem"; poor people can be like that—really have less to complain about because the "conventional wisdom" thought differently?

Krugman goes on:

Daily experience confirmed the sense of a fairly equal society. The economic disparities you were conscious of were quite muted. Highly educated professionals—middle managers, college teachers, even lawyers—often claimed they earned less than unionized blue-collar workers. Those considered very well-off lived in split-levels.[25]

The obvious drawbacks of that "fairly equal society" do not seem to occur to him. In terms of equality of opportunity, would blacks, Hispanics, gays, Asians, or women want to trade places with their counterparts in that land of his mandarin imaginings?[26]

Also out of sight and out of mind in that fairly equal society were millions of impoverished residents of Asia and Latin America. When President Lyndon B. Johnson signed the landmark Immigration Act of 1965 in the shadow of the Statue of Liberty, the symbolism of the gesture mattered far more than the substance. If the nation had even dimly imagined that over the next 35 years the door would swing wide to more than 20 million immigrants—about a third from Asia, and more than half from Latin America—the 1965 act would probably have died in committee.

But that is a subject for another book.

HOW TO COPE

Finally, I had planned a chapter of advice to the average reader. You'd like to know what's happening to the economy, but with all that econospinning out there, how do you cope?

In this case, I ended up having far *less* to say than I had thought. I conclude instead on an upbeat note: If the people attacked in this book actually read it, maybe their stuff will improve.

NOTES

Preface

1. George J. Stigler, *The Intellectual and the Marketplace* (Cambridge, MA: Harvard University Press, 1984).
2. See, for example, my July 8, 2002, *Barron's* column on the college history text, *Out of the Many: A History of the American People,* "team-written by four well-credentialed historians." To my embarrassment, the column is headlined, "1,000 Pages of Drivel"—a grotesque overstatement that I did not write, but unfortunately neglected to flag before it got printed. I focus only on the economic history, which takes up a relatively small but important part of this 1,000-page text.
3. Paul Krugman, *The Great Unraveling* (New York: Norton, 2004), p. xxxvii.
4. I had more than once included Krugman's 1998 collection, *The Accidental Theorist,* in one of my periodic columns on recommended books. I would still recommend that collection for some of its better pieces, even though the fissures already evident in the weaker efforts have in later work become chasms. Krugman, since joining the *Times,* seems to have experienced a great unraveling of his own.

   Those who love Krugman for his Bush bashing should not take his word on the economy, any more than those who hate him for it should reject everything he says on that topic. In the latter group, *National Review* online columnist Donald Luskin unfortunately makes it seem as though distaste for Krugman's economic reportage must split along party lines (not true in my case, since I voted for Bush's Democratic challengers both times).

   Finally, those who value Krugman for his critiques of U.S. foreign policy should ponder the implications of the following statement he makes on that subject in *The Great Unraveling:* "Since World War II the United States has built its foreign policy around international institutions, and has tried to make it clear that it is not an old-fashioned imperialist power, which uses military force as it sees fit" (p. 6). As an antidote, I recommend the 1984 book by the late *Wall Street Journal* reporter Jonathan Kwitny: *Endless Enemies: How America's Worldwide Interventions Destroy Democracy and Free Enterprise and Defeat our Own Best Interests,* and the 2005 book by independent scholar Gareth Porter: *Perils of Dominance: Imbalance of Power and the Road to War in Vietnam,* among many other titles.
5. See note 3.

6. Daniel Okrent, "13 Things I Meant to Write About but Never Did," *New York Times* (May 22, 2005).

7. Jonathan Chait, "Okrent's Last Word," *New Republic* (May 31, 2005), http://www.tnr.com/etc.mhtml?pid=2694.

8. Quote is from an e-mail sent by Krugman to Okrent on Sunday, May 22, 2005.

9. Lewis Carroll, *Sylvia and Bruno* (New York: Dover, 1998).

10. Eric Alterman, *What Liberal Media? The Truth About Bias and the News* (New York: Basic Books, 2003), p. xv.

11. See note 10, p. 121.

12. See note 10, pp. 121–122.

13. Edmund L. Andrews, "Fearing That a Gap Will Become a Chasm," *New York Times* (May 2, 2004).

14. Paul Krugman, "Social Security Scares," *New York Times* (May 5, 2004).

15. Paul Krugman "New Public Editor Hosts Paul Krugman—Daniel Okrent Debate: Krugman Lays Out Why He Believes Okrent Was Wrong," *New York Times Public Editor Web Journal,* no. 2 of 27 (May 31, 2005), http://forums.nytimes.com/top/opinion/readersopinions/forums/thepubliceditor/publiceditorswebjournal/index.html?offset=2.

Chapter 1: Eldercare Fraud

1. Hendrik Hertzberg, "Untrustworthy," *New Yorker* (March 28, 2005), p. 21.

2. See note 1.

3. Congressional Budget Office, "The Long-Term Budget Output" (December 2005), p. 22, http://www.cbo.gov/showdoc.cfm?index=6982&sequence=0.

4. See note 3, projections taken from Intermediate Spending Path.

5. See note 3

6. See note 3.

7. Congressional Budget Office, "The Future Growth of Social Security: It's Not Just Society's Aging," no. 9 (2003), http://www.cbo.gov/ftpdocs/43xx/doc4380/07-01-SocSec&Aging.pdf8.

8. The Concord Coalition describes itself as "a nonpartisan grassroots organization dedicated to informing the public about the need for generationally responsible fiscal policy."

9. See note 1.

10. Congressional Budget Office, "Comparing Budgetary and Trust Fund Measures of the Outlook for Social Security and Medicare," no. 10 (2003), http://www.cbo.gov/showdoc.cfm?index=4624&sequence=0.

11. "Shameless Photo-Op," *New York Times* (April 7, 2005).

12. See note 1, p. 21.

13. David Espo, "Your Retirement? It's in a File Cabinet by Ohio River," *Associated Press* (February 26, 2005). Confirmed via telephone by P. Hollenbach, U.S. Bureau of Public Debt spokesman, January 11, 2005.

14. See note 1, p. 22.

15. Douglas Holtz-Eakin, "The Economic Cost of Long-Term Federal Obligations," testimony to the Committee on the Budget, Washington, DC (July 24, 2003), p. 1.

16. Paul Krugman, "Who Lost the U.S. Budget?," *New York Times* (March 21, 2003).

17. See note 16.

18. See note 16.

19. Peter Orszag, Richard Kogan, and Robert Greenstein, "The Administration's Tax Cuts and the Long-Term Budget Outlook," Washington: Center on Budget and Policy Priorities (March 19, 2003), p. 3.

20. See note 19, p. 3.

21. See note 15, p. 10.

22. See note 15, p. 12.

23. See note 16.

24. See note 19, p. 1.

25. Paul Krugman, "Social Security Scares," *New York Times* (March 5, 2004).

26. Edmund L. Andrews, "Fearing That a Gap Will Become a Chasm," *New York Times* (March 2, 2004).

27. See note 26.

28. Jagadeesh Gokhale and Kent Smetters, "How to Balance a $43 Trillion Checkbook," *Wall Street Journal* (July 17, 2003).

29. Ron Suskind, *The Price of Loyalty: George W. Bush, the White House, and the Education of Paul O'Neill* (New York: Simon & Shuster, 2004).

30. Paul Krugman, "The Awful Truth," *New York Times* (January 13, 2004).

31. Jagadeesh Gokhale and Kent Smetters, *Fiscal and Generational Imbalances: New Budget Measures for New Budget Priorities* (Washington, DC: American Enterprise Institute Press, 2003), p. 4.

32. See note 26.

33. See note 25.

34. See note 25.

35. See note 25.

36. See note 25.

37. See note 25.

38. Paul Krugman, "Confusions about Social Security," *Economist's Voice,* vol. 2, article 1 (2005), http://www.bepress.com/ev/vol2/iss1/art1.

39. Paul Krugman, "America's Senior Moment," *New York Review of Books* (March 10, 2005).

40. See note 39.

41. See note 39.

42. See note 39.

43. Paul Krugman, "A Problem and a Crisis," *New York Review of Books* (April 7, 2005), http://www.nybooks.com/articles/17912.

44. Paul Krugman and Robin Wells, "The Health Care Crisis and What to Do about It," *New York Review of Books* (March 23, 2006), http://www .nybooks.com/articles/18802.

45. See note 44.

46. See note 44.

47. See note 44.

48. See note 3.

49. See note 44.

50. Strictly speaking, Krugman is celebrating Medicare Part A and B. not the drug benefit (Part D) added by the Bush administration, which he believes "works very differently from traditional Medicare" ("The Health Care Crisis and What to Do About It," *New York Review of Books*). But CBO cost projections he himself called "scary" ("America's Senior Moment," *New York Review of Books*) were made before the Medicare drug bill was passed.

51. Congressional Budget Office, "The Impact of Social Security and Medicare on the Federal Budget," no. 6 (2002), http://www.cbo.gov /showdoc.cfm?index=3982&sequence=0.

Chapter 2: Two Ways to Measure Employment

1. Paul Krugman, "Delusions of Triumph," *New York Times* (May 25, 2004).

2. See note 1.

3. Daniel Okrent et al., "New Public Editor Hosts Paul Krugman-Daniel Okrent Debate," *New York Times Public Editor Web Journal,* no. 2 of 27 (May 31, 2005), http://forums.nytimes.com/top/opinion/readersopinions /forums/thepubliceditor/publiceditorswebjournal/index.html?offset=2.

4. Quote is from e-mail sent by Krugman to Daniel Okrent and Editorial Page Editor, Gail Collins, on Sunday, May 22, 2005.

5. See note 3.

6. See note 3.

7. See note 1.

8. Bureau of Labor Statistics, U.S. Department of Labor, "BLS Handbook of Methods" (1997), Chapters 1 and 8.

9. See note 8, Chapters 2, 5, 6, and 7.

10. Bureau of Labor Statistics, U.S. Department of Labor, "The Employment Situation: April 2004," USDL 04-818 (2004), p. 1.

11. See note 10, p. 1.

12. See note 1.

13. See note 1.

14. See note 10, p. 7.

15. See note 10, p. 3.

16. See note 10, p. 1.

17. See note 10, p. 1.

18. See note 10, Table B-1.

19. See note 1.

20. Paul Samuelson and William Nordhaus, *Economics,* 16th ed. (New York: McGraw-Hill, 1998), p. 747.
21. Brad DeLong, "Why Oh Why Can't We Have a Better Press Corps? (Danny Okrent Jumps the Shark Once Again Edition)," *Brad DeLong's Semi-Daily Journal* (March 31, 2005), http://delong.typepad.com/sdj/2005/05/why_oh_why_cant_12.html.
22. See note 21.
23. See note 10, p. 3.
24. U.S. Census Bureau, "Monthly Population Estimates for the Unites States: April 1, 2000 to March 1, 2006," National Tables, http://www.census.gov/popest/national.
25. See note 1.
26. See note 3.

Chapter 3: Bush League Economics

1. Editorial, "Missing Jobs Found," *Wall Street Journal* (October 11, 2004).
2. Bureau of Labor Statistics, U.S. Department of Labor, "Table A-1: Employment Status of the Civilian Population by Sex and Age," http://www.bls.gov/webapps/legacy/cpsatab1.htm.
3. Paul Krugman, "Still a Baby Boom," *New York Times* (August 16, 2000).
4. Paul Krugman, "Spin the Payrolls," *New York Times* (August 10, 2004).
5. Paul Krugman, "Too Low A Bar," *New York Times* (October 24, 2003).
6. Editorial, "The Economy Unspun," *New York Times* (October 13, 2004).
7. Bureau of Labor Statistics, U.S. Department of Labor, "Table A-5: Employed Persons by Class of Worker and Part-Time Status," http://www.bls.gov/webapps/legacy/cpsatab5.htm. Last date of access: May 24, 2006.
8. Steven Hipple, "Self-Employment in the United States: An update," *Monthly Labor Review,* vol. 127, no. 7 (2004), p. 13.
9. Bureau of Labor Statistics, U.S. Department of Labor, "Current Employment Statistics Report Form-Service Providing: Instructions For Completing This Form," (revised July 2005).
10. Jon E. Hilsenrath, "The Outlook: Self-Employed Boost the Economic Recovery," *Wall Street Journal* (December 1, 2003).
11. See note 10.
12. Tim Kane, "Diverging Employment Data: A Critical View of the Payroll Survey," Heritage Foundation (March 4, 2004).
13. See note 12.
14. Allan H. Meltzer, "A Jobless Recovery?" *Wall Street Journal* (September 26, 2003).
15. See note 14.
16. See note 14.
17. Bureau of Labor Statistics, U.S. Department of Labor, "Assessing the Timeliness of Business Births in BLS Establishment Statistics," (April 7, 2004), p. 2.

18. See note 17, p. 2.
19. See note 1.

Chapter 4: Long-Term Unemployment Myths

1. Personal correspondence by Paul Krugman on May 24, 2005, in response to Daniel Okrent's column published in the *New York Times* (May, 22, 2005).
2. As produced, these three quotes omit the other reasons Krugman gave for objecting to the unemployment rate, which are quoted and discussed in later chapters.
3. Paul Krugman, "Our So-Called Boom," *New York Times* (December 30, 2003).
4. Paul Krugman, "Jobs, Jobs, Jobs," *New York Times* (February 10, 2004).
5. Paul Krugman, "No More Excuses on Jobs," *New York Times* (March 12, 2004).
6. Paul Krugman, "A Whiff of Stagflation," *New York Times* (April 18, 2005).
7. Anne Polivka and Stephen Miller, "The CPS After the Redesign: Refocusing the Economic Lens," Bureau of Labor Statistics, rev. (March 1995), p. 6.
8. Katherine Abraham and Robert Shimer, "Changes in Unemployment Duration and Labor Force. Attachment," Bureau of Labor Statistics (August 29, 2001).
9. Paul Krugman, "Reckonings: Reality Bites Again," *New York Times* (May 7, 2000).
10. See note 7, p. 23.
11. Paul Krugman, "Campaign 2004: Paul Krugman v. Ben Stein," *Capital Report,* CNBC (August 6, 2004).
12. See note 8, p. 5.
13. See note 8, p. 4.
14. Data compiled from BLS Series ID's LNU01000001 (Civilian Labor Force), LNU03000001 (Unemployed Level-Men), and LNU03008552 (Number of Unemployed for 15 Weeks and Over, Men).
15. See note 14.
16. Daniel Okrent et al., "New Public Editor Hosts Paul Krugman—Daniel Okrent Debate," no. 2 of 27, http://forums.nytimes.com/top/opinion/readersopinions/forums/thepubliceditor/publiceditorswebjournal/index.html?offset=9&page=previous.
17. Even Krugman's reference to the Anne Polivka and Stephen Miller study is misleading. The BLS economists did not merely "suggest" that the redesigned Household Survey "*might* have raised estimates of long-term unemployment," They provided specific quantitative estimates for this effect ("adjustment factors"), just as they did for all the other effects of the redesign that were covered in their comprehensive study. In their own study ("Unemployment Duration and Labor Force Attachment," pp. 407–411), Abraham and Shimer agreed that the redesign did have this effect, but ar-

gued that it was not quite as high as Polivka and Miller had found. When I mentioned this to Anne Polivka in an April 2005 telephone interview, she replied that she was still "quite comfortable" with her study's estimate. Either way, the BLS should post a warning on its web site about pre-1994 data on long-term unemployment.

18. See http://www.bls.gov/webapps/legacy/cpsatab5.htm.

19. See note 1.

20. See note 7, p. 41.

Chapter 5: The Case of the Phantom Dropouts

1. Bureau of Labor Statistics, U.S. Department of Labor, "Table A-12: Alternative Measures of Unemployment," and "Table A-13: Persons Not in the Labor Force and Multiple Jobholders by Sex, Not Seasonally Adjusted," http://www.bls.gov/cps/cpsatabs.htm. Last date of access: May 24, 2006.

2. Daniel Okrent et al., "New Public Editor Hosts Paul Krugman—Daniel Okrent Debate," *New York Times Public Editor Web Journal,* no. 2 of 27 (May 31, 2005), http://forums.nytimes.com/top/opinion/readersopinions /forums/thepubliceditor/publiceditorswebjournal/index.html?offset=2.

3. Paul Krugman, "Our So-Called Boom," *New York Times* (December 30, 2003).

4. Paul Krugman, "No More Excuses on Jobs," *New York Times* (March 12, 2004).

5. See note 4.

6. Paul Krugman, "The Vision Thing," *New York Times* (September 20, 2002).

7. Paul Krugman, "Twilight Zone Economics," *New York Times* (August 15, 2003).

8. See note 3.

9. See note 4.

10. Paul Krugman, "A Whiff of Stagflation," *New York Times* (April 18, 2005).

11. See note 4 and Paul Krugman, "Checking the Facts, in Advance," *New York Times* (October 12, 2004), with actual data derived in an article from the Economic Policy Institute, "Job Watch" (March 2004), http://www.epinet .org/content.cfm/webfeatures_ viewpoints_job_creation_numbers.

12. See note 4.

13. Paul Krugman, "Checking the Facts, in Advance," *New York Times* (October 12, 2004).

14. Anne Polivka and Jennifer Rothgeb, "Redesigning the CPS Questionnaire," *Monthly Labor Review,* vol. 116, no. 9 (1993), p. 24.

15. Monica D. Castillo, "Persons Outside the Labor Force Who Want a Job," *Monthly Labor Review,* vol. 121, no. 7 (1998), p. 35.

16. See note 15.

17. Anne Polivka and Stephen Miller, "The CPS After the Redesign: Refocusing the Economics Lens," p. 41 and Bureau of Labor Statistics, U.S.

Department of Labor (Revised March 1995), "Table A-13: Persons Not in the Labor Force and Multiple Jobholders by Sex, Not Seasonally Adjusted."

18. Bureau of Labor Statistics, U.S. Department of Labor, " Report 864: How the Government Measure Unemployment" (last modified October 16, 2001), http://www.bls.gov/cps/cps_htgm.htm. Last date accessed: May 24, 2006.

19. See note 17, p. 42.

20. See note 1.

21. See note 14, p. 24.

22. Paul Krugman, "The Dropout Puzzle," *New York Times* (July, 18, 2005).

23. See note 17, pp. 31–32.

24. See note 17, p. 41, and see note 18.

25. See note 10.

26. "A Strange Recovery," *Economist* (August 7, 2003).

27. Media Matter Action Network, *Misstating the State of the Union* (New York: Akashic Books, 2004), p. 28.

28. See note 15, p. 37.

Chapter 6: Participation Rate Follies

1. Paul Krugman, "The Dropout Puzzle," *New York Times* (July 18, 2005).

2. See note 1.

3. Bureau of Labor and Statistics, U.S. Department of Labor, "Employment Situation," http://www.bls.gov/schedule/archives/empsit_nr.htm#2006. Last date of access: May 24, 2006.

4. See note 1.

5. Katherine Bradbury, "Additional Slack in the Economy: The Poor Recovery in the Labor Force Participation during This Business Cycle," Federal Reserve Bank of Boston (2003), p. 1.

6. John Bregger and Steven Haugen "BLS Introduces New Range of Alternative Unemployment Measures," *Monthly Labor Review,* vol. 118, no. 10, October 1995, p. 23.

7. "Economics Focus: It's the Taking Part That Counts," *Economist* (July 28, 2005).

8. Jay Stewart, "What Do Male Nonworkers Do?" Bureau of Labor Statistics, U.S. Department of Labor, working paper 371 (April 2004), p. 2.

9. Bureau of Labor Statistics, U.S. Department of Labor, "Table A-12: Alternative Measures of Labor Underutilization," http://www.bls.gov/webapps/legacy/cpsatab12.htm. Last date of access: May 24, 2006.

10. See note 5.

11. Robert F. Szafran, "Chart 4: Age-Adjusted Labor Force Participation Rates, 1960–2045," *Monthly Labor Review,* vol. 125, no. 9 (2002).

12. Bureau of Labor Statistics, U.S. Department of Labor, "Table A-1: Employment Status of the Civilian Population by Sex and Age," http://www.bls.gov/webapps/legacy/cpsatab1.htm. Last date of access: May 24, 2006.

13. See note 1.

14. Stephanie Aaronson, Bruce Fallick, Andrew Figura, Jonathan Pingle, and William Wascher, "The Recent Decline in Labor Force Participation and Its Implications for Potential Labor Supply." Preliminary Draft, Division of Research and Statistics Board of Governors of the Federal Reserve System (March, 2006), p. 3–4.
15. See note 14, p. 4.
16. Lawrence Katz and Alan Krueger, "High-Pressure U.S. Labor Market of the 1990s," working paper 416 (Princeton, NJ: Princeton University, 1999), p. 1.
17. See note 16, p. 35.
18. See note 12.

Chapter 7: What Does the Employment–Population Ratio Tell Us?

1. Paul Krugman, "Bye-Bye Bush Boom," *New York Times* (July 6, 2004).
2. General Glut, "Four Out of Five Indicators Say the Job Market is Weak," *Brad DeLong's Semi-Daily Journal* (July 12, 2004), http://delong.typepad.com /sdj/2005/07/four_out_of_fiv.html.
3. See note 2.
4. See note 2.
5. Bureau of Labor Statistics, U.S. Department of Labor, "Table A-1: Employment Status of the Civilian Population by Sex and Age," http://www.bls.gov/webapps/legacy/cpsatab1.htm. Last date of access: May 24, 2006.
6. See note 5.
7. Brad DeLong, "The Employment/Population Ratio" *Brad DeLong's Semi-Daily Journal* (July 16, 2004), http://www.j-bradford-delong.net/movable _type/2004_archives/001212.html.
8. See note 1.
9. See note 1.

Chapter 8: May Average Hourly Earnings Rest in Peace

1. Testimony of Treasury Secretary John W. Snow before the House Financial Services Committee on the International Financial System and the Global Economy (May 17, 2006), http://www.treas.gov/press/releases/js4267.htm.
2. Bureau of Labor Statistics, U.S. Department of Labor, "Changes to the Current Employment Statistics Survey," press release (January 18, 2006), http://www.bls.gov/ces/cesww.htm.
3. Bureau of Labor Statistics, U.S. Department of Labor, "Real Earnings," press release (January 18, 2006), http://www.bls.gov/news.release /realer.toc.htm.
4. Paul Krugman, "Summer of Our Discontent," *New York Times* (August 26, 2005).

5. Paul Krugman, "The Joyless Recovery," *New York Times* (December 5, 2005).
6. Bureau of Labor Statistics, U.S. Department of Labor, "Current Employment Statistics Report Form: Service Providing," http://www.bls.gov/ces/bls790e .pdf. Last date of access: May 24, 2006.
7. Based on interviews with Bureau of Labor Statistics Supervisory Statistician and Branch Chief Kirk Mueller.
8. See note 2.
9. As explained by Bureau of Labor Statistics Research Assistant Michael Gorun:

   The data is easily available, but requires a bit of maneuvering to put it all together.

   First, the BLS's wage-and-salary data in the Quarterly Census of Employment and Wages is actually assembled by the Bureau of Economic Analysis's (BEA's) data under the "Personal Income and Outlays" tab (http://www.bea.gov/bea/dn/nipaweb/SelectTable.asp?Selected=N), Tables 2.2A and 2.2B. Then, I subtracted from the totals the earnings of agriculture, fishery, forestry, and hunting workers: Tables 6.3A through 6.3D. Next, I retrieved the Average Weekly Establishment data for Total, Private, and Service Employment (http://data.bls.gov/PDQ /outside.jsp?survey=ce). I multiplied each category by 52 to find the annual earnings, multiplied the annual earnings by the total workers in each category (data for production workers, http://data.bls.gov /PDQ/outside.jsp?survey=ce).

   Finally I divided the BEA data with the Establishment data to find the percentage share.

   The Household Survey also reports wage-and-salary data for all workers. But in this case, if you multiply the mean for all workers by the total number of employed workers (http://www.bls.gov/webapps /legacy/cpsatab1.htm), you find it comes to only 84% of the total reported by the BEA (which is in turn taken from the BLS's Quarterly Census) in 2004/2005.

   The data for number of part-time and full-time workers is from http://www.bls.gov/webapps/legacy/cpsatab5.htm, part-time worker earnings figures came from http://www.bls.gov/cps/cpsaat37.pdf, and usual mean earnings of full-time workers came from BLS Economist Joseph Meisenheimer.

Chapter 9: Hourly Compensation and the Unemployment Rate

1. Brad DeLong, "Four Out of Five Indicators Say the Job Market Really Is Weak," *Brad DeLong's Semi-Daily Journal* (July 12, 2005), http://delong .typepad.com/sdj/2005/07/four_out_of_fiv.html.
2. Bureau of Labor and Statistics, U.S. Department of Labor, "Changes to the Current Employment Statistics Survey," press release (January 18, 2006), http://www.bls.gov/ces/cesww.htm. Last date of access: May 24, 2006.

3. Bureau of Labor Statistics, U.S. Department of Labor, "Major Sector Productivity and Costs," http://data.bls.gov/cgi-bin/surveymost?pr. Last date of access: May 24, 2006.
4. Interview with BLS economist David Hiles, January 2, 2006.

Chapter 10: Wages and Productivity

1. David Nicklaus, "Paychecks Finally Are Getting Fatter," *St. Louis Post-Dispatch* (May 7, 2006).
2. Bill Barnhart, "Workers Reaping Little from Rising Profit Margins," *Chicago Tribune* (May 5, 2006).
3. There is another problem with comparing output and compensation figures through first quarter 2006 with the same data from much earlier periods: The more recent data is still subject to revision.

Chapter 11: The Record Profit Boom That Never Happened

1. "Breaking Records," *Economist* (February 10, 2005).
2. "A World Awash with Profits," *Economist* (February 10, 2005).
3. Louis Uchitelle, "A Recovery for Profits, but Not for Workers," *New York Times* (December 21, 2003).
4. Louis Uchitelle, "U.S. Growth May Hinge on Businesses," *New York Times* (December 30, 2005).
5. Paul Krugman, "The Joyless Economy," *New York Times* (December 5, 2005).
6. The Bureau of Economic Analysis's accounting excludes profits from capital gains and does not include write-offs. Also since the data refer to shares of gross *domestic* product (GDP), profits from overseas operations are also excluded, which can of course make a big difference for the oil and auto companies. But even if overseas profits were factored in, profits as a share of corporate sector GDP would still not be not be setting records for the corporate sector as a whole. National Income and Product Accounts "Table 6.16A: Corporate Profits by Industry," http://www.bea.gov/bea/dn/nipaweb/SelectTable.asp?Selected=N. Last date of access: May 24, 2006.
7. See note 2.
8. National Income and Product Accounts Table, "Gross Value Added of Domestic Corporate Business in Current Dollars and Gross Value Added of Nonfinancial Domestic Corporate Business in Current and Chained Dollars," "Table 1.14: U.S. Bureau of Economic Analysis," p. 3. http://www.bea.gov/bea/dn/nipaweb/SelectTable.asp?Selected=N. Last date of access: May 24, 2006.
9. See note 8, Table 1.1.5.
10. See note 8.
11. See note 8.
12. See note 8.

13. See note 8.
14. See note 8.
15. See note 2.
16. See note 1.
17. The Establishment Survey shows, for example, that in 2005, the average hourly earnings of nonsupervisory workers in the financial sector ran more 11% higher than in the private sector generally, and more than 8% higher than in the manufacturing sector, even including overtime (see www.bls .gov/webapps/legacy/cesbtab3.htm).

    While such data are surely approximate, the wage premium is both sizable and quite consistent historically. If anything, given the tendency for higher-paying service firms to leave this part of the Establishment Survey blank (see Chapter 8), the premium may even be understated.

Chapter 12: End the Monthly Madness: The Change in Payroll Employment Data

1. *Squawk Box,* CNBC (November 5, 2005, 8:24 A.M. EST).
2. Bureau of Labor Statistics, U.S. Department of Labor, revision data is from latest B-table series, "Table B-1: Employees on Nonfarm Payrolls by Industry Sector," http://www.bls.gov/webapps/legacy/cesbtab1.htm.
3. See the "Reliability of Estimates" under "Explanatory Note" in any Employment Situation Release, http://www.bls.gov/schedule/archives /empsit_nr.htm.
4. See note 1, 7:28 A.M. EST.
5. See note 1, 8:36 A.M. EST.
6. See note 1, 8:37 A.M. EST.
7. Bernard Baumohl, *The Secrets of Economic Indicators* (Upper Saddle River, NJ: Wharton School Publishing, 2005).
8. See note 2.
9. Bureau of Labor Statistics, U.S. Department of Labor, "Employment Situation: January 2006" (February 3, 2006), http://www.bls.gov/news.release /archives/empsit_02032006.pdf.
10. Bureau of Labor Statistics, U.S. Department of Labor, "Employment Situation: April 2003" (May 2, 2003), http://www.bls.gov/news.release /archives/empsit_05022003.pdf.
11. Eduardo Porter, "October Hiring Set Strong Pace of 337,000 Jobs," *New York Times* (November 6, 2004).
12. "New Jobless Claims Sink: Total Claims Lowest in 4 Years," *USA Today* (August 25, 2005), http://usatoday.com/money/economy/employment /2005-08-25-jobless_x.htm.
13. Kemba J. Dunham, "U.S. Payrolls Continue to Rise, But Pace of Hiring Slackens: Businesses Create Half as Many Jobs as Expected—Economists Are Unruffled," *Wall Street Journal* (December 6, 2004).

14. Joshua C. Pinkston and James R. Spletzer, "Annual Measures of Gross Job Gains and Gross Job Losses," *Monthly Labor Review,* vol. 127, no. 11 (November 2004), p. 5, http://www.bls.gov/opub/mlr/2004/11/art1full.pdf.
15. Gerard Baker, "Job and Wage Rises Put Pressure on Fed," *Financial Times* (February 6, 1999).
16. Louis Uchitelle, "U.S. Jobless Rate Hit 4.5% in April: 223,000 Jobs Lost," *New York Times* (May 5, 2001).

Chapter 13: End the Monthly Madness:
The Unemployment Rate

1. Mark Gongloff, "U.S. Job Growth Soars," CNNMoney.com (April 2, 2004), http://money.cnn.com/2004/04/02/news/economy/jobs/index.htm.
2. Louis Uchitelle, "Defying Forecast, Job Losses Mount for a 22nd Month," *New York Times* (September 6, 2003).
3. Greg Ip "Pace of Job Growth Picks up but Remains Less Than Robust," *Wall Street Journal* (February 9, 2004).
4. Bureau of Labor Statistics, U.S. Department of Labor, "Employment Situation: January 2003, July 2003, March 2004" (January 9, 2003), http://www.bls.gov/schedule/archives/empsit_nr.htm.
5. Bureau of Labor Statistics, U.S. Department of Labor, "Employment Situation Explanatory Note," last modified April 07, 2006, http://www.bls.gov/news.release/empsit.tn.htm.
6. Transcript of the National Press Club Meeting (December 18, 2003), Washington, DC.
7. See note 6.
8. John Berry, "Job Creation Picks Up Speed; Growth Is Called Sign of Sustainable Economic Expansion," *Washington Post* (November 9, 2003).
9. Bureau of Labor Statistics, U.S. Department of Labor, "Employment Situation: October 2003" (November 07, 2003), http://www.bls.gov/news.release/archives/empsit_11072003.pdf.
10. Louis Uchitelle, "Growth in Jobs Came to a Halt during December," *New York Times* (January 10, 2004).
11. Bureau of Labor Statistics, U.S. Department of Labor, "Employment Situation: December 2003" (January 9, 2004), http://www.bls.gov/news.release/archives/empsit_01092004.pdf.
12. See note 11.
13. Bernard Baumohl, *The Secrets of Economic Indicators* (Upper Saddle River, NJ: Wharton School Publishing, 2005), p. 30.
14. "Wharton School Publishing: Editorial Board Members," http://www.whartonsp.com/markets/detail.asp?st=46063.
15. See note 13, p. 30.
16. Bureau of Labor Statistics, U.S. Department of Labor, "The Employment Situation: March 2006" (April 7, 2006), http://www.bls.gov/news.release/archives/empsit_04072006.pdf.

17. Joseph Goldberg and William T. Moye, *The First Hundred Years of the Bureau of Labor Statistics* (Washington, DC: U.S. Government Printing Office, 1985).
18. Eileen Shanahan, "Reporting on Economy," *New York Times* (March 23, 1971).
19. Edwin Dale Jr. "Jobless Rate off Sharply, but Doubt Is Cast on Data," *New York Times* (July 3, 1971).
20. See note 19.
21. See note 19.
22. Nixon Presidential Material (June 17, 1971), cassette no. 775, Nixon and Haldeman, 2:42 P.M., Oval Office conversation.
23. Nixon Presidential Material (July 3, 1971), cassette no. 871, Nixon and Haldeman, 10:41 A.M., Oval Office conversation.
24. Nixon Presidential Material (July 5, 1971), cassette no. 876, Nixon, Haldeman, and Ziegler, 4:03 P.M., Oval Office conversation.
25. "The White House Memorandum for H.R. Haldeman from Fred Malek" (July 27, 1971).
26. Frank Porter, "Nixon Ousting Labor Analysts," *Washington Post* (September 29, 1971); "Chief of Labor Statistics Says His Bureau Is Being Reshaped," *New York Times* (September 29, 1971); and see note 19.
27. See note 19.
28. Nixon presidential materials: Memorandum for H.R. Haldeman from Charles Colson (December 8, 1971).
29. See note 18.
30. Conversation interview on May 19, 2004, with Joel Popkin, who was an assistant commissioner at the Bureau of Labor Statistics. Now, he is the president of economic consultants, Joel Popkin and Company.

Chapter 14:   Greenspan Idolatry

1. Greg Ip, "Fed Chief's Style: Devour the Data, Beware of Dogma," *Wall Street Journal* (November 18, 2004).
2. See note 1.
3. See note 1.
4. David Wessel, "Greenspan Sees an End to Rate Increases: Fed Chief Hints Restraint despite Some Inflation, Cheering Wall Street" *Wall Street Journal* (February 23, 1995).
5. Alan Blinder, *Central Banking in Theory and Practice* (Cambridge, MA: MIT Press, 1998), p. 19.
6. See note 1.
7. See note 1.
8. Federal Reserve, *Semi-Annual Monetary Policy Report,* testimony of Chairman Alan Greenspan before the Committee on Banking, Housing, and Urban Affairs, U.S. Senate (February 22, 1995).
9. See note 1.
10. See note 1.

11. Alan Greenspan at the Annual Dinner and Francis Boyer Lecture of the American Enterprise Institute for Public Policy Research, Washington, DC (December 5, 1996), http://www.federalreserve.gov/BOARDDOCS /SPEECHES/19961205.htm.

12. Federal Reserve, *Semi-Annual Monetary Policy Report,* testimony of Chairman Alan Greenspan before the Committee on Banking, Housing, and Urban Affairs, U.S. Senate (July 22, 1997), http://www.federalreserve.gov /boarddocs/hh/1997/july/testimony.htm.

13. See note 11.

14. Andrew Balls, "Greenspan's Record: An Activist Unafraid to Depart from the Rules," *Financial Times* (August 21, 2005).

15. See note 13.

16. See note 1.

Chapter 15: Best-Selling Myths: *Freakonomics*

1. "Unconventional Wisdom: Curiouser and Curiouser," *Economist* (May 12, 2005), http://www.economist.com/books/displayStory.cfm ?story_id=3960469.

2. Roger Lowenstein, "A Romp through Theories More Fanciful than Freaky," *New York Times* (June 19, 2005).

3. Steven E. Landsburg, "When Numbers Solve a Mystery," *Wall Street Journal* (April 15, 2005).

4. Cass R. Sunstein, "Super Freak," *New Republic* (July 21, 2005).

5. Steven D. Levitt in discussion with the author (June 9, 2005).

6. John J. Donahue III and Steven D. Levitt, "The Impact of Legalized Abortion on Crime," *Quarterly Journal of Economics,* vol. 116, no. 2 (May 2001), p. 1.

7. See note 6, p. 4.

8. See note 6, abstract.

9. See note 6, p. 9.

10. See note 5.

11. See note 6, pp. 13–14.

12. See note 6, p. 4.

13. See note 6, pp. 16–17.

14. See note 6, p. 17.

15. The data for the entire period (1989 through 2010) looks as follows:

Offspring of Black Unmarried Teenagers Who Would Have Been Ages 17 to 24 per 100,000 of the U.S. Population

1989	325.5	1995	386.6	2001	364.5	2007	354.8
1990	342.6	1996	387.5	2002	358.2	2008	358.0
1991	356.5	1997	384.7	2003	353.7	2009	360.4
1992	368.6	1998	380.2	2004	348.8	2010	361.6
1993	377.2	1999	375.5	2005	347.9		
1994	385.0	2000	370.7	2006	351.9		

16. See note 6, pp. 8–9.
17. Steven D. Levitt, "Understanding Why Crime Fell in the 1990s: Four Factors That Explain the Decline and Six That Do Not," *Journal of Economic Perspectives,* vol. 18, no. 1 (Winter 2004), pp. 181–182.
18. See note 5.
19. Steven D. Levitt and Stephen J. Dubner, *Freakonomics* (New York: Harper-Collins, 2005), p. 138.
20. See note 19, pp. 138–139.
21. See note 19, p. 139.
22. See note 19, p. 139.
23. See note 19, p. 72.
24. Steven D. Levitt and Chad Syverson, "Market Distortions When Agents Are Better Informed: The Value of Information in Real Estate," National Bureau of Economic Research (January 2005).
25. See note 24, p. 1.
26. See note 24, p. 1.
27. See note 24, p. 8.
28. See note 24, p. 3.
29. See note 24, p. 4.
30. See note 24, p. 1.
31. See note 24, p. 4.
32. See note 24, p. 9.
33. See note 24, p. 9.
34. See note 24, p. 4.
35. See note 24, p. 8.
36. See note 24, p. 9.
37. See note 24, p. 4.
38. See note 24, p. 3.
39. See note 24, p. 3.
40. See note 24, p. 3.
41. Office of Federal Housing Enterprise Oversight, the Latest House Price Index, "4Q 2005 Manipulatable Data for the Census Divisions and U.S.," http://www.ofheo.gov/media/pdf/4q05_hpi_reg.txt. Last date of access: May 24, 2006.
42. See note 24, p. 19.
43. See note 24. Abstract: "Agents Are Often Better Informed than the Clients Who Hire Them."
44. See note 24, p. 19.
45. See note 24, p. 19.
46. See note 24, p. 19.
47. See note 24, p. 1.
48. See note 5.
49. Jane Smiley, *Good Faith* (New York: Knopf, 2003), p. 9.
50. See note 49, p. 9.
51. See note 49, p. 10.

52. See note 49, pp. 64–65.
53. See note 49, p. 71.
54. See note 49, p. 72.
55. See note 49, p. 72.
56. See note 49, p. 67.

Chapter 16: Best-Selling Myths: *Nickel and Dimed*

1. Barbara Ehrenreich, *Nickel and Dimed* (New York: Holt, 2001), p. 200.
2. See note 1, p. 200.
3. See note 1, p. 221.
4. See note 1, p. 165.
5. See note 1, p. 166.
6. See note 1, p. 178.
7. See note 1, pp. 220–221.
8. See note 1, p. 220.
9. Conversation with Christopher Taber on June 13, 2001.
10. Tricia Gladden and Christopher Taber, "Wage Progression among Less Skilled Workers," JCPR working paper 72 (Chicago: Northwestern University, University of Chicago Joint Center for Poverty Research, February 9, 1999), p. 20, http://www.jcpr.org/wp/WPprofile.cfm?ID=72.
11. See note 1, p. 200.
12. See note 1, p. 115.
13. See note 1, p. 165.
14. See note 1, p. 199.
15. See note 1, p. 201.
16. See note 1, p. 201.
17. See note 1, p. 220.
18. "And Bear in Mind," *New York Times* (May 20, 2001).
19. See note 1, p. 203.
20. See note 1, pp. 203–204.
21. See note 1, p. 202.
22. See note 1, p. 203.
23. See note 1, p. 206.
24. Lawrence Mishel, "The State of Working America 2000–01," Economic Policy Institute, http://www.epinet.org/content.cfm/books_swa2000_swa2000.
25. See note 1, p. 193.
26. See note 1, p. 22.
27. See note 1, p. 212.

Chapter 17: Dobbs and Jobs

1. *Lou Dobbs Tonight,* CNN (December 8, 2005, 6:00 P.M. EST), http://transcripts.cnn.com/TRANSCRIPTS/0512/08/ldt.01.html.
2. *Lou Dobbs Tonight,* CNN (December 14, 2005, 6:00 P.M. EST), http://transcripts.cnn.com/TRANSCRIPTS/0512/14/ldt.01.html.

3. See note 2.

4. See note 2.

5. Rachel L. Swarns, "Dobbs's Outspokenness Draws Fans and Fire," *New York Times* (February 15, 2006).

6. Jeff Fleischer, "Exporting America: An Interview with Lou Dobbs" (February 7, 2005), http://www.motherjones.com/news/qa/2005/02/lou_dobbs.html.

7. See note 6.

8. Lou Dobbs, *Exporting America: Why Corporate Greed Is Shipping American Jobs Overseas* (New York: Warner Books, 2004), p. 167.

9. See note 8, p. 73.

10. See note 6.

11. Joshua C. Pinkston and James R. Spletzer, "Annual Measures of Gross Job Gains and Gross Job Losses," *Monthly Labor Review,* vol. 127, no. 11 (November 2004), http://www.bls.gov/opub/mlr/2004/11/art1full.pdf.

12. Bureau of Economic Analysis, "Trade in Goods and Services," http://www.bea.gov/bea/di/home/trade.htm. Last date of access: May 24, 2006.

13. See note 8, p. 67.

14. Bureau of Labor Statistics, U.S. Department of Labor, "Employment Status of the Civilian Noninstitutional Population, 1940 to Date," http://www.bls.gov/cps/cpsa2005.pdf. Last date of access: May 24, 2006.

15. See note 14.

16. See note 14.

17. See note 14.

18. See note 14.

19. See note 14.

20. See note 14.

21. Daniel Hecker, "Occupation Employment Projections to 2012," *Monthly Labor Review* (February 2004), p. 80.

22. See note 8, p. 105.

23. See note 21 p. 81.

24. See note 21, p. 100.

25. See note 21, p. 101.

26. See note 21, pp. 101–102.

27. Conversation Interview with Lou Dobbs on September 15, 2004.

Afterword

1. Malcolm Gladwell, "The Moral-Hazard Myth," *New Yorker,* vol. 81, no. 25 (August 2005), p. 44.

2. See note 1.

3. See note 1.

4. John C. Goodman, Gerald L. Musgrave, and Devon M. Herrick, *Lives At Risk* (Lanham, MD: Rowman & Littlefield Publishers, 2004), p. 2.

5. See note 1.

6. Paul Krugman and Robin Wells, "The Health Care Crisis and What to Do about It," *New York Review of Books* (March 23, 2006), http://www.nybooks.com/articles/18802.

7. See note 6.

8. Phillip Longman, "The Best Care Anywhere," *Washington Monthly,* (January/February 2005), http://www.washingtonmonthly.com/features/2005/0501.longman.html.

9. Congressional Budget Office, "The Potential Cost of Meeting Demand for Veterans' Health Care" (March 2005), p. 14. http://www.cbo.gov/showdoc.cfm?index=6171&sequence=0.

10. Paul Krugman, "Health Care Confidential," *New York Times* (January 27, 2006).

11. See note 9, p. 3.

12. See note 10.

13. See note 10.

14. See note 9.

15. See note 9.

16. See note 8.

17. See note 10.

18. See note 8.

19. See note 10.

20. Mortimer B. Zuckerman, "So Where Are All the Jobs?" *U.S. News & World Report,* vol. 135, no. 9 (2003), p. 86.

21. Kurt Richebacher, "America's Recovery Is Not What It Seems," *Financial Times* (September 4, 2003).

22. For more information see the testimony of Gordon R. Richards before the Subcommittee on the Census, "On the Quality of GDP Data, and the Bureau of Economic Analysis," Committee on Government Reform, United States Congress, http://www.bea.gov/bea/about/test-grr.pdf.

23. Paul Krugman, "For Richer," *New York Times Magazine* (October 2002), p. 62.

24. U.S. Census Bureau, "Table 2: Poverty Status of People by Family Relationship, Race, and Hispanic Origin: 1959 to 2004," http://www.census.gov/hhes/www/poverty/histpov/hstpov2.html.

25. See note 23.

26. See note 23.

INDEX

A

Abortion and crime, 164–174
Abraham, Katherine, 47, 51–52
Actuarial deficit, 8
Afghanistan, 210
Aging of the labor force, 81, 82
Alterman, Eric (*What Liberal Media?*), xv–xvii
Alternative Measures of Labor Underutilization, 70, 72, 73, 74
American Enterprise Institute, xi, 37
Andrews, Edmund, xvii, 10–14
Anecdotes versus evidence, 187
Asia/Asians, 212, 213
Associated Press, 6
Asymmetric information, 174–176, 182–184
Average hourly earnings, 91–100, 101–110, 112

B

Baby boomers, 46, 53–54, 103
Baumohl, Bernard, 132, 141
Benchmarking, 36, 95, 104–105
Benderly, Jason, 25–26, 101–102, 105–110
Bernanke, Ben, 150

Berry, John, 139
Blacks/African Americans:
    abortion and, 164–174
    equality of opportunity, 213
    women's wages, 187–188
Blinder, Alan, 152–153, 162
Blink: The Power of Thinking without Thinking (Gladwell), 208–209
Blogging/bloggers, xii, 86–88
Bond market, 125, 136, 137
Bonds, location of Social Security trust fund, 6
Boston Federal Reserve, 74
Boston Globe, 2
Bouroudjian, Jack, 126
Bradbury, Katherine, 74, 75, 77–81
Bureaucracy, 57
Bureau of Economic Analysis (BEA), 93, 104–105, 118, 211–212
Bureau of Labor Statistics (BLS):
    benchmarking, 36
    data (*see* Establishment Survey; Household Survey)
    employment-population ratio (EPR), 83–90, 102
    "Employment Situation" report, 18, 19–20
    hidden unemployed, 59–72, 89
    hourly earnings data, 91–100, 101–110, 112
    jobs, 199, 200, 201–203

Bureau of Labor Statistics (BLS)
  (Continued)
  labor underutilization measures,
     72, 73–77
  measures repudiated by, xviii, 99,
     102, 105
  measures that have outlived their
     usefulness, 91–92
  missed start-ups, 37
  monthly data, 127, 129, 146
  papers/studies/research, 47, 48, 57,
     76–77, 105, 201–203
  *Quarterly Census of Employment and
     Wages* (QCEW), 104, 135
  self-employment defined by, 32
  unemployment-gate scandal
     (1971), xix, 138, 146–149
Burns, Scott, 14, 15
Bush, George W./administration:
  ending Clinton era, 155
  jobs growth, 25, 30–43, 45
  Social Security, 1, 2, 4–5, 15
  spending increases, 2
  tax cuts, 2, 7, 13
  trust funds, personal knowledge of,
     4–5

C

Cable television news, xiii. *See also*
     CNBC's *Squawk Box*; CNN's
     Lou Dobbs
Cancer:
  deaths-from fallacy, 46, 118
  healthcare moral hazard myth, 208
Castillo, Monica D., 63, 72
Center on Budget and Policy
     Priorities, 7–10
Chain-weighting method, 211

Chait, Jonathan, xiv–xv
Chicago Tribune, 111
China, 193–196, 200
Clinton, Bill/Clinton era:
  Bush era replacing, and arbitrary
     wall between boom and
     aftermath, 155
  GDP, 119
  "It's the Economy, Stupid," xii
  job growth, 24, 31, 45, 47
CNBC's *Squawk Box,* xiii, xviii–xix,
     124–134
  described, 124–127
  fallacy, 130–134
     revision, 132
     sampling error, 131–132
     seasonal adjustment, 132–134
  as symptom of larger problem,
     127–130
CNN's *Lou Dobbs. See* Dobbs, Lou
Collins, Gail, xviii, 19, 57
Colson, Charles, 147, 148
Coming Generational Storm, The
     (Kotlikoff and Burns), 14, 15
"Comparing Budgetary and
     Trust Fund Measures of the
     Outlook for Social
     Security," 5
Compensation. *See* Labor
     earnings/wages
Computers, GDP, and productivity,
     210–212
Congressional Budget Office
     (CBO), 2–9, 14, 16–17,
     209–210
Consensus forecasts, 127,
     142–146
Consumer Price Index, 136
Cook County, Illinois, 176
Cooper Clinic, Dallas, 207

Corporate profit boom, 116–123

Credentialist fallacy, xv–xvii

Crime:

   prisoners, and labor participation
      rate, 82

   rates of, and abortion, 164–174

Cyclical determinism, 79–81

D

Data-noise, 127–130

DeLong, Brad, xiv, xviii, 19, 28–29,
   86–88, 102

Demographics, Social Security and,
   3, 14

Discouraged workers, 57, 71, 77

Dobbs, Lou, xiii, xix, 135, 193–203

   *Exporting America: Why Corporate
      Greed Is Shipping American
      Jobs Overseas,* 196–198, 200,
      202, 203

   main argument, 196–199

   misrepresenting BLS study,
      201–203

   outsourcing, 200–201

   real job destruction, 199–200

   telephone interview with, 203

Donahue, John J., III, 164–174,
   183

Dow Jones Survey of Forecasters,
   124

Drug benefit, Medicare Part D, 3, 4,
   8, 9

Drug prices:

   moral hazard myth, 206

   VHA bargaining, 210

Dubner, Stephen, 163, 174, 175,
   183

Dutta, Neil, xiii

E

Earnings. *See* Labor earnings/wages

"Economic man," 191–192

Economic Policy Institute, 186, 191,
   192

Economic slack, 77–81

Economist, xi, xviii

   on corporate profits, 116, 117,
      118, 120, 122

   on *Freakonomics,* 163

   on unemployment, 71, 74–77

Ehrenreich, Barbara (*Nickel and
      Dimed: On (Not) Getting By in
      America*), xiii, 185–192,
      212–213

Eldercare. *See* Medicare/Medicaid;
   Social Security

Employment-population ratio (EPR),
   83–90, 102

   arithmetical illustration, 85–86

   blogger's misleading trend, 85–88

   flattening trend, 88–90

   unemployment rate and, 85–86

Employment report, monthly (BLS),
   xvii–xix, 18–29. *See also* Bureau
   of Labor Statistics (BLS);
   Establishment Survey;
   Household Survey; Monthly
   figures

Engineering employment, 201

Entitlements, 9

Equality of opportunity, 213

Establishment Survey:

   benefits-related distortions, 104

   described, 20–24

   hours and earnings data generated
      by, 91–97

   versus Household Survey, xviii,
      18–29, 30–43, 103

Establishment Survey *(Continued)*
  apples-to-apples comparison,
    38–39
  description, 20–24
  job measurement (specialty),
    30–43
  Krugman confusing data from,
    xviii, 18–29
  nonsupervisory ratio, 93–100,
    103–104
  response rate, 94
*Exporting America: Why Corporate
  Greed Is Shipping American Jobs
  Overseas* (Dobbs), 196–198, 200,
  202, 203
Exxon Mobil, 117, 119, 198

F

Federal mortgage interest subsidies,
  189
Federal Open Market Committee
  (FOMC), 151
Federal Reserve:
  Boston, 74
  chairmen, 150
  interest rate cuts/hikes, 132, 137,
    144
  "Monetary Policy Report to
    Congress," 160
  short term data, 136
  studies published by, 74, 81
  Washington, 81
Federal spending, cost of, 7
Figueroa, Liz, 195, 196
Financial corporate sector, 119–120
Financial Times, 158, 210–211
Food, cost of, 185–186, 188
Ford, 117, 198
France, 200

Frank, Barney, 91, 99
Franken, Al, xiv
Freakonomics (Levitt and Dubner),
    xiii, xv, 163–184
  abortion and crime, 164–174
  real estate agents, 164, 174–183
Friedman, Milton, xvi
Full employment, defined, 25
Full faith and credit of the United
    States, 5
"Future Growth of Social Security:
    It's Not Just Society's Aging,"
    3, 14

G

Gender gap, 46, 49–52
"General Glut" (blogger),
    85–88
General Motors (GM), 117, 119
Germany, 200
Gladden, Tricia, 187–188
Gladwell, Malcolm, 205–209
Globalization and Its Discontents
    (Stiglitz), xvi
Gokhale, Jagadeesh, 10–11
Goldstein, Harold, 146–149
Great Depression, 119, 120
Greenberg, Leon, 148
Greenspan, Alan, xix, 150–162
  boom of 1990s, 154–156
  forecasting record, 156–162
  "irrational exuberance," 155
  quit rate and, 157–158
  slowdown that didn't have to
    happen, 151–154
Greenstein, Robert, 8, 10
Gross domestic product (GDP):
  calculation, 210–212
  deaths-from-cancer fallacy, 46, 118

forecasts by Federal Reserve, 160
government spending as percent
    of, 3
Medicare/Medicaid costs versus,
    2–3, 16
profits as proportion of, 116–119
quarterly versus monthly reporting
    of, 127

H

Haines, Mark, 124–127
Haldeman, H. R. ("Bob"), 147, 148
Healthcare, 205–212
    Medicare/Medicaid, 1–17
        cost of, xvii, 1–3
        drug benefit (Part D), 3, 4, 8, 9
        funding liabilities of, 5
        Hertzberg, 1–2
        journalists on, 1–2, 10–17
        Kennedy (Ted) on, 17
    moral hazard myth, 205–208
    preventive, 206–207
    single-payer system, 16, 17
    socialized medicine, 209
Hecker, Daniel, 201–203
Henle, Peter, 148
Heritage Foundation, xi, 34
Hertzberg, Hendrik, 1–2, 4–7
Hidden unemployment. See
    Unemployment
"High-Pressure U.S. Labor Market of
    the 1990s, The" (Katz and
    Krueger), 81–82
Hilsenrath, Jon E., 33
Hipple, Steven, 64, 65
Hispanics, 213
Hodgson, James D., 147, 149
Hollenback, Pete, 6
Holtz-Eakin, Douglas, 7, 9

Hoover, Herbert, 31
Hourly earnings figures, 91–100,
    101–110, 112
House Budget Committee on "The
    Economic Costs of Long-Term
    Federal Obligations," 6
Household Survey:
    versus Establishment Survey,
        xvii–xix, 18–29, 30–43, 103
    apples to apples comparison,
        38–39
    descriptions, 20–24
    job measurement (specialty),
        30–43
    Krugman confusing data from,
        xviii, 18–29
    three questions for analyzing
        trends, 46–54
        baby boomers, 46, 53–54, 103
        gender gap, 46, 49–52
        redesigned questionnaire, 46,
            47–49, 63, 64, 75
Housing/rents, 188–189

I

Immigration, 196, 198–199, 212, 213
Income distribution, 205, 212–213
Inflation:
    compensation adjusted for, 106–107
    food and, 185–186
    productivity measures, 112–113
Information:
    assumption of, 183–184
    asymmetric, 174–176, 182–184
Interstate commerce, 198
Involuntary part-timers, 57–58, 70
Ip, Greg, 150–162
Iraq war, 209, 210
"Irrational exuberance," 155

J

Jobs, xiii. *See also* Labor force;
  Payroll employment data;
  Unemployment
  CNN's *Lou Dobbs,* xiii, xix, 135,
    193–203
  creationist fallacy, 134–136
  destruction of, 199–200
  foreign competition for, 135
  outsourcing, 196, 200–201
Johnson, Lyndon B., 213
Johnson, Samuel, 35
Journal of Economic Perspectives, 173

K

Kane, Tim, 34
Katz, Lawrence, 81–82
Kennedy, Ted, 17
Kerry, John, 30
"Killer anecdotes," 187, 190
King, Larry, 207
Knowledge workers, 105
Kogan, Richard, 8–10
Kotlikoff, Laurence, 14, 15
Krueger, Alan, 81–82
Krugman, Paul:
  bestseller (*The Great Unraveling*),
    xiv, xv
  biographical profile, xiii–xv
  credentialist fallacy, xv–xvii
  employment measures, 18–20, 22,
    24–28
  employment-population ratio, 83,
    88–89
  healthcare, 7–10, 209, 210
  on impact of administration in
    office, 31

  income distribution, 212–213
  labor force participation rate,
    73–74, 75, 80
  1990s expansion, 100
  nonsupervisory wages, 93, 100
  Okrent and, xiv–xv, xviii, 19, 28,
    44–45, 56–57
  on O'Neill, 11
  partisan politics, xii
  profit boom, 116–117
  research credo, 56–58
  role in distorting policy debate,
    15–16
  Social Security and Medicare,
    xvii, 2, 7–17
  unemployment, hidden, 60,
    61–62, 64, 65, 67
  unemployment, long-term,
    44–58
  wages, and productivity, 111
Kudlow, Larry, 124, 125–126

L

Labor earnings/wages, xviii
  Ehrenreich on, 188
  employer resistance to increases,
    190
  hourly, 91–100, 101–110, 112
  inflation-adjusted compensation,
    106–107
  iron law of inertia governing
    increases, 108
  measures of, 91–100, 112
    downward bias, 98–99
    nonsupervisory workers,
      98–99
  productivity and, 111–115
  tight markets, 156

unemployment rate and, 99–100,
101–110
unskilled workers, 187–188
Labor force:
aging of, 81, 82
attachment, 52, 56, 63–64, 71,
81, 103
declines in, 140
"economic man," 193
employment-population ratio
(EPR), 83–90, 102
gender, 46, 49–52
iron law of math of, 30–31
jobs/joblessness (*see* Jobs;
Unemployment)
knowledge workers, 105
marginally attached, 63–64, 71
measuring, 20, 21, 23
nonsupervisory ratio, 93–100,
103–104
participation rate, 21, 23, 59, 60,
73–82
productivity, 111–115, 125, 200,
211–212
skilled workers, 202–203
underutilization measures, 70, 72–77
unskilled low-wage workers, 193
younger workers, 82
Labor Market Tightness Index
(LMTI), 101–102, 108–110
Laing, Jonathan, xiv
Latin America, 212, 213
Layoffs, 135
Leonhardt, David, xiv
Levitt, Steven:
credentials, xv, 163
Freakonomics (with Dubner), xiii,
xv, 163–184
abortion and crime, 164–174
real estate agents, 164, 174–183

semantics defense, 166, 173
telephone conversation with, 166,
172–174
Liesman, Steve, 126
Lives at Risk (Goodman et al.), 207
Longman, Philip, 210
"Long-Term Budget Outlook"
(December 2005), 3
Long-term unemployment. *See*
Unemployment, long-term
Low-income workers. *See Nickel and
Dimed: On (Not) Getting By in
America* (Ehrenreich)

M

Malek, Fred, 148
Marginally attached workers, 63–64,
71
Married male unemployment rate,
107, 109
Media Matters Action Network, 71
Medicare/Medicaid, 1–17. *See also*
Healthcare
cost of, xvii, 1–3
drug benefit (Part D), 3, 4, 8, 9
funding liabilities of, 5
Hertzberg, 1–2
journalists on, 1–2, 10–17
Kennedy (Ted) on, 17
single-payer system, 16, 17
Meltzer, Allan H., 35–36, 40, 159–160
Miller, Stephen, 47, 48, 50, 57, 63
Mishel, Lawrence, 191, 192
Monthly figures, xviii–xix
payroll employment data, 124–136
(*see also* Establishment Survey)
creationist fallacy, 134–136
revision, 132

Monthly figures *(Continued)*
  sampling error, 131–132
  seasonal adjustment, 132–134
  Squawk Box, 124–127,
    130–134
  real-time data versus revised data,
    xix
  unemployment rate, 137–149 *(see
    also* Unemployment)
  deconstructing the
    denominator, 139–141
  employment report and the
    bond market, 142–146
  false signals, 142
  irony, 139–140
  short-term obsession with, 141
  six-month moving average,
    141–142
  smoothing out, 141–142
  statistical insignificance,
    reporting, xii, 138–139
Monthly Labor Review, 63, 64, 72
Moore, Geoffrey, 147, 148
Moral-hazard myth, healthcare,
  205–208
Mueller, Kirk, 95

N

NAIRU. *See* Nonaccelerating
  inflation rate of unemployment
  (NAIRU)
Nardone, Tom, 105, 158
National Guard, 210
National Press Club, 139
New Republic:
  Chait, xiv
  on *Freakonomics,* 163
New Yorker, xvii, 1, 3, 6, 205–207
New York Review of Books, 16–17

New York Times:
  on Bush and jobs, 31–32
  columnist *(see* Krugman, Paul)
  Editorial Page Editor (Collins),
    xviii, 19, 57
  on *Freakonomics,* 163
  journalists/reporters:
    Andrews, xvii, 10–14
    Leonhardt, xiv
    Uchitelle, 116, 140, 141
  on *Nickel and Dimed,* 189
  ombudsman/Public Editor
    (Okrent), xiv–xv, xviii, 19,
    28, 44–45, 56–57
  partisan politics, econospinning,
    and errors, xi, xii, xiii
  on Social Security, 2, 5
  on Treasury study (2002), 12
Nichols, Rob, 11
*Nickel and Dimed: On (Not) Getting
  By in America* (Ehrenreich),
    xiii, 185–192, 212–213
9/11 terrorist attacks, 155–156,
  210
Nixon, Richard, xix, 138, 146–149
Nonaccelerating inflation rate of
  unemployment (NAIRU),
  106–109
Nonsupervisory ratio, 93–100,
  103–104
North American Free Trade
  Agreement (NAFTA), 199

O

"Occupation Employment
  Projections to 1992" (Hecker),
  201–203
Okrent, Daniel, xiii–xv, xviii, 19, 28,
  44–45, 56–57

O'Neill, Paul H., 10, 11
Orszag, Peter, 8–10
Orwell, George, 186
Outsourcing, 196, 200–201

P

Parker, Robert, 127
Participation rate, 73–82
"Participatory democracy,"
    95–196
Partisanship, xi, xii, xiii, xviii,
    30–31, 118
Part-timers, involuntary, 57–58,
    70
Pascal, Zachary G., 157–158
Payroll employment data, 124–136.
    See also Establishment Survey
    creationist fallacy, 134–136
    revision, 132
    sampling error, 131–132
    seasonal adjustment, 132–134
    Squawk Box, 124–127, 130–134
Payroll tax, 11, 192
Pearson, Hampton, 125
Perot, Ross, 135, 199, 207
Personal consumption expenditures
    (PCE), index of, 113
"Persons Outside the Labor Force
    Who Want a Job" (Castillo),
    63, 72
Peterson, Peter, 3–4
Phillips, Michael M., 157–158
Pilgrim, Kitty, 194–195
Politics, partisan, xi, xii, xiii, xviii,
    30–31, 118
Polivka, Anne, 47, 48, 50, 57, 63
Poor. *See Nickel and Dimed: On
    Not) Getting By in America*
    (Ehrenreich); Unemployment

Popkin, Joel, 148–149
Preventive healthcare, 206–207
Price determination, 188, 190,
    191
Price of Loyalty, The (Suskind), 11
Prisoners, 82
Production workers, 93
Productivity, 111–115, 125, 200,
    211–212
Profit boom, 116–123
Proxmire, William, 147

Q

*Quarterly Census of Employment and
    Wages,* 36, 42, 94–95, 97, 99,
    132
Quarterly Journal of Economics, 164
Questionnaires. *See* Establishment
    Survey; Household Survey
Quick, Rebecca, 126
Quit rate ("job leavers"), 157–158

R

Real estate agents, 164, 174–183
    asymmetric information and,
        174–176, 182–184
    as buyers, 182
    as deal makers, 181–182
    distorting information, 176–178
    representing buyers, 175–176,
        178–181
    representing sellers, 175, 180
    as sellers, 176–177, 182
Real-time (RT) data charts,
    128–131
Redesign of questionnaire, 46,
    47–49, 63, 64, 75

Reinhardt, Uwe, 206–207
Rents, problem of, 188–189
Reserves and National Guard, 210
Richebacher, Kurt, 210–211
Roe v. Wade, 167–168, 173, 174
Royal Dutch Shell, 117
Russia, 117

S

Sampling error, 131–132, 140–141
Samuelson, Paul, 25
School, young adults in, 81
Secrets of Economic Indicators, The (Baumohl), 132
Self-employment, 32–34, 57
Service-providing industries, 93
Shelter, 189
Shimer, Robert, 51–52
Single-payer system, 16, 17
Skilled workers, 200–201
Slack in the economy, 77–81
Smetters, Kent, 10–12
Smiley, Jane (*Good Faith*), 182
Snow, John, 91
Socialized medicine, 209
Social Security, xvii, 1–17
    bond redemption, 6–7
    demographics, 3, 14
    real value of benefit checks, 3
    saga of denial, 4
    trust fund, 2, 4–7
Solow, Robert, 154–155
Squawk Box. See CNBC's *Squawk Box*
St. Louis Post-Dispatch, 2, 111

Start-ups, missed, 37
States, trading among, 198
Statistical insignificance, reporting, xii, 138–139
Stewart, Jay, 76–77
Stigler, George, xiii
Stiglitz, Joseph, xvi
Structural changes and cyclical trends, 79
Suskind, Ron (*The Price of Loyalty*), 11
Sylvester, Lisa, 195–196
Syverson, Chad, 176–182

T

Taber, Christopher, 187–188
Terrorist attacks (9/11), 155–156, 210
Tightness index, labor market (LMTI), 101–102, 108–110
Timeliness, 92, 128, 136
Time magazine, 141
Times. See New York Times
Tipping Point, The (Gladwell), 208, 209
Trade deficits, 193–200
Trust fund, Social Security, 2, 4–7
Tucker, Bill, 193–194

U

Uchitelle, Louis, 116, 140, 141
Unemployment:
    hidden, 59–72, 73, 77
    discouraged workers, 57, 71, 74–77

measures of, as share of all
nonparticipants, 70–71
how to calculate, 68–70
U-1 (long-term
unemployment rate),
54, 55, 66–67, 70
U-2 (joblessness
unemployment rate),
55, 66–67
U-3 (official unemployment
rate), 54–55, 66–68,
77, 89, 90
U-4 (discouraged worker
unemployment rate),
6, 5, 66–68, 77, 89,
90
U-5 (marginally attached
unemployment rate),
66–68, 77
U-6 (marginally attached and
involuntary part-time
unemployment rate),
66–70, 77
U-7 ("want-a-job"
unemployment rate),
67, 69, 77
hourly compensation and rate of,
101–110
labor force participation rate,
73–82, 83–90
long-term, 44–58, 103
monthly measurement, 137–149
quit rate ("job leavers"),
157–158
rate, xix, 61, 71, 137–149
bond market and employment
report, 142–146
deconstructing denominator,
139–141
false signals, 142

irony, 139–140
short-term obsession with, 141
six-month moving average,
141–142
smoothing out, 141–142
statistical insignificance,
reporting, xii, 138–139
Unemployment-gate scandal (1971),
xix, 138, 146–149
USA Today, xiii
U.S. News & World Report,
210–211
Utgoff, Kathleen P., 139

V

Veteran's Health Administration
(VHA), 16, 209, 210
Volcker, Paul, 150

W

Wages. *See* Labor earnings/wages
Wall Street Journal:
on Levitt and *Freakonomics,* 163
Hilsenrath on self-employed, 33
Ip on Greenspan, xix, 150–162
ownership and connection to
Barron's, xi
partisan politics, xii, xviii, 30–31
on payroll employment, 30–31, 103
Quick on manufacturing
employment (as guest on
Squawk Box), 126
Wal-Mart:
Dobbs on, 194, 195, 196
Ehrenreich working at, 186–187,
188

Washington Monthly, 209, 210
Washington Post, 2, 139
Wells, Robin, 16–17
Wharton Business School, 141
"What Do Male Nonworkers Do?"
    (Stewart), 76–77
What Liberal Media? (Alterman),
    xv–xvii
Women, 52, 79, 103, 187–188,
    212, 213
Workers. *See also* Labor force:
    "economic man," 191
    knowledge, 105

low-wage, 191
skilled, 200–201
younger, 82
World Trade Organization, 195

Z

Zandi, Mark, 127
Zoning restrictions, 189, 192
Zuckerman, Mortimer B., 210–212